Statistics as Principled Argument

Statistics as Principled Argument

Robert P. Abelson
Yale University

LAWRENCE ERLBAUM ASSOCIATES, PUBLISHERS

1995   Hillsdale, NJ   Hove, UK

Lawrence Erlbaum Associates, Inc., Publishers
365 Broadway
Hillsdale, NJ 07642

Cover design by Mairav Salomon-Dekel

Library of Congress Cataloging-in-Publication Data

Abelson, Robert P.
Statistics as Principled Argument / Robert P. Abelson.
p. cm.
Includes bibliographical references and index.
ISBN 0-8058-0527-3 (acid-free). — ISBN 0-8058-0528-1 (pbk. : acid-free)
1. Statistics. I. Title.
QA276.A22 1995
001.4'22—dc20   94-34725
                                                            CIP

Books published by Lawrence Erlbaum Associates are
printed on acid-free paper, and their bindings are chosen for
strength and durability.

Printed in the United States of America
10 9 8 7 6 5 4 3 2

This book is dedicated to Willa Dinwoodie Abelson and to John Wilder Tukey, who in their special ways have encouraged me in seeking wisdom's direction.

Contents

Preface

This book arises from 35 years of teaching a first-year graduate statistics course in the Yale Psychology Department. When I think back over this time span I am struck both by what has changed in teaching statistics, and by what has remained the same.

The most obvious changes are effects of the computer revolution. In the 1950s a Computing Laboratory was a room containing a large collection of mechanical calculators—ungainly Monroes and Marchants with push buttons for entering data, and an interior assembly of ratchets for carrying out arithmetic operations. From the clickety-clack, you could usually tell at a considerable distance how many students were working on their data late at night. I confess to occasional nostalgia for this period of earnest, pitiful drudgery, but then I come to my senses and realize that in the old days, statistical analysis was not merely noisy; it also took forever, and was filled with errors. Nowadays, of course, computing facilities and statistical packages for both mainframes and PCs have vastly enlarged the possibilities for fast, complex, error-free analysis. This is especially consequential for large data sets, iterative calculations, multifactor or multivariate techniques, and—as heralded by the founding of the *Journal of Computational and Graphical Statistics* in 1992—for the use of computers in connection with graphical procedures for exploring data (see also Cleveland, 1993; Schmid, 1983; Wainer & Thissen, 1993). I do not mean to suggest that computers eliminate stupidity—they may in fact encourage it. But well-conceived analyses can be done with extraordinarily greater speed and in much greater detail than was possible a few short decades ago.

Other noteworthy developments in the last 20 years are: Exploratory Data Analysis (Hoaglin, Mosteller, & Tukey, 1983, 1985, 1991; Tukey, 1977), which sharply shifts emphasis away from statistical significance tests toward freewheeling search for coherent patterns in data; log-linear models (Goodman, 1970; Wickens, 1989) to analyze the frequencies of cases appearing in the cells of multiway tables; the Pandora's box of applications of the LISREL program (Jöreskog, 1978) for structural equations and confirmatory factor analysis; the family of techniques called "bootstrapping" (Efron, 1992) for dealing with sampling variability; and the explosion of interest in "meta-analysis" (Glass, 1978; Hedges & Olkin, 1985; Mullen, 1989; Rosenthal, 1991; Wachter & Straf, 1990) for drawing generalizations across sets of studies.

Despite many new developments and the intensity of statistical training offered in several university departments, students generally seem as bemused as ever. From long observation of student struggles with statistics, I conclude that the difficulties lie not so much with computational mechanics as with an overall perspective on what they are doing. For many students, statistics is an island, separated from other aspects of the research enterprise. Statistics is viewed as an unpleasant obligation, to be dismissed as rapidly as possible so that they can get on with the rest of their lives. Furthermore, it is very hard to deal with uncertainty, whether in life or in the little world of statistical inference. Many students try to avoid ambiguity by seizing upon tangible calculations, with stacks of computer output to add weight to their numbers. Students become rule-bound, thinking of statistical practice as a medical or religious regimen. They ask questions such as, "Am I allowed to analyze my data with this method?" in the querulous manner of a patient or parishioner anxious to avoid sickness or sin, and they seem to want a prescriptive answer, such as, "Run an analysis of variance according to the directions on the computer package, get lots of sleep, and call me in the morning."

For years, I always responded to students who asked, "Can I do this?" by saying something like, "You can do anything you want, but if you use method M you'll be open to criticism Z. You can argue your case effectively, however, if you use procedure P and are lucky enough to get result R. If you don't get result R, then I'm afraid you'll have to settle for a weaker claim."

Eventually, I began to appreciate an underlying implication of the way I found myself responding: namely, that the presentation of the inferences drawn from statistical analysis importantly involves rhetoric. When you do research, critics may quarrel with the interpretation of your results, and you had better be prepared with convincing counterarguments. (These critics may never in reality materialize, but the anticipation of criticism is fundamental to good research and data analysis. In fact, imagined encounters with antagonistic sharpsters should inform the design of your research in the first place.) There are analogous features between the claims of a statistical analyst and a case presented by a lawyer—the case can be persuasive or flimsy (even fishy), the style of inference may be loose or tight, prior conventions and rules of evidence may be invoked or flouted, and so on.

I have always wanted to write a statistics book, full of tips, wisdom, and wit—most of it fairly simple, as befits a first-year graduate or advanced undergraduate course in statistics for psychology or other social sciences. My mock title was, "Lots of Things You Ought to Know About Statistics, but Are Too Stupefied to Ask." Unfortunately, I had lacked an underlying theme to tie together all the bits of advice, and I did not want to do just another cookbook. When I hit upon the notion of statistics as principled argument, I knew that I had a unifying theme.

Beyond its rhetorical function, statistical analysis also has a narrative role. Meaningful research tells a story with some point to it, and statistics can sharpen the story. Students are often not mindful of this. Ask a student the question, "If your study were reported in the newspaper, what would the headline be?" and you are likely to receive in response a rare exhibition of incoherent mumblings, as though such a question had never been even remotely contemplated.

By continually posing the newspaper headline question, I have been led to consider what kinds of claims a statistical story can make, and what makes a claim interesting. Interestingness seems to have to do with changing the audience's beliefs about important relationships, often by articulating circumstances in which obvious explanations of things break down. Thus my image of the ideal statistician, already conceived as a good (but honest!) lawyer and a good storyteller, also includes the virtues of a good detective. All three roles can be fun. The detective work (Tukey, 1969) is playful as well as logical, and the sleuth should be open to unanticipated clues and unexpected relationships in the data.

Putting this all together, I have arrived at the theme that the purpose of statistics is to organize a useful argument from quantitative evidence, using a form of principled rhetoric. The word *principled* is crucial. Just because rhetoric is unavoidable, indeed acceptable, in statistical presentations does not mean that you should say anything you please. I am not advocating total relativism or deconstructionism in the field of statistics. The claims made should be based clearly on the evidence. And when I say "argument," I am not advocating that researchers should be surly and gratuitously combative. I have in mind spirited debate over issues raised by data, always conducted with respect for the dignity of all parties.

My theme cannot be advanced in a technical vacuum. Particular statistical methods must be discussed, albeit I have minimized the use of formulas and heavy data sets. In most of the book, the ideas revolve around elementary probability theory, *t* tests, analysis of variance, and simple issues of research design. It is therefore assumed that the reader has already had some access to systematic coverage of elementary statistics, such as occurs in an undergraduate course. Chapters 1 through 5 review and interpret basic material, and chapters 6 through 10 develop several topics that have received insufficient attention in statistics and research design texts, or have not been viewed in connection with debates about research claims. I have tried to make the presentation accessible and clear, but some readers may find a few sections cryptic (especially in chaps. 6 and 7). Use your judgment on what to skim. If you don't follow the occasional formulas, read the words. If you don't understand the words, follow the music and come back to the words later.

I have included many examples, not for cookbook instruction on how to calculate this or that, but to explain the connection of statistics to substantive claims about the real world. These examples are often from the research domain I know best, experimental social psychology. (Many of these examples are somewhat old—but then again, so am I.) The remaining examples are sprinkled widely throughout a number of empirical disciplines. I hope that all readers who want to sharpen their understanding of statistical arguments will feel welcome. I also hope that statistical and research experts will treat with forbearance my pedagogical oversimplifications of technical issues, and find at least as many pithy thoughts in the book as they do errors of omission and commission.

Teachers and researchers may find this book valuable as a source of material outside the usual range of things that appear in standard texts. Students may use the book as a supplement to a standard statistical text, or as stand-alone reading. Research groups may find it valuable to discuss the issues in the book as they occur in their own research domain. It has been my observation that most students do not *really* understand statistical material until they have been through it three times—once for exposure, once for practice, and once for the dawn of genuine insight. This book is designed for the third pass-through, and I hope that readers will carry what they learn into their research programs.

I am pleased to thank the many people who offered comments on various drafts. I list them alphabetically (an ordering principle that has been kind to me throughout my life): Robert M. Abelson, Willa Dinwoodie Abelson, Irene Blair, Jacob Cohen, Peter Frensch, Eric Gold, Jack Glaser, Anthony G. Greenwald, Dave Kenny, John Pawelek, Deborah Prentice, Robert Rosenthal, Alex Rothman, Laurie Snell, John W. Tukey, and Doug Whalen. Of these, special thanks go to Willa Dinwoodie Abelson, whose fine sense for felicity of expression was extraordinarily helpful; Irene Blair, who brought missing references out of hiding; Jacob Cohen, who upon discovering that I was saying many of the same things that he had for years been crying in the wilderness, responded with encouragement rather than pride of place; Dave Kenny, whose many interesting comments led me to include additional material; and to Deborah Prentice, who as a star teacher of statistics suggested a number of changes that made the statistical material more understandable. Judith Amsel of Lawrence Erlbaum Associates was unfailingly enthused about this project, and highly tolerant of my pokey rate of writing. For any flaws in the book, the usual rule of blame applies: *Mea culpa.*

Abelson's Laws

1. Chance is lumpy.

2. Overconfidence abhors uncertainty.

3. Never flout a convention just once.

4. Don't talk Greek if you don't know the English translation.

5. If you have nothing to say, don't say anything.

6. There is no free hunch.

7. You can't see the dust if you don't move the couch.

8. Criticism is the mother of methodology.

1 Making Claims With Statistics

MISUNDERSTANDINGS OF STATISTICS

The field of statistics is misunderstood by students and nonstudents alike. The general public distrusts statistics because media manipulators often attempt to gull them with misleading statistical claims. Incumbent politicians, for example, quote upbeat economic statistics, whereas their challengers cite evidence of wrack and ruin. Advertisers promote pills by citing the proportion of doctors who supposedly recommend them, or the average time they take to enter the bloodstream. The public suspects that in the interest of making particular points, propagandists can use any numbers they like in any fashion they please.

Suspicion of false advertising is fair enough, but to blame the problem on statistics is unreasonable. When people lie with words (which they do quite often), we do not take it out on the English language. Yes, you may say, but the public can more readily detect false words than deceitful statistics. Maybe true, maybe not, I reply, but when statistical analysis is carried out responsibly, blanket public skepticism undermines its potentially useful application. Rather than mindlessly trashing any and all statements with numbers in them, a more mature response is to learn enough about statistics to distinguish honest, useful conclusions from skullduggery or foolishness.

It is a hopeful sign that a considerable number of college and university students take courses in statistics. Unfortunately, the typical statistics course does not deal very well, if at all, with the argumentative, give-and-take nature of statistical claims. As a consequence, students tend to develop their own characteristic misperceptions of statistics. They seek certainty and exactitude, and emphasize calculations rather than points to be drawn from statistical analysis. They tend to state statistical conclusions mechanically, avoiding imaginative rhetoric (lest they be accused of manipulativeness).

It is the aim of this book to locate the field of statistics with respect to rhetoric and narrative. My central theme is that good statistics involves principled argument that conveys an interesting and credible

1

point. Some subjectivity in statistical presentations is unavoidable, as acknowledged even by the rather stuffy developers of statistical hypothesis testing. Egon Pearson (1962), for example, wrote retrospectively of his work with Jerzy Neyman, "We left in our mathematical model a gap for the exercise of a more intuitive process of personal judgment" (p. 395). Meanwhile, Sir Ronald Fisher (1955) accused Neyman and Pearson of making overmechanical recommendations, himself emphasizing experimentation as a continuing process requiring a community of free minds making their own decisions on the basis of shared information.

Somewhere along the line in the teaching of statistics in the social sciences, the importance of good judgment got lost amidst the minutiae of null hypothesis testing. It is all right, indeed essential, to argue flexibly and in detail for a particular case when you use statistics. Data analysis should not be pointlessly formal. It should make an interesting claim; it should tell a story that an informed audience will care about, and it should do so by intelligent interpretation of appropriate evidence from empirical measurements or observations.[1]

CLAIMS MADE WITH STATISTICS: COMPARISON AND EXPLANATION

How are claims developed in statistical tales? For most of this book, we treat statistics in connection with systematic research programs, but to begin, let us discuss the case in which purportedly newsworthy statistical "facts" are picked up by roving reporters and presented in the media.

Stand-Alone Statistics

Many of these statistics are isolated, stand-alone figures such as: "The average life expectancy of famous orchestral conductors is 73.4 years" (Atlas, 1978), or "adults who watched television 3–4 hours a day had nearly *double* the prevalence of high cholesterol as those who watched less than one hour a day" (Tucker & Bagwell, 1992), or "...college-edu-

---

[1]There is a different light in which some people view the field of statistics. Data gathering may be seen as the archival activity of assembling "facts," which at some later time may be used according to the needs of particular investigators or administrators. Historically, statistics began with the collection of tax and census records, and the term *statistics* derives from the description of *states* (Cowles, 1989). Prime modern examples of archives that can later be used for various research purposes are census data, and public opinion survey data banks such as the General Social Surveys (Davis & Smith, 1991). Resources like these are important, and I do not underestimate their value. Nevertheless, data banking is but the beginning of certain research enterprises, not their culmination. It is the theoretical and applied payoff of data analysis that engages my attention in this book.

cated women who are still single at the age of thirty-five have only a 5 percent chance of ever getting married" ("Too Late," 1986; discussed by Cherlin, 1990; and Maier, 1991). The point of the life-expectancy statistic was supposedly that conducting an orchestra is so fulfilling that it lengthens life. The cholesterol story was somewhat puzzling, but the implication was that increased junk food consumption accompanied heavy TV watching. The marriage statistic was based on shaky projections of future trends, and could be variously explained or dismissed, depending on who was doing the explaining or dismissing.

A problem in making a claim with an isolated number is that the audience may have no context within which to assess the meaning of the figure and the assertion containing it. How unusual is it to live until age 73.4? Does "nearly double" mean I shouldn't watch TV? If one can't answer such questions, then a natural reaction to this type of numerical pronouncement would be, "So what?"

The Importance of Comparison

In the example about women and percentage marrying, a background context is readily available, and most people would regard 5% as a startlingly low marriage rate compared to the general average (or compared to what was true 50 years ago). The idea of *comparison* is crucial. To make a point that is at all meaningful, statistical presentations must refer to differences between observation and expectation, or differences among observations. Observed differences lead to why questions, which in turn trigger a search for explanatory factors. Thus, the big difference between the 5% future marriage rate for 35-year-old, college-educated single women and one's impression that some 80% or 90% of women in general will marry, evokes the question, "I wonder why that is? Is it career patterns, the lack of appeal of marriage, or a shortage of eligible men?... Or maybe the 5% figure is based on a faulty statistical procedure." Such candidate explanations motivate the investigators (or their critics) to a reanalysis of existing evidence and assumptions, or the collection of new data, in order to choose a preferred explanation.

Apart from the standard statistical questions of why there is a difference between one summary statistic and another, or between the statistic and a baseline comparison figure, there occasionally arises a need to explain a lack of difference. When we expect a difference and don't find any, we may ask, "Why is there *not* a difference?" Galileo's fabled demonstration that heavy and light objects take the same time to fall a given distance is a case in point. The observed constancy stands in contrast with a strong intuition that a heavy object should fall faster, thus posing a puzzle requiring explanation.

Standards of Comparison

At the outset of the explanation process, there is a complication. Given a single statistic, many different observations or expectations may be used as standards of comparison; what is compared with what may have a substantial influence on the question asked and the answer given. Why questions are said to have a *focus*.[2] The longevity datum on famous orchestral conductors (Atlas, 1978) provides a good example. With what should the mean age at their deaths, 73.4 years, be compared? With orchestral *players*? With *nonfamous* conductors? With the general public?

All of the conductors studied were men, and almost all of them lived in the United States (though born in Europe). The author used the mean life expectancy of males in the U.S. population as the standard of comparison. This was 68.5 years at the time the study was done, so it appears that the conductors enjoyed about a 5-year extension of life— and indeed, the author of the study jumped to the conclusion that involvement in the activity of conducting *causes* longer life. Since the study appeared, others have seized upon it and even elaborated reasons for a causal connection (e.g., as health columnist Brody, 1991, wrote, "it is believed that arm exercise plays a role in the longevity of conductors" [p. B8]).

However, as Carroll (1979) pointed out in a critique of the study, there is a subtle flaw in life-expectancy comparisons: The calculation of average life expectancy includes infant deaths along with those of adults who survive for many years. Because no infant has ever conducted an orchestra, the data from infant mortalities should be excluded from the comparison standard. Well, then, what about teenagers? They also are much too young to take over a major orchestra, so their deaths should also be excluded from the general average. Carroll argued that an appropriate cutoff age for the comparison group is at least 32 years old, an estimate of the average age of appointment to a first orchestral conducting post. The mean life expectancy among U.S. males who have already reached the age of 32 is 72.0 years, so the relative advantage, if any, of being in the famous conductor category is much smaller than suggested by the previous, flawed comparison. One could continue to devise ever and ever more finely tuned comparison groups of nonconductors who are otherwise similar to conductors. Thoughtful attention to comparison standards (usually "control groups") can substantially reduce the occurrence of misleading statistical interpretations.

---

[2]A shift in the focus of question and answer is well illustrated by a joke beloved among 10-year-old children: "Why did the turkey cross the road?" ... "Because it was the chicken's day off." The reader who doesn't understand children's jokes can get the idea of focus by studying the effect of underlining different words in a why question. See Lehnert (1978).

Choosing Among Candidate Explanations

For any observed comparative difference, several possible candidate explanations may occur to the investigator (and to critics). In a given case, this set of explanations may include accounts varying widely in their substance and generality, ranging from a dismissal of the observed difference as a fluke or an artifactual triviality to claims that the observations support or undermine some broad theoretical position. In our orchestra conductors example, the set of candidate explanations includes at least the following: (a) The result arose fortuitously from the particular sample of conductors included; (b) the comparison standard is still flawed, as it does not account for subpopulations with shorter life spans who are also ineligible to become conductors (e.g., the chronically ill); and (c) conductors *do* live longer, because of some common genetic basis for longevity and extraordinary musical talent, health benefits from the activity of conducting (or from a larger class of activities that includes conducting), or health benefits from something associated with conducting, such as receiving adulation from others, or having a great deal of control over others.

It is the task of data analysis and statistical inference to help guide the choice among the candidate explanations. The chosen explanation becomes a *claim*. (If this term implies more force than appropriate, we may use the blander word *point*.) In the conductor example, it is risky to make a claim, because of a lack of relevant data that would help winnow the set of explanations. It would be helpful to have information on such matters as the life expectancy of well-known pianists, actors, professors, lawyers, and so forth; the life expectancy of eminent conductors who retire early (for reasons other than health); the life expectancy of siblings of famous conductors (ideally, twin siblings—but there would not be enough cases); and the comparative life expectancies of elderly people who stay active and those who are inactive (for reasons other than poor health).

Experimentalists would despair at the vagueness of specification of the needed evidence (how should one define "poor health," "active" "retire"), and the sinking feeling that there are just too many variables (some of them unknown) that might be associated with longevity. The experimental investigator would be in a much more comfortable position if he or she could isolate and *manipulate* the factors assumed to be relevant in one or more of the proposed causal accounts. An experimenter, as distinct from an observer, tries to *create* (or re-create) comparative differences rather than just to observe them passively.

Consider the possible explanation that orchestral conducting is so personally satisfying or otherwise beneficial that it extends life beyond the age at which the individual would have died in the absence of this activity. The standard experimental way to try to recreate such an effect would be to assemble a group of potentially outstanding conductors, arrange for a random half of them to have prestigious orchestra posts whereas the other half have less involving career activities, and then collect longevity data on all of them. Of course this test would be absurdly impractical. I mention it because it suggests the possibility of conceptually similar experiments that might be feasible. For example, one could recruit a group of elderly people, provide a random half of them with social or physical activities, or social control, and monitor their subsequent feelings of well-being and state of health relative to that of the other half, who had received no intervention.[3] The bottom line for the conductors example, though, is that casual, one-shot tabulations of statistical observations will almost certainly be difficult to interpret. Therefore it is rhetorically weak to make claims based on them, and such claims deserve to be regarded with great skepticism. Well-justified explanations of comparative differences typically depend on well-controlled comparisons such as can be provided by careful experiments, and therefore we emphasize experimental data in this book. (Sometimes, one can also do well by the sophisticated collection of converging lines of evidence in field observations.) The quality of explanation improves dramatically when there are many interrelated data sets, some of them repeated demonstrations of the core result(s) or of closely related results, some of them ruling out alternative explanations, and yet others showing that when the explanatory factor is absent, the result(s) fail to appear.

Systematic Versus Chance Explanations

To understand the nature of statistical argument, we must consider what *types* of explanation qualify as answers to why questions. One characteristic type, the *chance* explanation, is expressed in statements such as, "These results could easily be due to chance," or "A random model adequately fits the data." Indeed, statistical inference is rare among scientific logics in being forced to deal with chance explanations as alternatives or additions to systematic explanations.

In the discussion to follow, we presume that data are generated by a single measurement procedure applied to a set of objects or events in a given domain. We suppose that the observations comprising the data set differ, some from others, and we ask why. A *systematic factor* is an influence that contributes an orderly relative advantage to particular subgroups of observations, for example, a longevity gain of a certain number of years by elderly people who stay active. A *chance factor* is an

---

[3]There is in fact a growing literature in the field of health psychology that speaks to precisely this idea (Langer & Rodin, 1976; Okun, Olding, & Cohn, 1990; Rodin, 1986).

influence that contributes haphazardly to each observation, with the amount of influence on any given observation being unspecifiable.

The Tendency to Exaggerate Systematic Factors

Inexperienced researchers and laypeople alike usually overestimate the influence of systematic factors relative to chance factors. As amateur everyday psychologists and would-be controllers of the world around us, we exaggerate our ability to predict the behavior of other people. We have difficulty thinking statistically about human beings.

Kunda and Nisbett (1986) showed that in matters of human *ability*, especially athletic ability, there is some degree of appreciation of inexplicable variations in performance from one occasion to the next. We understand, for example, that a tennis player might be on his game one day but flat the next, so that a sample of performances is necessary to make a reliable judgment of ability. Even so, the relative importance of chance influences is seriously underestimated in many athletic contexts. Abelson (1985) asked baseball-wise psychologists to consider whether or not a major league batter would get a hit in a given turn at bat, and to estimate the proportion of variance in this event explained by differences in the skill of different batters, as opposed to chance factors affecting the success of a given batter. The median estimate was around 25%, but the true answer is less than one half of 1%! In part this is due to the highly stingy properties of "explained variance" as a measure of relationship between two variables (Rosenthal & Rubin, 1979), but more interestingly, it is because we as baseball fans are prone to regard a .330 hitter as a hero who will almost always come through in the clutch, and the .260 hitter as a practically certain out when the game is on the line.

The underappreciation of chance variability extends to other domains. For events such as lottery drawings in which skill plays no objective role whatever, subjects under many conditions act as though some control can be exerted over the outcome (Langer, 1975). Kunda and Nisbett (1986) concluded that in matters of *personality*, inferences based on a single encounter are made with undue confidence, ignoring the possibility of situational influences that vary over time and place. We tend to feel, for example, that the person who is talkative on one occasion is a generally talkative person (the "fundamental attribution error," Ross, 1977).

The upshot of all this is a natural tendency to jump to systematic conclusions in preference to chance as an explanation. As researchers, we need principled data-handling procedures to protect us from inventing elaborate overinterpretations for data that could have been dominated by chance processes. We need to understand that even though statistical calculations carry an aura of numerical exactitude, debate necessarily surrounds statistical conclusions, made as they are against a background of uncertainty. A major step in the winnowing of explanations for data is to make a judgment about the relative roles played by systematic and chance factors.

Inasmuch as chance is not well understood—even by those who have had a bit of statistical training—we introduce whimsical, hopefully memorable metaphors for the operation of chance factors (chap. 2).

LANGUAGE AND LIMITATIONS OF NULL HYPOTHESIS TESTS

A staple procedure used in psychological research to differentiate systematic from chance explanations is the significance test of a null hypothesis. Elementary statistics texts describe many varieties of them, but students often regard null hypothesis testing as counterintuitive, and many critics (e.g., Cohen, in press; Falk & Greenbaum, in press; Tukey, 1991) find much to fault in null hypothesis tests. It is worthwhile to set forth here the quirky logic of these tests, so that later on when we refer to their application, the reader will be well informed about their role in statistics, and the reasons for complaint about them.

Consider the simplest type of laboratory experiment, in which subjects are assigned at random to either an experimental group or a control group. Members of the two groups perform the identical experimental task, except for the additional manipulation of a single factor of interest in the experimental group—say, the receipt of prior information or training, or the administration of a drug. The experimenter wishes to test whether the experimental factor makes a systematic difference on some appropriate measure of task performance.

Presumably, performance measures on the task differ from individual to individual, and we ask a rhetorical why question. The systematic explanatory factor is the manipulation introduced by the experimenter. To say that this factor is systematic is to assume that on average it improves (or damages) task performances in the experimental group by some unknown amount over and above performances in the control group. We can try to estimate the magnitude of this systematic effect simply by calculating the difference between the mean performance scores of the two groups.

But there are also chance factors in this situation—things that add noise to individual measurements in an unknown way. We mention two categories here: sampling errors and measurement errors. Sampling errors arise from the "luck of the draw" in randomly assigning subjects to the two groups; the experimental group may contain a predominance of people with somewhat higher (or lower) task ability than members of the control group, thus introducing a mean difference that could be mistaken for a systematic effect. Measurement errors refer to unknown and unrepeatable causes of variability in task performance over time, place, and circumstance. The laboratory room may be too warm when Subject 17 performs the task; Subject 42 may have a headache that day; and so on.

In qualitative terms, there are three possible accounts for the data arising from this experimental design: (a) The variability of task scores can be entirely explained by the systematic factor, (b) the variability of task scores can be entirely explained by chance factors (sampling and measurement errors), or (c) the variability requires explanation by both chance factors and the systematic factor.

The first and the second accounts are simpler, and parsimony would suggest that they be tested before falling back on the third account. Why tell a complicated story if a simpler story will do? The third account can be held in reserve if both of the first two accounts are inadequate. The first possibility, completely systematic data with no chance variability, would be immediately apparent in the data set: All the scores in the experimental group would be equal, and different from all the equal scores in the control group. This outcome may be approximated in the physical and biological sciences, where chance variability is typically very small. With psychological data, however, this outcome is quite rare—but if and when it occurs, statistical inference is not used (Skinner, 1963).

Setting aside these rare, errorless cases, we are left with the choice between the all-chance explanation, and the systematic-plus-chance explanation. We can tell if we need to invoke a systematic factor by first testing the all-chance explanation; if chance factors do not adequately account for the data, then systematic factor is needed. This is in essence the justification for significance tests of the null hypothesis.

The Language of Null Hypothesis Testing

A null hypothesis test is a ritualized exercise of devil's advocacy. One assumes as a basis for argument that there is no systematic difference between the experimental and control scores—that except for errors of sampling and measurement the two groups' performances are indistinguishable. If (according to a formal procedure such as a t test) the data are not sharply inconsistent with this conception, then an all-chance explanation is tenable, so far as this one data set is concerned. This is often described as "accepting the null hypothesis." If, on the other hand, the data are inconsistent with the all-chance model, the null hypothesis is rejected, and the systematic-plus-chance model is preferred.

An important caveat here is that the standard terms, "accept" or "reject" the null hypothesis, are semantically too strong. Statistical tests are aids to (hopefully wise) judgment, not two-valued logical declarations of truth or falsity. Besides, common sense tells us that the null hypothesis is virtually never (Cohen, 1990; Loftus, 1991) literally true to the last decimal place. It is thus odd to speak of accepting it. We often use other terms for this outcome, such as "retaining the null hypothesis" or "treating the null hypothesis as viable."[4] Similarly, rejection can be softened with alternative phrases like, "discrediting the null hypothesis."

In any case, the investigator wanting to show the influence of some experimental factor proceeds by discrediting the assumption that it doesn't matter. The backhandedness of this procedure reflects the fact that null hypothesis tests are motivated by rhetorical considerations. Suppose an experimental investigator announces that the data demonstrate—despite considerable variability from case to case—the systematic efficacy of a particular educational or medical intervention or the operation of a particular theoretical principle, but a critic counters that the data could easily have arisen from fortuitous sampling or measurement errors. Who wins this scientific debate? The critic does, unless the investigator can come up with a *counter*-counter, to the effect that the data are in fact quite unlikely to be explained entirely by chance factors. With such a rebuttal, the investigator discredits the null hypothesis (and therefore the critic will in practice usually be deterred from raising this argument in the first place).

Significance Tests Provide Very Limited Information

The answer to the simple question, "Is there some systematic difference between the experimental group and the control group?" is not usually electrifying. As mentioned earlier, there is virtually always some difference caused by sensible experimental manipulations. Indeed, the only examples where the exact satisfaction of the null hypothesis is worth considering occur when there is widespread disbelief that some strange phenomenon exists at all. For example, the null hypothesis is interesting when discrediting it implies that mental telepathy is possible, or that stimuli below the level of conscious awareness can have reliable effects on attitudes and behavior. The complementary case is also interesting, in which everybody believes beforehand that an effect must exist. For instance, virtually everyone who follows sports believes that there is such a thing as "streak shooting" in basketball, and it caused a considerable furor when Gilovich, Vallone, and Tversky (1985) argued from a set of sensitive statistical tests on sequences of shots that the null hypothesis of no streak shooting is tenable.

---

[4]A good way to think about what it means to retain a null hypothesis of no mean difference is that the analyst is insufficiently confident to assert which mean is larger (Tukey, 1991). See chapter 3, footnote 1.

Single Studies Are Not Definitive

Even in these rare cases, though, where the outcome of a simple significance test may have scientific (and possibly popular) news value, a single study never is so influential that it eliminates all argument. Replication of research findings is crucial. After all, if a result of a study is contrary to prior beliefs, the strongest holders of those prior beliefs will tend to marshall various criticisms of the study's methodology, come up with alternative interpretations of the results, and spark a possibly long-lasting debate.

Sometimes critics prove right in the long run, and sometimes they prove wrong. To take an example from the physical sciences, skepticism about the existence of "cold fusion" prevailed after a year or two of debate (Pool, 1988) over a claim of success. The opposite outcome of debate is illustrated by the reality of "subliminal perception"—meaningful stimulus registration without awareness—that after a period of skepticism has been widely accepted (Kihlstrom, 1987).

Debate about the existence of extrasensory perception (ESP) went on for years in an inconclusive, rather sterile fashion (Hyman, 1991; Utts, 1991). Argument had not progressed much beyond the "mere existence," null-hypothesis-testing stage to a more interesting, focused examination of the strength and generality (if any) of ESP, the conditions that encourage it, and the process by which it may operate. (Recently, the debate has become more usefully focused on the properties of a particular type of demonstration, the *Ganzfeld* procedure [Bem & Honorton, 1994; Hyman, 1994].)

Thus even in the rare cases where the literal truth of the null hypothesis is at issue, and especially in the preponderance of cases where the null hypothesis is a straw man, the investigator wants to formulate a position going beyond a primitive test of a single null hypothesis. Scientific arguments are much more rich than that. Before working up to the issues in some typical debates, however, we stay at an elementary level and discuss in detail what makes statistical arguments rhetorically forceful and narratively compelling.

PERSUASIVE ARGUMENTS: THE MAGIC CRITERIA

There are several properties of data, and its analysis and presentation, that govern its persuasive force. We label these by the acronym MAGIC, which stands for *magnitude, articulation, generality, interestingness,* and *credibility*.[5]

[5]There are other schemes for classifying the quality of statistical evidence and its presentation. The enumeration of various forms of *validity* (internal, external, construct, trait, discriminant, ecological, predictive, etc.) is a well-known alternative (Campbell,

Magnitude

The strength of a statistical argument is enhanced in accord with the quantitative magnitude of support for its qualitative claim. There are different ways to index magnitude, the most popular of which is the so-called "effect size" (Cohen, 1988; Glass, 1978; Hedges & Olkin, 1985; Mullen, 1989; Rosenthal, 1991). In the basic case of the comparison between two means, effect size can be simply given as the difference between the means; often, however, this difference is divided by the standard deviation of observations within groups. In chapter 3, we bring up a number of alternatives, and introduce the concept of "cause size," which also bears on the interpretation of magnitudes of effects.

Articulation

By articulation, we refer to the degree of comprehensible detail in which conclusions are phrased. Suppose, for example, that the investigator is comparing the mean outcomes of five groups: A, B, C, D, E. The conclusion "there exist some systematic differences among these means" has a very minimum of articulation. A statement such as, "means C, D, and E are each systematically higher than means A and B, although they are not reliably different from each other" contains more articulation. Still more would attach to a quantitative or near-quantitative specification of a pattern among the means, for example, "in moving from Group A to B to C to D to E, there is a steady increase in the respective means." The criterion of articulation is more formally treated in chapter 6, where we introduce the concepts of *ticks* and *buts*, units of articulation of detail.

Generality

Generality denotes the breadth of applicability of the conclusions. The circumstances associated with any given study are usually quite narrow, even though investigators typically intend their arguments to apply more broadly. To support broad conclusions, it is necessary to include a wide range of contextual variations in a comprehensive research plan, or to cumulate outcome data from many interrelated but somewhat

---

1960; Cook & Campbell, 1979). The analysis of validity has been very useful, but it has never caught on as a coherent whole. It strikes the student as rather formal and esoteric. Another system has been given in an exquisitely sensible little book on the importance of statistical analysis in medical research (Hill, 1977). This author named but did not elaborate on criteria similar to mine. If my approach has any claim to novelty, it is that I have chosen and developed my criteria within the unifying premise of statistics as argument, and I know of no previous source that has systematically pursued such an approach.

different studies, as can be done within the context of meta-analysis (Mullen, 1989; Rosenthal, 1991). In chapter 7, we present an analysis of variance framework for interpreting generalization.

High-quality evidence, embodying sizeable, well-articulated, and general effects, is necessary for a statistical argument to have maximal persuasive impact, but it is not sufficient. Also vital are the attributes of the research story embodying the argument. We discuss two criteria for an effective research narrative: interestingness, and credibility.

Interestingness

Philosophers, psychologists, and others have pondered variously what it means for a story to be interesting (e.g., Davis, 1971; Hidi & Baird, 1986; Schank, 1979; Tesser, 1990), or to have a point (Wilensky, 1983). Our view in this book is that for a statistical story to be *theoretically interesting*, it must have the potential, through empirical analysis, to change what people believe about an important issue. This conceptual interpretation of statistical interestingness has several features requiring further explanation, which we undertake in chapter 8. For now, the key ideas are *change of belief*—which typically entails surprising results—and the *importance* of the issue, which is a function of the number of theoretical and applied propositions needing modification in light of the new results.

Credibility

Credibility refers to the believability of a research claim. It requires both *methodological* soundness, and *theoretical* coherence. Claims based on sloppy experimental procedures or mistaken statistical analyses will fall victim to criticism by those with an interest in the results. Clues suggested by funny-looking data or wrongly framed procedures provide skeptics with information that something is amiss in the statistical analysis or research methodology. (Of course, you might yourself be in the role of critic, whereby you can track these clues in other people's research reports.)

Many extensive catalogs of methodological and statistical errors already exist in the literature (Aronson, Brewer, & Carlsmith, 1985; Campbell & Stanley, 1963; Evans, 1991; King, 1986). Our discussions differ from standard ones in two ways. We classify statistical errors "bottom up"—that is, in terms of various odd appearances in data, from which types of error may be induced (chap. 5); and we treat a selection of research design errors in the context of how they might affect the ongoing debate between an investigator and a critic (chap. 9).

The credibility of a research claim can sustain damage from another source—the claim may violate prevailing theory, or even common sense. The research audience cannot bring itself to believe a discrepant claim, such as a purported demonstration of extrasensory perception, which would require vast revision of existing views. In such cases, debate tends to occur on two fronts simultaneously. The critic will typically pick on suspected methodological errors, thus accounting for the claim as a methodological artifact. The investigator must be prepared to try to rule out such accounts. Also, a theoretical battle will develop, in which the investigator is challenged to show that her alternative theory is *coherent*, that is, capable of explaining a range of interconnected findings. If result A requires explanation X, result B calls forth explanation Y, and result C explanation Z, where explanations X, Y, and Z have little relation to each other, the narrative of results A, B, and C is incoherent (Thagard, 1989). On the other hand, if a single explanatory principle accounts for several different results, the story is coherent. When the results would be unrelated were it not for sharing the same explanation, the story is not only coherent, it is *elegant*. In chapter 9, we refer to coherent bundles of results as *signatures*.

The outcome of a theoretical debate depends on the comparative adequacy of the respective accounts of existing data. But the contest may also hinge on who has the *burden of proof* in the exchange of criticisms and rebuttals. Usually, this burden rests with the investigator, especially at the outset. Critics are often freewheeling in their invention of counterexplanations: It could be this, it may be that, it's merely such-and-so. Some types of counterexplanations are so vague as to be untestable—which gives the critic a substantial debating advantage. Nevertheless, despite occasional abuse of the ability to criticize, science is better off being tolerant of kibitzers and second-guessers. The critic is often right. Anyway, science should have both a conservative bias—which prevents rapid and bewildering shifts of views—and ultimate openness, such that persistent innovators can ultimately triumph if their claims are indeed meritorious. These issues are discussed more deeply in chapter 9.

The requisite skills for producing credible statistical narratives are not unlike those of a good detective (Tukey, 1969). The investigator must solve an interesting case, similar to the "whodunit" of a traditional murder mystery, except that it is a "howcummit"—how come the data fall in a particular pattern. She must be able to rule out alternatives, and be prepared to match wits with supercilious competitive colleagues who stubbornly cling to presumably false alternative accounts, based on somewhat different clues. (This is analogous to the problems faced by heroic fictional detectives who must put up with interference from cloddish police chiefs.)

STYLE AND CONVENTION

Our five major criteria for an effective statistical argument depend on the quality of the data and on the skill of the investigator in designing research and presenting results. There are other aspects of statistical arguments that depend hardly at all on data or on skill—instead, they are matters of taste and convention.

Style

For our purposes, the *style* of the statistical argument within a research presentation can be loosely represented by a dimension along which different possible presentations of the same results can be arrayed: At one extreme is an assertive and incautious style, running toward reckless and excessive claims; at the other extreme is a timid and rigid style, with an unwillingness to make any claims other than the most obvious ones. In practice, styles are not usually at the extremes, but rather at intermediate positions nearer to one pole than the other. We label these the *liberal* style and the *conservative* style (chap. 4).

The liberal style is oriented more toward exploration of data and discovery of possibly systematic effects. By contrast, the conservative style reflects a confirmatory attitude toward research results, where one is willing to forego claims about marginal or unexpected findings in order to be more confident about the remaining claims.

It might seem that one should be able to calibrate just how liberal to be if one could place relative costs on making too many claims versus making too few claims. Indeed, there are times when research is explicitly exploratory, with open season on speculations, and times when it is explicitly confirmatory, requiring the utmost prudence. But most research falls somewhere in the middle, and even in explicit cases, the required decision calculation is impractical because the costs of the two types of errors are not sensibly quantifiable. There is a boundary in data interpretation beyond which formulas and quantitative decision procedures do not go, where judgment and style enter.

Conventions

Sometimes this subjective element is disguised by the use of *conventions*. There are many such, the most prominent of which is the notorious $p = .05$ as the "conventional" significance level. If everyone follows the conventions, individual investigators are freed from the responsibility (but denied the opportunity) for using their own judgment. This is relatively benign as long as conventions are reasonable, and everyone realizes that they are conventions rather than commandments.

The Inevitability of Uncertainty

An analogy can be drawn with a legal system. The dispensation of justice is fraught with uncertainty. There are imponderable costs associated with declaring a guilty person innocent, or an innocent person guilty. The balance between these two types of mistake is set by the legal conventions of a society, in particular, how weighty the evidence of a defendant's guilt must be to justify convicting him. In the Anglo-American tradition for capital offenses, guilt must be established "beyond a reasonable doubt." Such a convention, though it may convey a reassuring illusion that the decision policy is exact (provided that nobody is lying), is itself subject to ambiguity and alternative interpretation. By and large, nonetheless, wise use of this imprecise tradition serves us well.

In applications of statistics in the social sciences, some element of subjectivity is always present, and the research investigator is cast in a role analogous to that of a legal advocate. In this metaphor, the scientific audience plays the part of judge or jury hearing the testimony of the investigator and of those who may disagree. Though it may take several judicial proceedings, a judgment is eventually reached.

THE BOTTOM LINE

A research story can be interesting and theoretically coherent, but still not be persuasive—if the data provide only weak support for the rhetoric of the case. On the other hand, a lot of high-quality rhetoric can be squandered by a poor narrative—for example, if the research is so dull that no one cares which way the results come out. Thus rhetoric and narrative combine multiplicatively, as it were, in the service of persuasive arguments based on data analysis. If either component is weak, the product is weak. The argument is strong only when it has the MAGIC properties of forceful rhetoric and effective narrative. In making his or her best case, the investigator must combine the skills of an honest lawyer, a good detective, and a good storyteller.

2 Elementary Arguments and the Role of Chance

I have proposed that the proper function of statistics is to formulate good arguments explaining comparative differences, hopefully in an interesting way. In this chapter the four most elementary kinds of statistical arguments are introduced, with a pithy illustration of each. All four are affected by some manifestation of chance. The first two arguments each involve a comparison between a set of observations and a chance expectation; the arguments differ in whether or not a comparative difference is claimed. The next pair of arguments compare the means of two sets of observations with each other; one argument claims that the observed mean difference could have been due to chance, whereas the other claims a systematic difference on top of chance effects.

Common sense tells us that an explanatory argument is better if concise, with overexplanation giving grounds for skepticism. If John excuses his absence from work by claiming that his grandmother died, and besides, he had a bad cold, we are inclined to doubt his sincerity. He has violated one of Grice's (1975) axioms of normal discourse, namely that a speaker should give sufficient information to be understood, but no more.

As with everyday explanations, even more so with scientific explanations. The ideal of parsimony gives preference to the simplest explanation adequate to account for a given corpus of data. In chapter 1, we noted that in the social sciences, part of the job of the investigator is to sort out the relative contributions to data from chance factors and from systematic factors. The most parsimonious (though often not the most welcome) kind of explanation is that the data can be attributed entirely to chance factors. This case of pure chance serves as a very low-level, baseline explanation that may be altered to include systematic factors if statistical analysis shows them to be necessary. The role of chance in the four simple arguments (and more complex ones to come later) is not entirely transparent, and requires discussion. In this chapter we offer two conceptions of chance—random *generation* and random *sampling*—

each taking advantage of a different descriptive metaphor. A third process, random *assignment*, enters our discussion briefly.

RANDOM GENERATING PROCESSES

To picture the vagaries of chance, I like to imagine a committee of leprechauns responsible for producing data on demand. They tinker around with odd ingredients and secret processes, chuckling to themselves as they send bits and pieces of data from Glocca Morra to the investigator. They may or may not include systematic ingredients, but they always throw in chance variations. It is not easy to tell what they are doing, but sometimes their eccentric procedures for manufacturing randomness contain characteristic regularities, and an investigator can learn much by being alert to clues of assembly-line chance production, leprechaun style.

One type of whimsical regularity is a *random generating process*. This term denotes the repetitive production of variable observations with characteristic properties of uncertainty. Unpredictable mechanical procedures such as the flipping of coins, the rolling of dice, and the spinning of a roulette wheel are common examples of these repetitive processes. A classic early article on probability by Bayes (1764) used the imagery of an invisible hand rolling balls on a square table, and an observer noting whether the ball stopped before reaching an arbitrary line. In most such examples, the data are sequences of categorical outcomes (e.g., random strings of heads and tails). Sometimes there are symmetries such that on every repetition (trial), each outcome has the same probability (heads and tails are 50/50). In other examples such as Bayes' table, the outcomes may not be equally likely. Coins and dice, for that matter, can be loaded to favor one or another outcome; any mechanical device can have asymmetries that have unexplored consequences (imagine, e.g., the procedure of flicking a thumbtack with a forefinger along a table top to see whether it lands point up or point touching the table). Even more exotic unpredictable physical processes can be imagined. Our leprechauns could toss shamrocks, or roll apples over a cliff, seeing whether or not each object landed in a brook below.

The Binomial Process

Suppose that there are two qualitative outcomes, a "positive" outcome and a "negative" outcome (say, the apple either does or does not land in the brook), and the probabilities of these two outcomes are constant for every repetition of the process. Suppose further that the outcomes are *independent* from trial to trial, meaning that the actual outcome on any given trial does not affect the probability of any later outcome. Coin flips are usually considered independent of one another, because there is no physical influence, or residue of information from a given flip that will carry over to the next flip.[1] The coin doesn't "remember" how it came out before. Day-to-day weather events provide a clear example of *non-independent* outcomes. Because weather patterns tend to persist for a few days, a rainy day is more likely to occur following a rainy day than following a sunny day.

The two conditions of constant outcome probability and trial-to-trial independence define a *binomial* process. This type of random generating process creates its characteristic *patterns* of outcomes, albeit the individual outcomes are unpredictable. Consider the sequence of outcomes as represented by a string of symbols, a (1) representing a positive outcome, and a (0), a negative outcome. A surprising and important feature of these patterns is that in principle they are unrelated to the exact physical nature of the process. Statistically speaking, a binomial process is a binomial process is a binomial process. Just from observing the outcomes, we will be unable to tell whether the leprechauns were flipping loaded coins, or rolling apples. When a process obeys the defining conditions of the binomial, its long-run statistical properties are completely characterized.

Long-Run Properties of Binomial Processes.   One of the long-run properties of binomial processes is that the relative frequency of positive outcomes in a long series will closely approach the single-trial probability of a positive outcome. If each apple has a 7 in 10 chance of landing in the brook, then over a long series of trials, the relative occurrence of this event will be 70%, plus or minus a small margin of error.[2] Turning this statement around, we can regard the relative occurrence of positive outcomes in the data as an estimate of the constant per-trial probability, a feature of the process that may have been unknown before any data were gathered.

Other long-run properties characterize the trial-by-trial sequence of positive (1) and negative (0) outcomes. Consider a string of heads (1) and tails (0), say, [1100010100001110...]. A given string contains runs of like outcomes; the aforementioned string starts with a run of two heads

---

[1] To be careful about this assertion, some assumption needs to be made about the variability from trial to trial of the blows imparted to the coin by the flipper's thumb. The reason for this is that some dextrous conjurors are able to achieve such constancy of the flip stroke that they can make heads come out every time. Without going into the subtleties of the necessary assumption, suffice to say that our hypothetical flipper is highly variable and erratic.

[2] An appropriate version of the "central limit theorem" (see Adams, 1974) states that as the number of independent events increases, the observed proportion of successes almost certainly gets arbitrarily close to the per-trial probability. For any specified degree of closeness (say .1%, or .01%), one can attain any desired odds (say, 99 to 1) of getting that close by taking a large enough sample.

followed by a run of three tails. Because binomial processes are mathematically well specified, it is possible to calculate for a sequence of given length the expected frequency of occurrence of runs of length two, three, four, and so on, for both the positive and negative outcomes. A powerful mathematical analysis of several types of run counts is given by Fu and Koutras (1994).

The Gambler's Fallacy.   There are two interrelated popular misconceptions of the nature of binomial sequences. One of these is the "gambler's fallacy." If there has been a long run of one outcome, an observer might reason that because the two outcomes are destined to come out in a given ratio in a lengthy set of trials, the outcome that has not appeared for a while is temporarily advantaged. Upon seeing six straight occurrences of black from spins of a roulette wheel, a gambler suffering from this illusion would confidently bet on red for the next spin. This fallacy also occurs among baseball fans. A hitter with a batting average of .250 gets a hit one time in four, on average. The fan, reacting to the information that a .250 hitter has made an out his first three times up in a game, is wont to say that the batter "is due." A hit his fourth time up would mimic his general average of one out of four.

Why is it fallacious to think that sequences will self-correct for temporary departures from the expected ratio of the respective outcomes? As a kid, years before I was exposed to formal statistical training, I used to puzzle about this question in the form of the following paradox: Suppose that John and Bill each flip coins known to be fair; John gets five heads in a row, and Bill five tails in a row. Then they switch coins. On John's next flip, this time with Bill's coin, should the outcome tend to be tails (to even up John's record) or heads (to even up the record of Bill's coin)? As one thinks about this conundrum, more riddles tend to come to mind. Suppose a coin yields 10 heads in a row, and then you wait before the 11th flip. Maybe you even bury the coin for a year, or put it in a time capsule. When unearthed, how will it know to have a preference for tails?[3] No, the gambler's fallacy can't be right.

Chance is Lumpy.   Does this mean, then, that randomly generated sequences *don't* balance out to the proper ratio? In a way, yes, but only by trivial amounts when the sequence gets really long. Ten extra heads

---

[3]In a test of psychological (though surely not logical) behavior when confronted by such riddles, Eric Gold (personal communication, September 1991) found that when the next flip after a run of four heads was made with a new coin, the gambler's fallacy sharply diminished. Also, when a pause of 24 minutes was introduced following a run, the fallacy also dropped. Intuitively, people seem to regard chance behavior (here, the putative compensatory tendency) as residing in the coin in use. Interestingly, in games of bridge or poker, particular chairs are often thought to embody consistent (rather than compensatory) good or bad luck. How we imbue inanimate objects with our superstitions!

won't distort a 50/50 ratio much after a half million or so more heads and a half million or so tails. Local imbalances of one or the other outcome are like undigested lumps in the long stream of data. This is an illustration of Abelson's First Law of statistics: *Chance is lumpy.*[4] People generally fail to appreciate that occasional long runs of one or the other outcome are a natural feature of random sequences. It has repeatedly been demonstrated that when subjects are asked to write down a series of chance outcomes such as might result from a succession of flips of a fair coin, they tend to avoid long runs of either outcome. The sequences they write usually alternate back and forth too quickly between the two outcomes (Wagenaar, 1972). This appears to be because people expect random outcomes to be *representative* (Kahneman & Tversky, 1972) of the process that generates them, so that if the trial-by-trial expectations for the two outcomes are 50/50, then the person will everywhere make the series come out almost evenly divided. A related psychological error is to judge sequences that have in fact been generated by a binomial process to be nonrandom, that is, to be attributable to systematic causal factors. These natural errors make it very important to be careful in explaining sequences of qualitative outcomes, resisting the temptation to claim systematicity unless chance explanation is insufficient.

The first two simple arguments we consider, then, are: (a) the modest proposal that a set of data could simply represent the expression of a

---

[4]Statements about randomness can readily lead into a metaphysical quagmire, but it is worthwhile to risk the bog with an amplification of this statement. By "chance" I mean an output from a mathematically *idealized*, hypothetical random generating (e.g., binomial) or sampling process. The reason for the warning about lumpiness is that people generally assume too much local regularity in their concepts of chance. People are lousy random number generators, as discussed in the paragraph after this footnote.

But serious issues are raised when one asks what natural or artificial mechanism could *in practice* perfectly simulate chance behavior. Scientists in many fields need sequences of random numbers for modeling phenomena with probabilistic features. And they are needed in creating random samples or random assignments for social science research. The standard way to produce such sequences has been to have a computer repeatedly multiply varying many-digit numbers together, each time selecting scattered digits of the product. It has recently been discovered, however, that although such sequences obey simple tests for true randomness, they fail more elaborate, finicky tests by manifesting too much lumpiness (Ferrenberg, Landau, & Wong, 1992). This finding has caused considerable consternation, and a pessimistic review of possible alternatives for random number generation (Browne, 1993). It is conceivable that both artifice and nature are intrinsically incapable of generating sequences of events that mathematical statisticians will accept as ideally random.

Such a metaphysical catastrophe would not have damaging consequences, however, for the social science research discussed in this book. The anxieties of the physicists and mathematicians over randomness are akin to worrying about atomic clocks drifting by .01 seconds per century, whereas social scientists typically operate at a level of precision more appropriate for an alarm clock that gains or loses 6 hours a week.

random generating process; (b) the more forthcoming claim that some systematic explanation of the data is required, above and beyond the operation of a random generating process.

Argument 1: The Data Could Come From a Random Generating Process

We have pointed out that "pure chance" can be a parsimonious account for a data set. If the data are consistent with such an account, but the investigator doesn't offer it, then a critic surely will, and the investigator will be in an embarrassingly weak rhetorical position.

We have also noted that data strings coming from very different physical realizations of random generating processes can be indistinguishable. Different animals, so to speak, leave the same statistical footprints. There are even cases of sequential events not often considered to be in the realm of chance, which nevertheless produce data strings with the characteristic features of randomness.

Chance as a Factor in Manifestly Skilled Behaviors.   Confusion between chance (in the sense we have been discussing) and systematic effects is great when skilled performances are at issue. For example, if an athlete is *trying* to produce a given outcome, it goes against the grain to call the result of the effort chance. Yet at the same time, we accept as natural some variation in the success of repeated attempts.

When is it appropriate to invoke systematic factors in explaining sequences of athletic performances, say, basketball players repeatedly attempting to score baskets? In general, systematicity can be claimed when some meaningfully identifiable portions of the data set are markedly different from one another. Sequences aside, if some individuals (and some teams) are fairly consistently more successful than others, then we are inclined to believe that they are really better, rather than just lucky. Also, when it is observed that a given player gradually increases his or her rate of success, the reasonable supposition is that the player is systematically improving in skill. Third, there are certain external conditions that are coherently associated with the rate of success, for example, playing on one's home court (Cooper, DeNeve, & Mosteller, 1992; Harville & Smith, 1994).

The effects of other external conditions, however, may be murky. Athletes might claim that playing four games in five nights is detrimental. Or that the team is predictably worse on Sundays, or when their biorhythms are unfavorable. At some point, statisticians might scrutinize performance data to try to adjudicate between real effects and apparent effects more parsimoniously attributed to chance.

Example: The Hot Hand in Basketball. One such investigation (Gilovich, Vallone, & Tversky, 1985) has concerned the so-called "hot hand" in basketball. When a player runs off a string of successful shots, aficionados of the game are apt to say that the player is hot, and when in the midst of a series of misses, cold. These popular terms—which also arise in other competitive sports and games—connote supposedly causal influences of unknown, perhaps unknowable origin. The trained statistical investigator, having learned that data-generating processes can be realized by all sorts of physical mechanisms, thinks abstractly about sets of observations, temporarily stripping away the context in which they arose.

Thus with the hot hand, what the investigator examines are the strings of hits and misses by each of a number of basketball players over a large number of games. For purposes of statistical examination, the data might as well have come from apple rolls by leprechauns as from shots by basketball players. The feature of interest in the data is whether successive shots by given players are nonindependent, tending to run in systematic streaks with hits following hits (and misses following misses).

When appropriate data sets were examined, what did the investigators of the hot hand conclude? Surprisingly, they found no evidence whatever to support the notion of unusually hot streaks by players. The data for each player were entirely consistent with a random generating process, in particular, a binomial process (constant probability for success on each shot, and independence between shots; Gilovich et al., 1985). To reach this conclusion, the investigators conducted several analyses, including a comparison of the probabilities of making shots after having made or missed one, two, or three previous shots, a count of the number of runs of hits and misses in strings of consecutive shots, and a comparison with chance expectation of the variability of success across games. Such analyses were conducted for each member of the Philadelphia 76ers on both field goals and free throws, and for sequences of practice shots by members of the male and female teams from Cornell. (Analyses were later conducted on other pro teams, with the same conclusion.)

Reactions to the Lack of Evidence for Hot Hands. Basketball players, coaches, writers, and fans who have heard about this conclusion generally find it incredible. They profess to *know* that hot streaks exist. Why? Gilovich (1991) proposed that the persistent belief in the reality of streakiness, as opposed to randomness, is associated with the failure to appreciate what random strings look like. People do not realize that chance is lumpy, and attribute the occasional lumps to mysterious, supposedly systematic processes such as hot hands. Also, many people may be unwilling to believe that whether or not a shot goes in is absolutely unrelated to the success or failure of the previous shot. Don't players have periods of feeling relaxed and in a groove? Don't offenses use successful plays repeatedly, until the defense gets wise?

There is indeed a certain fragility to the argument that the features of a data string are indistinguishable from those of a well-defined random generating process. Finite data strings cannot be *guaranteed* to be random. It requires a controversial metaphysical leap, in fact, to claim that specific *data* are random, as opposed to making the inference that their generating *process* is random. The most circumspect statement is that given strings are not inconsistent with the hypothesis of an underlying random process. But if one were to look at new data, or previously unanalyzed features of old data, it is conceivable that some evidence of nonrandomness would emerge. This possibility sustains the hopes of those who are true believers in a given phenomenon, and are frankly annoyed that spoilsport statisticians try to tell them that their belief is wrong-headed. They are ready to leap in with a counterargument should the opportunity arise.

Larkey, Smith, and Kadane (1989) did in fact pounce on the hot hand issue, claiming that the previous investigators had neglected the *timing* of shots in true manifestations of hot hands. A reanalysis considering only runs of shots closely spaced in time, they said, would reveal the hidden phenomenon. Larkey et al. presented such an analysis, purporting to show a hot hand for at least one player—Vinnie Johnson, nicknamed "Microwave" because of his fabled hot streaks.

Tversky and Gilovich (1989), in rebuttal, emphasized that the reanalysis failed to uncover any hot players other than Johnson, and that Johnson's statistically remarkable streakiness depended entirely on a single run of seven baskets. Furthermore, that single run of seven could not even be found on the videotape provided by Larkey et al.! Instead, there was a run of four good shots, a miss followed by a score off his own rebound, and then one more hit. Correcting for this tabulation error, even the Microwave didn't depart from randomness.[5] Undaunted by this setback, other believers in hot hands may yet try coming up with a convincing reanalysis.

Argument 2: Unspecified Factors Cause Departures From Randomness

Attributing a data set to mere chance is often deflating. It is an argument that something or other (such as the hot hand) doesn't exist.[6] Rejecting the null hypothesis of mere chance, by contrast, supports the argument that something or other *does* exist. We may not know what the responsible systematic factor is, but we can feel some assurance that there is one.

---

[5]Johnson was found to be more likely to shoot again shortly after a hit, making the psychological impact of the hot hand illusion more compelling.

[6]There are exceptions to the general idea that chance accounts are vacuous and nihilistic. One exception arises from the concept of efficient markets in economics, which requires

Extrasensory Perception: A Good Illustration.   Experiments on extrasensory perception (ESP), especially of mental telepathy or clairvoyance, provide appropriate illustrations. In one often-used setup (Whitten, 1977), an assistant selects randomly shuffled symbol cards one by one. The potential psychic in another place records his impressions of the sequence of symbols. Typically in such experiments, there are five possible symbols. They may sometimes be equally often represented in the symbol deck, but for purposes of our discussion, let us assume that the five symbols could occur different numbers of times in a deck of, say, 25 cards.

For each run through the deck the success of telepathy or clairvoyance is scored by matching the impressions of the psychic against the actual cards, tallying the number of correspondences. The skeptical, wet blanket model of this situation is that ESP does not exist; the apparent successes are entirely due to a binomial process with a probability of one out of five, or .2, on each of 25 independent trials. (The successive symbol impressions are not usually independent of one another, but the cards themselves, if well shuffled, would be independent over trials, and thus also would be the matches between the cards and the impressions.)

Example: A Famous Series of Clairvoyance Tests.   In the celebrated Pearce–Pratt Series of tests conducted at Duke University in 1933–1934 (see Rhine & Pratt, 1954), the overall percent correct over 70 separate runs through a deck was 30%. The binomial process model predicts close convergence to 20% in a long series of trials, so the data seem a rather poor fit to this chance model. Because the expected variability of the chance process depends only on the number of trials and the probability of success on each (both of which are known here), one can in fact precisely assess the odds against getting a 30% success rate by chance. These odds are so steep they run off the available statistical tables—we might as well call them a skintillion to one. Therefore the original investigators felt supremely confident in rejecting the mere chance binomial model. It was inferred that something else was involved in the causation of success: something labeled *clairvoy-*

(Otherwise, rational analysts would predict the trend, and their investment behavior would make the trend disappear.) Relevant sequential data have been much analyzed (DeBondt & Thaler, 1990) to see whether a random generating process gives an adequate account. In several small ways, it doesn't, creating some difficulty for economic theorists. Here we have the oddity of a systematic theory predicting chance data.

Quantum theory in physics is another peculiar case. Quantum theory postulates a subatomic microworld in which systematic events and states are inherently probabilistic. Though the theory is now accepted, it still seems counterintuitive. "I cannot believe that God would play dice with the universe," Albert Einstein is supposed to have said. In any case, in virtually all social science applications, chance as a complete explanation of raw data is a rival to systematic explanation, not its embodiment.

ance, the ability to gather stimulus information through other than normal sensory channels.

ESP has long been controversial. Sure enough, there is a counterargument against the Pearce–Pratt claim, which we present in chapter 5. For the moment, we note that there was no analysis of the day-to-day variability of the success rate or of the sequential properties of the data. Because the level of success was higher than could reasonably be expected from an appropriate random generating process, there seemed no need to examine further properties of the data. Such an omission could be unfortunate, for the reason that if a binomial process is not the explanation, one would at least like some clues as to what is going on instead. Merely labeling the presumed systematic process as clairvoyance is not of itself a very helpful explanation. Does clairvoyant success come in streaks, like hypothetical hot hands? Does it improve with practice? How variable is it? Do people who believe in ESP have more of it? Further elaborations such as this are important in the *articulation* of systematic processes (chap. 6), and in the *credibility* of claims (chap. 9).

Remarks on the First Two Argument Types

Summing up the first two argument types, each one takes advantage of the statistical regularities of a random generating process—a somewhat lumpy, patterned randomness with a specifiable rate of success in a very long series. We used the binomial model as the simplest illustration of a random generating process. Given the per-trial probability of success, and the assumption of independent trials, all the statistical regularities of the process are mathematically known. This is very important, because it immediately provides a rich set of expectations against which data can be tested.

In our first example, it was argued on the basis of analysis of the sequential properties of the hot hand data that the chance model was a sufficiently good fit. The argument in our second example was that chance alone could not explain the data, at least not the overall success rate. (It was accidental that the chance model was accepted when sequential properties were examined, but was rejected when overall success rate was the criterion. Examples going the other way around could just as well have been given.)

RANDOM SAMPLING PROCESSES

The first way to think about chance was to imagine a random generating process. There is another way, using the idea of a *random sampling process*. Suppose that for a large number of individuals in a "population," measurements (or *scores*) are written on slips of paper by our busy leprechauns, and dropped into a hat. There is no patterning to the scores in a hat, such as was the case with the binomial generating process. All we can assume is that there is some *distribution* of these scores. The leprechauns know the shape and various summary properties of the distribution in any hat, such as the mean, but they don't tell us. They merely shuffle slips without peeking at them, and deliver one or more samples of them. The bemused investigator who requested these samples of scores must make inferences about the populations from the samples he sees.

Appreciating the Omnipresence of Variability

Psychologically, there is a tendency to underestimate the degree to which means (or other calculated statistics) may vary from one sample to another. We are inclined to endow quantities we calculate with an aura of exactitude and finality, not worrying enough about the results that might obtain were other samples to be drawn. This proclivity is particularly misleading when the size of the sample is small. Tversky and Kahneman (1971) coined the phrase, "The law of small numbers," to refer to the tendency to impute too much stability to small-sample results. In like fashion, Kunda and Nisbett (1986) noted that in some everyday situations, observation of a few isolated behaviors leads too readily to judgments of stable personal characteristics such as friendliness or introversion. Here it is likely that observations of the behavior of another person are not perceived as potentially variable samples over time, but as direct indicants of stable traits. The perceiver is especially likely to be misled if the sample is biased with respect to time and place (say, the other person is seen only on Saturday evenings at parties). To be mindful of the ever-present possibility of limited, quirky samples leading to runaway intuitions, let us coin Abelson's Second Law: *Overconfidence abhors uncertainty.*[7] Psychologically, people are prone to prefer false certitude to the daunting recognition of chance variability.

Comparing the Means of Two Groups

The uncertainty attached to statistical summaries is surprisingly great in comparing results from two groups (A and B), each represented by a sample of individuals. A standard inferential task in this situation is to decide whether or not the two groups of scores could plausibly be

---

[7]The tendency to overlook or downplay chance variability is but one instance of a pervasive "overconfidence bias" (Fischhoff, Slovic, & Lichtenstein, 1977)—the tendency for people to believe themselves to be more often correct than is objectively the case.

regarded as two samples from the same population. The scores could be the results of a test, such as an IQ test. Or they could be physical measurements such as individuals' weights. Or they could be scores derived in some fashion from other scores, say, the differences between average reaction times to identify words with positive versus negative meaning. The important features for our purposes are simply that every one of a large number of individuals in a population has an actual or potential score, and that two subsets of randomly sampled individuals are given special attention.

Imagine that we are concerned with the weights of 18-year-old women. We want to compare the average weights of two subgroups, say, those who jog regularly with those who never jog. If we are to make a judgment about whether or not a particular systematic factor makes a difference, we need to appreciate the way that chance factors make their appearance in this situation.

Unlike the data sets used in Arguments 1 and 2 discussed previously, weight data[8] do not seem representable by a simple random generating process. The pound-by-pound details of weight accretion to a particular level are complex and ill-understood. But even though we cannot find an appropriate generating process, we can imagine leprechauns shuffling a hatful of weights, each identified with a distinct 18-year-old woman, and conducting some sampling operation(s) leading to the creation of data sets for Groups A and B.

There are two major variations in the way that samples are used in simple comparisons of two groups. In a *true experiment*, the investigator compares average scores in two groups that differ on a factor that has been *manipulated* by the investigator. This case is treated in Argument 4, later.

The other case is an *observational study*, where the intent lies in comparing two natural groups on some feature of interest. In our illustration, we are interested in knowing if the average weight of 18-year-old women is systematically different for those who jog regu-

---

[8]If we were willing to assume that the weight of a young adult results from the aggregation of a large number of independent causes, each of which could be present or absent during preadult physical development, then it can be shown that the distribution of adult weights would have the shape of the *normal distribution*. Interestingly, this type of assumed aggregation can be visualized as a random generating process: A large group of leprechauns, each carrying an apple, walk single file past a large wooden barrel. Each one in turn decides with his own characteristic probability whether or not to put his apple into the barrel. When the last leprechaun has passed by, the weight of the barrel is noted. Then the barrel is emptied, and each elf retrieves his apple. The group comes round again, repeating its random behavior, and creating a new load of barreled apples; then again, and again. If this process is repeated indefinitely, the distribution of barrel weights will have the shape of a normal curve. It is unreasonable, however, to assume that the process determining biological height is analogous to this random generating process, and indeed, observed weights are not normally distributed (Shils & Young, 1988).

larly and those who have never jogged. This is a *population* question; if it were feasible to gather the information on *all* 18-year-old women[9] who either jog regularly or have never jogged, a hard-working lunatic might do that. In practice, it is much more reasonable to take samples for the two groups.

"Representative" Samples: An Attractive Illusion.   How ought an investigator go about this? Informally speaking, she wants her samples to be representative of the joggers and nonjoggers, respectively. The concept of representativeness, however, is an appealing but misguided idea (much as it was when applied to random sequences). It relies on the image of a microcosmic population, a cleverly selected sample that is an exact replica of the larger universe of individuals. It is a Noah's Ark sort of conception, with *proportional* representation of different types of individuals.

If we knew exactly what measurable attributes were most predictive of systematic weight differences among 18-year-old women, we might try to design proportionalized ("stratified") samples only on these attributes. But often we don't have such information. And we would enter a labyrinth if we tried to select sets of people with various *combinations* of these attributes. Anyway, we would still have to decide how to sample individual members.

Random samples come to the rescue. These are samples in which each member of the relevant population has an equal chance of being chosen, and all possible samples are equally likely. The individual members of a random sample are unpredictable, but the process has statistical regularity that allows probabilistic statements to be made about the average scores of sample members. The variability from sample to sample of the average score depends only on the variability of individual cases and the size of the sample.

How Can Random Numbers Be Produced?   Procedures for creating random samples are nontrivial. A popular misconception is that haphazardness is involved, so that all you need do, for example, is to put on a blindfold and stick pins into a master list. This is a flawed procedure. If you blindly stick a pin into each page of a phone book, say, names near the middle of the page will be more likely to be chosen than those at top or bottom, violating the equal-chance definition of random samples. Other informal schemes have similar difficulties.

There are computer algorithms for producing random numbers, which can be attached to individuals in various ways, say, by dialing

---

[9]All?! Do we include Eskimos? Bulimics? Pygmies? Once we raise the question of who belongs in the population, we realize that there are boundaries to the universe of cases to which we intend to generalize.

random phone numbers. Most academic and commercial organizations draw samples for telephone interviewing by refinements of random digit dialing (see Crano & Brewer, 1986).

However, there are a number of obstacles to the achievement of perfectly random samples. (In surveys of the population of people with telephones, e.g., what do you do about answering machines [Tuckel & Feinberg, 1991])? What about interview *refuseniks*? How do you prevent oversampling of people with several phone numbers, or undersampling people in large households with only one phone? Etc.) For the present discussion, we imagine that the investigator subcontracts the job of drawing random samples to Leprechauns Inc., an upscale firm that promises to produce unpredictability of precisely the style you request. The data for the samples are guaranteed not to be biased on any property of the population(s) from which the samples are drawn—but of course the customer has to be aware that chance is lumpy.

The investigator wishing to compare the weights of joggers and nonjoggers requests two random samples, one for each group. Leprechauns Inc. happens to have a hatful of the weights of all 18-year-old female joggers, and a hatful for the weights of all nonjoggers. They draw a random sample from each of these hats, and present it to the investigator. She must decide if there is a systematic mean weight difference associated with jogging. Suppose that in her data the average jogger weighs 118 lbs., and the average nonjogger 123 lbs. Can she be confident that this direction of difference is a reliable result?

If the samples were small and/or the variance of cases *within* the samples were large, a 5-lb. difference could conceivably be an accident of sampling variation. With larger samples or smaller within-sample variation, at some stage a 5-lb. difference would become convincing evidence that joggers (of given age and gender) on average weigh systematically less than nonjoggers.[10] A formal statement corresponding to this intuition provides a statistical test procedure.

The t Test.   The alert reader will long since have said never mind the leprechauns, here we just do a t test. That of course is the standard textbook recommendation for testing whether the difference between the means of two groups departs significantly from zero. But textbook

---

[10]Were a systematic weight difference associated with jogging to be claimed, there would still arise a serious problem of interpretation. For starters, we would not know whether the joggers weighed less before they started jogging, or lost weight due to jogging. Furthermore, we would be at the mercy of critics who might suggest that social categories, such as yuppies, could both encourage jogging and be disproportionately composed of thin people. Such problems of causal interpretation were discussed in chapter 1 in connection with the supposedly long-lived conductors, and are treated in more detail in chapter 9 in connection with research debates.

readers are often in the position of Dylan Thomas' (1954) autobiograph-ical child who was told "everything about the wasp except why" (p. 25).

The t ratio is a convenient and cogent measure: It is the observed mean difference between two samples, relative to an estimate of sampling variability. Consider the null case where the two groups of scores are randomly sampled from the same population. Here, it is as though the leprechauns draw a double-sized random sample of slips from *one* hat, and deal them like cards into two piles representing Group A and Group B, respectively. In this case of no systematic difference between the As and the Bs, the value of t will tend to come out relatively small; but if the two samples differ because on top of chance variability the Statistical Imp has added a systematic increment for one group or the other, t will tend to come out relatively larger.

The tables of critical values of t are derived assuming that the overall distribution of scores from which samples are drawn is known to be the normal distribution. Now, a great many raw data distributions depart in some respect from the normal distribution (Mandlebrot, 1965; Micceri, 1989). Fortunately, the p values based on the t test (especially those near the .05 significance level) are insensitive to the actual shape of the underlying distribution for many types of realistic non-normal distributions (Sawilowsky & Blair, 1992). The t test is said to be "robust" (Kirk, 1982; Tukey, 1962) against variations in the shape of the distri-bution.[11] For rhetorical purposes, there are basically two possible out-comes to a simple t test. A skeptical account based on pure random sampling can either survive, or else be discredited in favor of an account that also includes a systematic group difference in mean score. Each outcome houses an elementary argument, as we now illustrate.

Argument 3: The Data Could Come from a Random Sampling Process

Example: Power to the Students.   Our next example (with slight alteration) is from a student research project at Yale in 1992, exploring the psychology of participation in a campus-wide agitation by graduate students for several university concessions, including union recognition.

A questionnaire designed to tap the correlates of commitment to the graduate students' cause was administered to 52 randomly chosen students from three departments. Twenty-nine of them participated in a well-planned campus demonstration a couple of days later; the other 23 did not. The mean ratings by the participants and nonparticipants

---

[11]Contrary to prevailing supposition, however, the t test is not very robust against violation of the assumption of equal variances within groups. When the variances of the two groups are rather different (say, in a ratio of at least 3:1) the t test tends to give somewhat inflated values, and modifications may be in order (Wilcox, 1987).

on a number of attitude and self-rating scales from the questionnaire were compared.

The data in Table 2.1 come from a much larger table, filled with comparisons between the participant and nonparticipant groups. The mean self-ratings in answer to the question, "On a political spectrum going from very liberal to very conservative, where would you place yourself?" are given in the table for the two groups. This question (along with related others) was asked because the investigators anticipated that ideological differences might be among the correlates of participation in such a campus demonstration; in particular, they thought that liberals would be more likely than conservatives to press for student union recognition. The usual stereotype of student demonstrators is that they are driven by fervent devotion to political and social causes aimed at changing the established order.

However, the difference between the means on the liberalism/conservatism question turned out to be in the "wrong" direction. The participants were on average more conservative than were the nonparticipants. However, the difference between the means was only .02—two hundredths of a scale point on a 7-point scale. The trivial size of this difference can be appreciated by noting that if 1 of the 29 people in the participant group had given himself a rating of 2 rather than 3, say, the mean rating for participants would have been lower by $1/29$, or .03 (rounded), altogether nullifying the difference between participants and nonparticipants. In practice, one could hardly find a mean difference smaller than this, and the t of .07 and corresponding p over .90 reflect the virtual equality of observed means in the two groups. Self-placement on a liberalism–conservatism scale, then, bore no systematic relation to participation in this campus demonstration, as though liberalism scores were sampled from a single distribution and assigned randomly to participants or nonparticipants. This is a bit surprising.

Limitations to the Conclusion.   What are we to make of this? Has the investigator established the literal conclusion that the liberalism of nonparticipants in campus demonstrations is exactly the same as for participants?! No. Although the null hypothesis is stated as an exact equality of the means of two groups, chance factors blur the outcome.

TABLE 2.1
Mean Self-Ratings of Liberalism by Participants and Nonparticipants in a
Campus Demonstration

Participants (N = 29)	Nonparticipants (N = 23)
2.72	2.70

Note. On a 7-point scale, 1 = very liberal, 7 = very conservative.
$t(50) = .07$, $p > .90$.

Hypotheses that the difference was +.25, +.50, or even −.50 would have been accepted by t-tests also. We can only specify a band of plausible true mean differences in the population of graduate students from which the samples came. In this example, such a band can be given by the 95% confidence limits, which run from −.54 to +.61. The range of plausible true differences thus includes zero, but no logic compels it to *be* zero. It appears, nonetheless, that the true difference is very apt to be no larger than about half a scale point.

From another direction comes a further limitation on what conclusions can be drawn. The study was extremely narrow in scope—two groups from three departments at one university, based on participation in one demonstration. We consider questions of generality of claims in chapter 7, but for the moment we may simply note that one study certainly cannot establish a sweeping general claim. Yet a third problem with the claim of no systematic relation between ideology and participation is that the self-rating measure of liberalism may have been unreliable or inappropriate. How do we know, for example, that the students took the liberalism question seriously? Or that the range of liberalism on a predominantly liberal campus is meaningful?

Strengthening the Argument.   In recruiting all these doubts, we seem to be virtually dismissing the results of the study. But this is too precipitous a collapse in the face of criticism. There were in fact several pieces of collateral evidence serving to bolster the basic claim. There were very small and nonsignificant differences between participants and nonparticipants on other ideology-related questions, such as attitudes toward unions, or toward the Gulf War. Yet these questions and the self-rating of liberalism correlated significantly with one another, undercutting the arguments that respondents might have been indifferent and inattentive while answering the questions, or that the liberalism scale made no meaningful distinctions. Furthermore, on attitudes toward campus issues, including those that motivated the demonstration, there was no evidence of difference between participants and nonparticipants!

The two groups did differ significantly and substantially, however, on questions concerning the desirability and likely effectiveness of a demonstration. For example, for the statement, "It is important that every student stand up and be counted on the day of the demonstration," the mean score for the participants was 1.58 units higher than for the nonparticipants on a 7-point scale of agree/disagree. On predictions for the likely turnout for the demonstration, 80% of the participants but only 20% of the nonparticipants said it would be heavy.

Taken together, the results in this modest study were coherent, and give credibility (see chap. 9) to the following argument: Under the circumstances of this particular demonstration, ideological and campus issue positions had minimal bearing on participation; what mattered instead was belief in the efficacy of such action. Generalization to other campus demonstrations is hazardous, but nevertheless suggest a cautionary tale: Observers of political demonstrations should not automatically assume that participants are more extreme in their political attitudes than is typical for their interest group. They may be distinguishable in their endorsement of political means rather than political ends.

Random Assignment and Experimental Manipulation.   In the previous example, the investigator had no control over the causal influences in the situation. The causes of the behavior of interest were unknown, and remained somewhat arguable even after a lot of good detective work. Causal claims can be crisper when the groups are defined entirely by some property introduced experimentally by the investigator. In order to ensure that the groups do not differ in some other systematic way, the experimenter uses *random assignment* of individuals to the two groups. In acting thus, the experimenter co-opts the sampling scheme of the leprechauns in the null case: Individuals are drawn from a *single pool* of subjects, and at random each one is labeled an A or a B. Thus at the outset the As and the Bs differ only by chance. On top of this foundation, the experimenter also attempts to take over the role of the Statistical Imp by treating the A's differently from the B's in some single key aspect—say by paying the As more than the Bs—and measures the degree of group difference on some subsequent behavior or judgment. The beauty part of this strategy is that if a significant difference is found, it permits the experimenter to claim that the experimental treatment caused the group difference in behavior. The reasoning is that because the groups differed only by chance before the manipulation, a systematic difference afterwards implies that the experimental manipulation was responsible.[12] (For a brief and especially readable discussion of the distinction between experimentation and observation, see Mosteller & Tukey, 1991; for a more extended discussion of experimentation in social psychology, see Aronson, et al., 1985.)

Loopholes in the Logic of Experimental Manipulation.   Most textbooks convey the impression that the logic of the "true experiment" is airtight. But it must be confessed that there are leaks in the this logic, too. As we show in the example in the next section, and several examples

---

[12]There is another excellent property of random assignment followed by an experimental manipulation. When the original pool of subjects constitutes a biased, rather than random sample from a population (say, by taking volunteers only), the claim of a causal role for the experimental manipulation is unaffected. What changes is that this claim attaches to a *biased population*: for example, only to the subpopulation of those who tend to volunteer.

in chapter 9, there is a set of loopholes through which critics can slip alternative causal explanations. The problem is that causal force can be claimed either for the treatment itself, or for something about the treatment, usually something unintended and overlooked by the experimenter. The problem is usually more circumscribed in experiments with random assignment than in comparisons of observed groups, but it doesn't go away, as treatments are never totally pure. Let us see how this can come about, using a famous experiment in social psychology.

Argument 4: A Known Cause Produces Departure From Randomness

Example: A Paradoxical Effect of Reward.   Social psychologist Leon Festinger, in his development of cognitive dissonance theory (Festinger, 1957), put forward an interesting analysis about what would happen if you induced someone to defend a position they didn't believe in, promising them a reward for doing so. He predicted that the *smaller* the reward, the greater the tendency for the speaker to change belief to conform to his insincere behavior. The reasoning behind this prediction is that arguing against your own beliefs creates the need to rationalize your inconsistency. If you have been given a large reward, you can say to yourself that you are only doing it for the money; but a small reward provides insufficient justification for the insincerity, and your main line of excuse comes from altering your beliefs to conform to your behavior.

In the first of many experimental tests of this prediction, Festinger and Carlsmith (1959) set up a situation in which the subject, after performing two very boring tasks, was asked to tell the next subject that the tasks had been interesting. The pretext given by the experimenter for this request was that he was studying the psychological effects of expectations about tasks, and his randomized schedule called for the next subject to expect the tasks to be interesting. However (the experimenter explained in evident embarrassment), the confederate who usually planted these expectations had just called and said he couldn't come in, so the experimenter needed someone else. The experimenter said that he could pay $1 (or, for other subjects, $20) if the subject would play the needed role, and agree to be a back-up if the situation ever arose again.

Subjects typically were disarmed by this request, and of the 71 asked, 68 complied. In conversation with the next "subject" (who was really a confederate), they found themselves making up various claims of how they had enjoyed the tasks. Following this, they were thanked by the experimenter, who casually reminded them that the psychology department was conducting an interview of some sort in a room down the hall, and would they mind stopping in? (The experimenter professed not to know any details of this, other than the fact that such an interview had been announced in class—as indeed it had been.)

In this subsequent interview, subjects were asked four questions about the tasks performed in Dr. Festinger's lab. The key question was, "Were the tasks interesting and enjoyable?" Subjects were encouraged to talk about the matter, and then asked to rate the tasks on a scale from −5 (extremely dull) to +5 (extremely interesting). The mean response by the 20 subjects offered $1 was 1.35, whereas for the 20 subjects offered $20, it was −.05. The value of the t statistic given for the difference between these group means was 2.22, with $p < .03$.

The authors therefore rejected the skeptical interpretation that the difference between the means was due solely to accidents of random sampling, and concluded that the $1 group was systematically different from the $20 group, in the direction predicted by dissonance theory. The statistical aspects of this example seem straightforward. Using a t test, the null hypothesis of sheer random sampling variability was dismissed as implausible, and the systematic prediction by dissonance theory of a bigger effect in the $1 condition was considered supported. We should note here, however, that even though the statistical argument is apparently strong enough, the $1 versus $20 manipulation entails many convolutions in the experimental procedure that provide opportunities for alternative, nondissonance interpretations of the systematic group difference. For example, one critic (Rosenberg, 1965) argued that the ratings of task enjoyability in the $20 condition were lowered by many subjects because they felt guilty about accepting an apparent bribe. Twenty dollars, the argument went, must have seemed excessive for only 5 minutes of work, and the distressed subjects used the final ratings as a statement that they were not to be bribed into *believing* that the tasks were interesting. In chapter 9, we discuss further elaborations in alternative narrative accounts of the Festinger–Carlsmith (1959) experiment. Additionally, we raise in chapter 5 two quibbles with the t test presented in the authors' report of this experiment. (Is nothing sacred?)

SUMMARY

I have given an example for each of four elementary arguments: the "hot hand" data that fit a simple random generating process model; the clairvoyance data that depart from a random generation model; a questionnaire study of participation in a campus demonstration, where responses on one or more questions are consistent with a simple random sampling model; and the experiment on the effect of small reward, where a simple random sampling model is insufficient. (For the latter two arguments, I have arbitrarily chosen an observational study for an illustration of a chance result, and an experimental study for a case of a systematic result. It could easily have been the other way around.)

All four studies produce results that to many people are counterintuitive. My choice of studies with some surprise or kick to them was deliberate: such examples are more interesting and more memorable. (See chap. 8.) They motivate more extensive searches for flaws and counterarguments, and as a result of such attention and debate, stimulate theoretical extensions, generalizations, and qualifications.

Operationally, to test the adequacy of a pure-chance account of the comparative differences in your data, you must begin by conceptualizing the operation of chance. In some situations, analogous to coin flipping or other repeatable generating processes, the nature of the process determines certain statistical regularities in that type of data. By testing the approximate conformity of the data to the regularities of the chance process, you are able to decide whether to maintain the null hypothesis (perhaps reluctantly), or to argue that it is implausible under an all-chance model. The latter rhetorical flourish clears the way for a claim of a systematic factor contributing to the comparative differences in the data. The sequence of steps is much the same when chance is embodied by a random sampling model, except that in that case our ignorance of the underlying distribution of scores forces us to rely on assumptions about its approximate shape. For the simple arguments we have considered here, these approximations are usually adequate.

Caveat

In the examples presented earlier—and elsewhere in the book—the data analyses provide relatively reasonable grounds for making the categorical arguments that have become standard in null hypothesis testing, that is, either accepting or rejecting the existence of a systematic factor differentiating the means of two groups. It is often the case, however, that a given research study yields ambiguous results: There may be some indication of a systematic factor at work, but too weakly to reject a chance explanation definitively. The p value attaching to a t test may be something insipid like $p = .15$, say. Such situations are extremely common, especially in view of the low power (Cohen, 1962, 1988) typical of t tests in psychological research.

The student who encounters this situation in his or her own research project may well become paralyzed, not knowing how to write up such an outcome. My aim in this book is to highlight and encourage the essential role of argument in social science research, but how can you make an argument without a supportable premise?

The student required to submit a research report in this situation has six options, the first four of them unsatisfactory, the fifth honest but a bit nebbish, and the sixth effortful and essential. He or she can: (a) try to manufacture a forced argument that the p value is really better than it looks; (b) give the insipid p value and then proceed to ignore it in a discussion that presumes the operation of the systematic factor; (c) limply shrug off the results as possibly due to chance; (d) tell the statistical facts with no attempt to interpret what they might mean; (e) tell and comment on the statistical facts, being straightforward and nondefensive about the uncertainties involved; or (f) do more research.

The silliness and flummery associated with the first four of these options should greatly temper our reliance on p values. The accept–reject dichotomy has a seductive appeal in the context of making categorical statements such as in the four examples of this chapter. But these examples were carefully chosen to encourage simple categorical claims, and for that reason alone are atypical. Every researcher should play the part of a ruthlessly clear-headed analyst who considers the *magnitude* of effects, along with the other MAGIC criteria. Such an analyst should be capable of treating his own research outcomes with humility, for example by acknowledging that the systematic results that have been claimed are in truth rather weak, inconsistent, or hard to understand.

Of course, student research projects do not faithfully reflect the context within which serious research is conducted and published. Moreover, we have been considering only the most elementary statistical arguments, based on isolated studies. In practice, real research investigations usually involve multiple studies conducted as part of an ongoing conceptual elaboration of a particular topic. This permits a richer variety of possible assertions about outcomes than those we have considered in this chapter. In any case, serious investigators do not ordinarily submit articles without some form of interpretive argument. If they did, such articles would be unlikely to be accepted for publication, or if published, to be read. In cases of inconclusive or messy data in an uncharted area, experienced researchers will usually withhold attempts at publication until further research either clarifies what is going on, or leads the investigator to abandon the line of research entirely.

As outlined in chapter 1, there are other criteria for a good argument beyond having strong data. These are discussed in later chapters. We turn next to a detailed examination of measures of the magnitude of systematic effects.

3 Magnitude of Effects

The examples of the previous chapter were selected to lend themselves to fairly straightforward conclusions. To get us started, focus was placed on tests of statistical significance. Truth to tell, however, the information yield from null hypothesis tests is ordinarily quite modest, because all one carries away is a possibly misleading accept–reject decision. Furthermore, the categorical mode of thinking encouraged by significance tests can lead to misinterpretations of comparative results (see chap. 4; see also Cohen, 1990; Gigerenzer, 1993).

For this among other reasons, it is wise to supplement or replace the qualitative outcome of the null hypothesis test with something more quantitative, indicative of the degree of difference between two means, or of other types of effects. There are several candidates for such measures, each with its own advantages and disadvantages.

The simple idea of using the obtained p value is not satisfactory, for reasons to be indicated, and we discuss several other approaches: indices of *effect size* (Cohen, 1988), now in common use in meta-analysis (Rosenthal, 1991); the *ratio of effect size to "cause size,"* by analogy with dose-response analysis in biostatistics (Goldstein, 1964); and *confidence limits.* We also consider *Bayesian analysis* (Edwards, Lindman, & Savage, 1963; Winkler, 1972). Here we concentrate on the simple situation of a single comparison, deferring to chapter 7 a discussion of the aggregation of results over many studies.

PROBABILITY MEASURES

The p Value from a Significance Test

The particular level (p value) at which the null hypothesis is rejected (.05, .02, .01, etc.) is often used as a gauge of the degree of contempt in which the null hypothesis deserves to be held. Rhetorically and qualitatively, this is perfectly reasonable. Clearly it should be hard for a skeptic to maintain the null hypothesis when the data have only one chance in a thousand of having arisen from it. As a magnitude measure, the significance level has the attraction that statistical computer packages commonly provide the precise p values for a variety of test procedures. Significance levels also have the nice (though not unique) feature that it is easy to combine p values from several independent tests of the same null hypothesis to generate an overall significance test (Rosenthal, 1978).

But these virtues are dangerous. A major difficulty with simply using the significance level is that the p value depends not only on the degree of departure from the null hypothesis, but also on the sample size. Thus with very large samples, small effects can readily achieve extreme significance levels. With tens or hundreds of thousands of cases, as in mass aptitude or ability tests, or millions of cases, as with census data, significance tests are almost totally uninformative; whether the p value comes out .0001 or .00001 or .000001 is not a useful distinction.[1]

A Common Confusion.   There is also a common confusion when using the significance level as an indicator of the merit of the outcome. When the null hypothesis is rejected at, say, the .01 level, a correct way to state what has happened is as follows: "If it were true that there were no systematic difference between the means in the populations from which the samples came, then the probability that the observed means would have been as different as they were, or more different, is less than one in a hundred. This being strong grounds for doubting the viability of the null hypothesis, the null hypothesis is rejected." It is only a short misstep from this clumsy but correct statement of the null hypothesis logic to the more pithy but incorrect summary, "The probability that the null hypothesis is true is less than one in a hundred." Students and even some experienced researchers make this kind of misstatement very frequently (Cohen, in press; Oakes, 1986). It is a very seductive mistake, because the second statement is both simpler and seemingly more definite, and it is hard to see what is wrong with it.

The error arises from a general confusion about *conditional* probabilities (Dawes, Mirels, Gold, & Donahue, 1993), whereby the probability

---

[1]This effect of large samples seems to trivialize the whole enterprise of significance testing. A Yale graduate student once put the matter this way in presenting his research: "I did not carry out any significance tests on my results, because all of them would be significant just by having the samples be large enough." This methodologically blasphemous statement was so suddenly and casually delivered that the audience (myself included) was momentarily stunned, and unable to mobilize an immediate rejoinder. The statement is misguided, but can the reader say why?... (For the answer, see the following note.)[2]

[2]The appropriate challenge to the student should have been, "Will you guarantee that the direction of each of your results would be as you state if you had had a larger sample?"!

of the data given a hypothesis is mistakenly equated with the probability of the hypothesis given the data. (Illustration: compare the probability of testing positive for a very rare disease if you have it with the probability of having it if you test positive for it. If you think these two probabilities are the same, you have failed to take the "base rates" into account. The second probability is typically less than the first, because it is very unlikely for *anybody* to have a very rare disease, even those who test positive.)

The Probability (?) of a Greenhouse Effect.   As an example of this error in an important practical context, consider a scientist discussing the potential reality of the greenhouse effect, after an unusually hot summer. He testifies that the average absolute value of yearly change in mean measured temperature over the globe is historically on the order of .2°F, with a standard deviation of about .25, but that the change during the past year had been a rise of .75°F. When referred to the historical distribution of mean temperature changes, a jump of as much as .75 has less than one chance in a hundred of belonging to that distribution, and therefore the null hypothesis that the rise in temperature that particular year was due to a random sampling process can be rejected at the .01 level. He then goes on to say that it is therefore 99% certain that the warming trend was caused by the greenhouse effect. If the chance explanation had only a 1% probability, then the alternative, systematic explanation of the greenhouse effect must have a 99% probability....

Sounds reasonable. What's wrong with this reasoning? At least three things: First of all, increased focus was placed on the temperature change data mainly because the rise was so unusual, and if the only time you test the null hypothesis is on those rare occasions when it looks obviously false, then of course you increase your chances of declaring it false—even if it were true. This phenomenon of post hoc focusing is an example of the "hocus focus" trick discussed in chapter 4. Second, no consideration was given to the probability that the same temperature rise would have occurred under a hypothetical greenhouse model. Third, there might be *other* systematic forces at work, unrelated to the greenhouse effect, to create a big rise in temperature.

The Whodunit Analogy.   Let us clarify the second of these problems. The null hypothesis is always, implicitly or explicitly, in competition with alternative hypotheses, and if one wants to make a quantitative statement about the probability that the null hypothesis is the appropriate one, the *relative* abilities of the competing hypotheses to explain the data at hand must be considered. One cannot simply convert the significance level at which the null hypothesis has been rejected into a quantitative index of its truth value. An analogy may be drawn with the situation faced by a detective solving a whodunit, who estimates that if the butler did it, there was only one chance in a hundred he could have made his escape unseen. Should the detective therefore conclude that there is only one chance in a hundred that the butler is the murderer? Well, though it might seem so at first, reflection reveals a problem. Suppose that the only other suspects are the maid and the chauffeur. If the maid did it, the chances that she would have escaped unseen were only one in a thousand. And for the chauffeur, even less. But somebody must have done it. Thus when unlikely hypotheses are in competition with each other, the potential truth value of each must be enhanced (see Einhorn & Hogarth, 1986). In the next section, we consider a potential fix for this problem.

The Bayesian Approach

For many years, there has existed in the statistical community an alternative to classical significance testing. It involves the use of Bayes' Theorem, and devotees of this approach are called Bayesians (Edwards et al., 1963).

The theorem addresses the problem introduced earlier, namely, how to take account of the competition between a hypothesis and its alternatives. A given set of data is seen as altering the odds (i.e., the relative likelihood) that a hypothesis is true, compared to its alternatives. To apply Bayes' Theorem, one needs some estimate of these odds *before* the data are collected. The data then may tip the balance in these odds, depending on the relative likelihood of the data under the hypothesis and its alternatives. To simplify the discussion, we take H to be a substantive hypothesis based on some systematic model (e.g., the greenhouse effect), and consider only a single alternative—not-H, the null hypothesis (e.g., chance variation in temperatures). (Bayesian analysis extends to the case of several distinct alternatives to H, and even to the case of a continuum of alternatives, but for clarity of the present discussion, we set these complications aside.)

We use the following notation: $P(H/D)$ = the probability that hypothesis H is true, given data D; $P(-H/D)$ = the probability that not-H is true, given data D; $P(H)$ = the *prior* probability that H was true (before the data); $P(-H)$ = the prior probability that not-H was true; $P(D/H)$ = the probability of the data occurring, given H as true; $P(D/-H)$ = the probability of the data, given not-H as true.

The *odds-ratio* form of Bayes' Theorem (Winkler, 1972, p. 412):

$$\frac{P(H/D)}{P(H/-D)} = \frac{P(H)}{P(-H)} \times \frac{P(D/H)}{P(D/-H)} \tag{1}$$

says that: *posterior odds = prior odds × relative likelihood.*

The ratio on the left of the equation represents the odds favoring hypothesis H over not-H after the data are gathered—the *posterior odds*. The first ratio on the right gives the odds favoring H over not-H *prior* to the data collection—the *prior odds*; the last ratio specifies the *relative likelihood* of the data under H versus under not-H. The formula says that the posterior odds in favor of a hypothesis, given the data, are equal to the odds beforehand, multiplied by the relative likelihoods of the data under H versus not-H.

Example. The Greenhouse Effect.   In principle this is a swell scheme, as it promises to address the butler/maid and greenhouse interpretive problems discussed previously. Take the greenhouse problem. Suppose reasonable people believed the odds were 2:1 in favor of the greenhouse hypothesis before the scientist's testimony was introduced. Now his analysis, properly interpreted, says that *if no greenhouse effect existed*, the rise in yearly temperature he observed had a probability of 1 in 100. What he did not supply, but we also need, is the probability of the same temperature rise *if the greenhouse effect held*. Let us pull a number out of a hat, and suppose that this probability was 3 in 100. Then the relative likelihoods of the temperature data with versus without the greenhouse effect would be 3:1. Multiplying this ratio by the prior odds (2:1) favoring greenhouse, we end up with posterior odds of 6:1 in its favor. Odds can be converted back into probabilities by the relationship (probability = odds/(1 + odds)). Thus the probability of greenhouse in this hypothetical case would be (6/7) = .857.

A Bayesian Magnitude Measure.   In this example, we came to the (hypothetical) conclusion that the increase in global temperature raised the odds favoring the existence of a greenhouse effect from 2:1 beforehand to 6:1 afterwards. We might wonder what index of strength to assign to the data in this case—and in general, how to use Bayesian analysis for measuring the magnitude of a data effect. The posterior odds on hypothesis H do not seem to yield a reasonable index of the strength of the data, as these odds are a function of both the data and the prior odds. A better index would seem to be the *change in odds* in favor of H brought about by the data D. A convenient measure of this change is simply the posterior odds divided by the prior odds, and we find by rearranging Equation 1 that this ratio equals the relative likelihood of the data under H and not-H: Therefore one might propose this relative likelihood as a measure of the strength of the data in support of H (and against not-H).

Difficulties With the Bayesian Approach.   In the context of testing the difference between two means, not-H represents the null hypothesis of no difference, and $P(D/-H)$ is the ordinary p value. Hypothesis H

represents a systematic alternative to the null hypothesis, and $P(D/H)$ the probability of the data under *that* hypothesis. A major problem is that $P(D/H)$ is typically a composite hypothesis over different possible degrees of systematic effect. For each possibility, $P(D/H)$ is different, and we will not know nor feel comfortable guessing how to weight them.[3]

A nagging second problem is that dividing the posterior odds by the prior odds would be arithmetically illegitimate should $P(H)$, the prior probability that H is true, be zero. The $P(H) = 0$ case raises interesting issues.

Hypotheses That Can't Be True: The Philpott Example.   A curious argument over an obscure British experiment sharply illustrates the issue of the zero prior probability. In the late 1940s, a British psychologist named S. J. F. Philpott reported a series of experiments that he claimed as strong support for the existence of a fundamental constant of mental processing time, 40.76 *septillionths* of a second (Philpott, 1950). His reasoning was based (never mind the details) on the distribution of times to completion of sets of arithmetic problems by experimental subjects. He constructed an experimental comparison from which he argued that if the null hypothesis of chance between-group differences were rejected, the only alternative would be to accept his fundamental constant. Philpott then presented data that purportedly required rejection of the null hypothesis at the .01 level, and touted this as strong evidence in favor of his proposed constant.

In a telling critique, the redoubtable L. F. Richardson (1952) argued that the natural variability of the latency of each component process would be orders of magnitude greater than the purported constant, and measurement errors would swamp the investigation of Philpott's (1950) assumption, anyway. This theory was so incredible, in Richardson's opinion, that it deserved to be assigned a prior probability, $P(H)$, of zero. If the value $P(H) = 0$ is inserted into the Bayesian Equation 1, then inexorably, $P(H/D)$ will be zero. (The only loophole would occur if $P(D/-H)$ were also zero, but that would have required that Philpott's data had achieved the .00000000... significance level.) In other words, if a hypothesis is certainly false to begin with, then no finite set of data can add any credence to it.

In the Philpott–Richardson debate, Richardson was articulate, polite, and undoubtedly right—indeed, Philpott's research has faded into obscurity. But one should appreciate that Richardson's line of argument could become mischievous if applied by an irresponsible critic to any

---

[3]When the hypothesis H is a discrete choice among two possibilities, Bayesian analysis proceeds with greater facility. Mosteller and Wallace (1964) carried out a famous Bayesian application to the question of whether Alexander Hamilton (H) or James Madison ($-H$) wrote several disputed *Federalist Papers*. The posterior odds came out very heavily in favor of Madison. This study is discussed in further detail in chapter 8.

novel hypothesis. In essence the argument says, "The data be damned, you're obviously wrong"—hardly an attitude in the true scientific spirit.[4] Thus the introduction of prior probabilities, the core of the Bayesian approach, highlights the vulnerability of the results of a single experiment to a debate that degenerates when a vocal critic or cabal believes that $P(H) = 0$.

The Bayesian Reply on Impossible Hypotheses.   Bayesians might reply that priors should be based on logic or on previous data, not on mere opinion. Anyway, $P(H) = 0$ is an extreme case that would stunt debate whether or not a Bayesian argument were made. In other cases what the "priors" do is to permit investigators to reach their own short-run judgment of $P(H/D)$, which then becomes a prior probability awaiting the next set of data. In the long run, evidence from data sets $D_1, D_2, D_3,...$ will in principle cause $P(H/D_1,D_2,D_3,...)$, the probability of the hypothesis given *all* the data, to converge on a consensual value, independent of the starting preconception P(H). In chapters 7–9, we will discuss repeated research tests. For the case of the single study, what the Bayesian approach does is to raise the important issue of the *change in relative belief* in a hypothesis from before to after the data collection.

Having said this, however, we may be led to wonder whether change in belief is a measure of the magnitude of an effect, or of something else. A piece of research that radically changes our beliefs in alternative hypotheses is certainly influential, and in that sense "strong," but one could have a strong belief in a small effect, or a weak belief in a large effect. Change of belief seems to have something to do with *interestingness*, which we discuss in chapter 8. We turn next to measures of effect size per se.

EFFECT SIZES

The Raw Effect Size

Setting aside thorny considerations of probability, the most obvious candidate for quantifying the strength of a conclusion from a simple significance test is the raw magnitude of the effect: in the case of a t test of a mean difference, the size of the observed mean difference. On the

---

[4]An interesting example of the conflict between scientific open-mindedness and the presentation of what seems to be a totally ridiculous hypothesis occurs in an exchange of data (Orme-Johnson, Alexander, Davies, Chandler, & Larimore, 1988) and commentary (Duval, 1988; Orme-Johnson, Alexander, & Davies, 1990; Russett, 1988; Schrodt, 1990) on the "Maharishi effect." The hypothesis was that the frequency and severity of wars, crimes, and accidents decreases as a direct function of the number of people engaged in transcendental meditation at an isolated site within the geographical region.

face of it, big effects are more impressive and important than small effects.

One advantage of the raw effect size as a measure is that its expected value is independent of the size of the sample used to perform the significance test. A second advantage is that it is expressed directly in the units of the scale of the dependent variable, and sizes of difference along that scale ought to be meaningful to the investigator.

On the other hand, it could be argued that with a smallish sample, one might obtain a big apparent effect without being able to reject the null hypothesis. In other words, an effect size ought not be judged totally in isolation, but in conjunction with the p value (which in turn depends on the sample size and the within-group variability). For fixed n, an observed mean difference is more impressive to the extent that it is statistically more reliable, that is, the within-group variability is smaller. In the end, of course, what the investigator would like to know about an effect size measure is how consistently big it is over a series of experiments.

There may be a more telling disadvantage to the raw effect size measure. Even though one might think that the investigator ought to be familiar with his or her response scale, it is frequently the case in psychology that new scales are developed for new research purposes, and the units along the scale have not acquired much meaning. It takes experience with the research area to have a good feeling for what magnitude of difference along the response scale would be truly consequential. Is a between-group mean difference of three quarters of a point on a 7-point attitude scale a big difference? Is a difference of 25 milliseconds noteworthy in a novel type of reaction time experiment? A one-shot study in a new area may thus suffer from the rhetorical weakness that the effect size is not readily interpretable.

The Standardized Effect Size

In view of this, it is useful to have an index that is conceptually independent of the response scale. Such an index is the standardized effect size, defined as the raw effect size divided by the standard deviation of scores (within groups) on the response scale. Thus if on a 21-point scale, the experimental group has a mean of 13, the control group has a mean of 11, and the standard deviation of individual scores around their group means is 3.0, the standardized effect size is .667. This type of standardized measure first arose in power analysis (Cohen, 1962, 1988), where effect sizes need to be scale independent.

The standardized effect size is one index favored by devotees of meta-analysis (see chap. 7). Its independence of response scale is especially advantageous when combining studies with different response scales. Other dimensionless indices, such as a correlation coefficient r, also arise in the meta-analytic family (Mullen, 1989), and may be more adaptable to results arising from a mish-mash of different significance tests. The measure r is the ordinary Pearson product–moment correlation coefficient between the independent and dependent variables. In the case where the means of two groups are compared, r is the "point biserial" correlation (Mullen, 1989, p. 96). Its value can be ascertained readily as a function of the sample sizes and the standardized effect size (or the value of t in the between-group t test; Rosenthal, 1991). Another possible magnitude measure is r^2—the proportion of explained variance—but as we noted in chapter 1, this tends to convey too pessimistic an impression.

Like raw effect size, we should note, the value of the standardized effect size (or one of its variants) does not by itself tell us that the null hypothesis can be rejected. That outcome depends not only on the effect size, but also on the sample sizes in the study (Mullen, 1989). However, as social scientists move gradually away from reliance on single studies and obsession with null hypothesis testing, effect size measures will become more and more popular.

Causal Efficacy

In an insightful article entitled "When Small Effects are Impressive," Prentice and Miller (1992) argued that striking and memorable research results in psychology sometimes can come from studies in which effect sizes are small. They cited two circumstances in which this can happen: (a) when the manipulation of the independent variable is minimal, and (b) when the dependent variable seems difficult to influence.

An example of the first case is Isen and Levin's (1972) study of the effects of good mood on helping behavior, wherein students casually given a cookie while studying in the library were subsequently much more generous in volunteering to help another student than were students not given a cookie. (The average offers of helping time in the experimental and control groups were 69 minutes and 17 minutes, respectively.) This study makes its point pithily because a cookie seems a trivial and irrelevant influence on altruistic behavior.

An example of the second case is Milgram's (1963) famous obedience paradigm. Milgram's studies feature both a seemingly small manipulation—an authority figure telling the subjects to continue in the experiment—and the unthinkable response of shocking a helpless victim beyond the level of clear mortal danger.[5] What these examples have in common is that the research audiences presumably did not expect the effects to come out at all, much less to be as big as they were. (Working

---

[5]Prentice and Miller (1992) did not cite the Milgram (1963) example. They were concerned primarily with impressive *small* effects, and of course the Milgram effect was large.

52 extra minutes per cookie does not translate into a living wage!) We propose that the rhetorical impact of a research result is a direct function of the raw effect size divided by the "cause size," a ratio that we call *causal efficacy*. A large effect from a small variation in the cause is the most impressive, whereas a small effect arising from an apparently large causal manipulation is the most anticlimactic and disappointing. Causal efficacy is akin—in the military jargon of the late Cold War—to "bang for the buck."

Example of Low Causal Efficacy: Saccharin and Cancer.   To articulate this concept further, it will help to consider an example with an extremely low value of causal efficacy. When the investigator labors mightily to bring forth a mouse, the audience is likely to be unimpressed to the point of scorn. This indeed happened in the study of the effects of saccharin on bladder cancer. The Food and Drug Administration is enjoined by the Delaney Amendment (National Research Council, 1979) to ban all substances that have been "found to induce cancer when ingested by man or animal" (chap.2, p. 10). The reason animals are included in this injunction is that it is extraordinarily difficult to carry out conclusive toxicity studies on humans (true experiments with random assignment of subjects to toxic conditions being out of the question). Experiments with (say) rats are easy to run except for one catch: The cancer rates are generally so small that an impractically large sample of animals is required to reliably demonstrate effects of small toxic dosages.

The usual research strategy adopted in such circumstances is to use a modest number of animals and hype up the dosage. The most frequently quoted study on saccharin used such a strategy (Food and Drug Administration, 1973). The diet of the experimental rats was 7.5% saccharin daily, for a period of 2 years. At the end of that time, 7 of 23 experimental rats had contracted bladder cancer, whereas only 1 of 25 saccharin-free rats had done so—a statistically significant difference. This study was taken to be respectable and important by reputable scientific judges (National Research Council, 1978), but was greeted by public ridicule. Someone in the diet soda industry (which had a self-interest in keeping saccharin in their sodas) calculated that the dosage for the experimental rats was the equivalent of the saccharin in 800 cans of diet soda per day for a human. The study was editorially chastised ("Overstated Risks," 1979), partly on the grounds that such a huge intake would be preposterous even for the most devoted soda fiend, and therefore that the risk had been wildly exaggerated. A person drinking 800 cans of soda a day would die from hyperextended innards long before succumbing to cancer, argued the study's detractors.

The Dose Response Curve.   There are indeed difficulties in applying animal research results to the danger of cancer in humans, not least of which is the large variability in the susceptibility of different species to different forms of cancer. But the large-dosage strategy with rats is not as lunatic as it might sound. The scientific community is accustomed to thinking about systematic variations in the strength of causes, and how this bears upon effects. The most persuasive evidence establishing smoking as a cause of cancer was not simply the finding that smokers had higher cancer rates than nonsmokers, but the systematic climb in cancer rates with increases in smoking rates, among other things (see chap. 9).

Biostatisticians refer to the probability of disease or death as a function of the rate of toxic exposure as the *dose response curve*. With an appropriate transformation of the probability scale,[6] the curve often becomes a straight line. If dose response is in fact linear for rats ingesting saccharin, then the morbidity probability at very high dosages can be scaled back to get an estimate of the small probability that would obtain at lower, more typical dosages. If we accept this logic, and take the rat results to be relevant to humans, the conclusion is that saccharin increases the risk of bladder cancer, but not by much.

The linearity assumption is fragile, and my point is not to defend it in this particular case. I cite the example simply to elaborate on the concept of causal efficacy, and to illustrate how unimpressed the public can be by research results with apparently very small efficacy.

Objective Causal Efficacy.   Dose response studies have the special property that the independent variable is physically quantified, so that cause size can be precisely specified (say, in milligrams per day). Meanwhile, the raw effect size is a simple function of the relative proportions of death or disease in treated versus control animals. Because both causes and effects are objectively quantifiable, the ratio of effect size to cause size in this case can be termed *objective causal efficacy*.

Subjective Causal Efficacy.   How are we to operationalize cause size in the common type of psychological study with *qualitative* variation in the independent variable, such as giving the subject a free cookie? With respect to its effect on altruistic behavior, we should not really be reckoning the cause size of a free cookie by the economic value of the cookie. Isen and Levin (1972) hypothesized that the effect is mediated by good mood, and one would like to be able to scale the goodness of cookie-induced mood relative to other good mood inducers such as receiving praise for performance on a test, or finding a dime left in a telephone booth. One way to try this is by eliciting ratings from subjects,

---

[6]The most common transformations of p are the cumulative normal ogive (the probit) and the logistic function (the logit). Both transformations act so as to "stretch the tails" of p, so that the difference between the transforms of, say, .01 and .02 is a good deal larger than that between .49 and .50. The formula for the logit is $\ln[p/(1 - p)]$.

as is done with *manipulation checks* (Aronson et al., 1985). These ratings are used to check that subjects have registered the intended manipulation of the independent variable (e.g., good or bad mood). Applying such ratings to the assessment of causal efficacy would permit calculation of the ratio of effect size to *experienced* differences on the causal variable (e.g., a 10% increase in helping behavior per point on a 7-point rating scale of pleasantness of mood). Such an index might be called *subjective causal efficacy*. In forming such an efficacy ratio, both effect size and cause size should be *raw* mean differences.

Example. A Bias in Judgments of Manuscript Quality.   To illustrate, consider an experiment by Wilson, DePaulo, Mook, and Klaaren (1993). They hypothesized that a group of scientists reading flawed research studies about important topics (e.g., prevention of heart disease) would rate them as more methodologically rigorous than would an equivalent group of scientists reading identical research studies about unimportant topics (e.g., prevention of heartburn). Six pairs of topics differing in importance were used. Each scientist rated three important and three unimportant studies on 9-point scales for methodological rigor and perceived importance.

The manipulation of importance (e.g., heart attack vs. heartburn) did register with the subjects. The mean rating of perceived importance of the supposedly important studies was 7.15, and of the supposedly unimportant studies, 4.44, yielding a huge mean difference of 2.71.

In the test of the hypothesized bias, the overall mean ratings of methodological rigor were 2.91 for the important studies, and 2.61 for the unimportant studies, a (statistically significant) difference of .30. The subjective causal efficacy is (.30/2.71) = .11 units of increase in judged rigor per unit of judged importance. This coefficient should be interpreted like a (raw) regression coefficient.[7] This subjective causal efficacy of .11, although significantly different from zero, is rather

---

[7]Judd, McClelland, and Culhane (in press) discussed effect size estimates entirely in terms of the slope of the regression of the dependent on the independent variable. Formally, this is equivalent to the ratio we have called causal efficacy. However, for the very common case of the comparison of the means of two conditions differing on an unquantified variable, the conditions variable must be "dummy coded" (say, +1 vs. −1). However subtly, this practice serves to discourage thinking about the extent to which the conditions differ in their cause size. It is extraordinary that the causal variable has been largely ignored in treatments of effect size.

In this vein, it is interesting to compare regressionlike coefficients, such as causal efficacy, with correlational measures such as the r recommended by Rosenthal (1991) for meta-analysis. Although correlation and regression are often conflated in the minds of social scientists, there is an important difference. Correlation coefficients are sensitive to an artifact called "restriction of range" (Cohen & Cohen, 1983, pp. 70–72): When the distribution of scores on variable X is for some reason truncated so as to eliminate the tails, the correlations between X and other variables decline. The same is not true for linear

modest. It signifies that even if the most extremely important study (a rating of 9) were compared with the most extremely unimportant study (a rating of 1), the difference in the expected judgment of rigor would only be $[.11 \times (9 - 1)] = .88$, less than one unit on the 9-point scale. (Still, as the authors argued, judgments of rigor ought not to be influenced by perceived importance at all.)

Unexpectedly Big Effect Sizes: The Milgram Study.   There remain cases of qualitative variations in the independent variable that cannot sensibly be rated by subjects. In the famous Milgram (1963) study, for example, what is the cause size of an authority figure in a white coat telling an experimental subject that it is necessary to continue shocking the screaming man in the next room? The cause is not physical, and it is not reasonable to ask subjects how obedient they feel. Although there is no way in such cases to attach a number to the cause size, the observed effect size can still be compared to a useful baseline figure, namely the expected effect size. One can ask interested observers what size of raw effect they expect, and calculate the mean of these expectations. In the Milgram study a number of students were in fact asked what percentage of subjects would deliver the maximum shock. These worthies gave a mean estimate of 1.2%, whereas the actual result was 65% (Milgram, 1963).

Intuitively, the discrepancy between the observed raw effect size and the expected raw effect size is directly related to the *surprisingness* of the result. In chapter 8 we define a *surprisingness coefficient* (S), primarily as it relates to interestingness, although it might also be regarded as a magnitude measure. We postpone the details, other than to say that in the Milgram (1963) case, the surprisingness coefficient is 1.28—where 1.0 represents a highly surprising result, and 2.0 the maximum possible surprise. (The latter value would arise if the expected effect were 0% and the obtained effect 100%, or vice versa.) Milgram asked for subjective estimates as a public relations device, but it is reasonable to imagine less sensational experiments for which the experimenter asks particular research audiences for subjective estimates of raw effect sizes.

Expected Effect Sizes are Like Bayesian Priors.   Note that this line of thinking uses effect sizes to do something like what Bayesian

---

regressions, however. The slope (b) of the regression line giving the expected magnitude of some variable as a function of X is not systematically affected by truncation.

The relevance of this point is that small cause sizes are analogous to restricted ranges. Rosenthal's (1991) measure r is therefore apt to come out too small whenever the independent variable is experimentally manipulated only modestly. By contrast, causal efficacy measures will (assuming linearity) tend to come out the same whether the cause sizes are small or large.

reasoning does with probabilities. The expected effect size acts like a Bayesian prior probability, and for any given effect, different investigators and commentators may have different priors. The obtained outcome of a well-conducted study will modify the expected effect size away from the prior toward the observed result. Upon replication, new data may impel a further adjustment in the expected effect size, and so on. In well-behaved cases, the expected effect size will converge to the true effect size, independent of the original prior. The research community will have learned what to expect, and the surprisingness coefficient will approach zero. People who have been exhaustively informed about the Milgram (1963) study and related research now should realize that having an authority figure tell an experimental subject to continue a behavior is in fact an extremely powerful influence. Sophisticated observers asked to predict the fraction of the population harming others at the instruction of a high-status authority figure will presumably no longer say 1%, but something closer to 65%.

CONFIDENCE LIMITS

Thus far we have discussed two types of criteria for assessing the magnitude of the effect in a simple study comparing the means of two groups: probabilities and effect sizes. The latter category includes raw and standardized mean differences. If we also take into account prior expectations or cause sizes, then we can countenance still further variations, namely Bayesian posterior probabilities or various estimates of causal efficacy.

Another way of representing effect magnitude arises through the use of *confidence limits*. One makes statements of the form, "With 95% confidence, the true experimental effect lies somewhere between A and B." Confidence limits on mean differences have the property that they bracket zero if and only if the null hypothesis is retained (at the significance level expressed as 100% minus the confidence level). When the null hypothesis is dismissed, one can be confident of the *direction* of the effect, and then use the confidence limits to establish boundaries on the likely size of effect. Confidence limits have been enthusiastically recommended (e.g., by Bailar & Mosteller, 1988; Cohen, in press; Tukey, 1991; and many others) as an alternative to p values in statements of results, because the confidence limits give more information: In particular, they specify a plausible minimum and maximum degree of departure of the mean difference from zero.

It takes two quantities, the lower boundary and the upper boundary, to specify confidence limits. If we use two-index summaries, the choice would be between confidence limits on the one hand, and p value accompanied by effect size on the other. Another possibility is to use confidence limits on some measure of effect size.

As Tukey (1991) pointed out, confidence limits on raw effect sizes are particularly valuable when there are interesting benchmarks along the scale of measurement. In many applied areas where new programs or therapies are being evaluated, one may want to know not just whether the average improvement for the recipients is greater than zero. More relevant may be whether the improvement is above a specified threshold given by economic, political, or practical considerations, or by comparison with a historically typical improvement. Or, in testing a treatment that costs less or has fewer side effects than the conventional therapy, one might want to know if the new treatment were at least (say) 90% as effective as the conventional one.

In later chapters, particularly chapter 7 covering meta-analysis, we analyze tabulations containing one magnitude index per study, and therefore fall back on effect sizes. The emphasis on an effect size strategy entails no intended criticism of confidence limits. Indeed, with clever graphical techniques for representing confidence limits jointly for multiple studies (Tukey, 1991), having two measures per study entails no serious loss of conciseness.

In the next two chapters, we discuss styles of statistical rhetoric (chap. 4), and detective work (chap. 5), before returning to the exposition of the last four of the MAGIC criteria.

4 Styles of Rhetoric

The investigator's usual desire to have strong results can exert a biasing influence on his or her presentation of a study's outcomes. The indicators of effect magnitude discussed in chapter 3 can often be exaggerated in the telling, and investigators differ in their tendencies toward exaggeration or understatement of results. Stylistic variations are most obvious in the treatment of p values. Despite warning the reader of overattention to ps, this chapter devotes attention to them because they are ubiquitous in the social science literature. It is clear, though, that over- or underexaggeration tendencies also apply to other magnitude indicators. Some researchers, for example, call correlation coefficients of .35 "modest," whereas others label them "substantial." Furthermore, investigators have a great deal of leeway to pick and choose which aspects of the results to emphasize. As Rosenthal (1991) said in reference to the reporting of studies, "a fairly ambiguous result often becomes quite smooth and rounded in the discussion section" (p. 13).

BRASH, STUFFY, LIBERAL, AND CONSERVATIVE STYLES

Consider the situation of the investigator obsessing over prospective significance tests. Aside from a few rare examples such as those given in chapter 2, acceptance of the null hypothesis is usually a dull outcome that seems to brand the research a waste of time. On the other hand, rejection of the null hypothesis suggests that some systematic, explanatory factor is causing the groups to be different. "Yes, there is a group difference favoring Group A over Group B" is clearly a more satisfying statement than "there could be a difference favoring Group A over Group B, but that result cannot be claimed with confidence."

It is only natural for researchers to prefer saying something of substance to saying something vapid. Negative results often do not even get written up. Students may abandon dissertations because null hypotheses cannot be rejected. Faculty members, journal editors, and other readers of manuscripts often react less kindly toward accepted than rejected null hypotheses (see Greenwald, 1975, and Rosenthal, 1979, for a discussion of these attitudes and their consequences). Given all this, it is very tempting for people to try desperately to make their results come out statistically significant. In the peculiar language of American politics, one might say that investigators try to exert "spin control" over the interpretations of their results. This is especially true for outcomes that are *almost* significant, say, $.05 < p < .10$. The game then becomes one of somehow pushing the results toward or beyond the conventional $p = .05$ level.

The Brash Style

What devices are available to the desperate researcher for arguing that the results look good, when a dispassionate observer would say they are marginal or worse? There are at least five:

1. Use a one-tailed test.
2. When there is more than one test procedure available, use the one producing the most significant result(s).
3. Either include or exclude "outliers" from the data, depending on which works better.
4. When several outcomes are tested simultaneously, focus on the one(s) with the best p value(s)—the "hocus focus" trick.
5. State the actual p value, but talk around it.

Sophisticated readers of research reports are of course aware of these devices, and will recognize blatant attempts by the author to make weak p values sound strong. The net result of the usual built-in motivation to reject null hypotheses is thus to create a temptation to overstate one's results, balanced by the risk that one will be found out, at some loss to one's immediate case and long-run reputation. In terms of our legal analogy, this is the dilemma faced by a lawyer who is offered a sizable fee to defend a client of questionable virtue. With enough inventiveness, a case may be drawn in defense of almost any client; but to manufacture flimsy arguments may eventually justify the attribution that one is a shyster. This is an especially damaging attribution for a scientific researcher, which is why we emphasize that researchers should be like *honest* lawyers.

We refer to the rhetorical style that overstates every statistical result as *brash*. Investigators who use the five devices previously listed, freely and inappropriately, invite skepticism and disfavor.

The Stuffy Style

Life would be simple if one could give the unqualified advice to the statistics user, "Never be brash." Among other things, this would imply total abstinence from any of the five devices that enhance the argument for rejection of the null hypothesis. Indeed, some statistics texts and some statistics instructors come close to this flat-out admonition. Taking the five devices one by one, the most complete injunction against brashness would be as follows:

1. Never use one-tailed tests.
2. Only use a single, predetermined analysis for any data set.
3. Never exclude outliers.
4. Avoid special focus on any particular result, especially if it is favorable.
5. Stick strictly to a fixed significance level, for example, .05, and make no distinctions between outcomes that nearly beat it ($p <$ .06, say), and those far from significance.

When such proscriptions are packaged together, the net effect is to make statistical analysis into a set of legal or moral imperatives, such as might be announced at a public swimming pool. (ABSOLUTELY NO DOGS OR FRISBEES ALLOWED. VIOLATORS WILL BE PROS-ECUTED.) The teaching and learning of statistics as a series of "don'ts" can be so intimidating that students are often heard to ask the question, "Can I do this analysis?" as though seeking permission from a higher authority who will guarantee their immunity from prosecution. This style of thinking about statistics goes to the oppo-site extreme from the excesses of brashness. We refer to it as the *stuffy* style of rhetoric. In Tukey's (1969) terms, this approach views statistics as a ritual of *sanctification*, destroying the exercise of statistical detective work.

As we see in this and subsequent chapters, there are sometimes good reasons to depart from the stuffy style, and the student who acts on these reasons should not be "left with feelings of dishonesty and guilt at having violated the rules" (Gigerenzer, 1993, p. 326). To the student who asks, "Can I do this?" a reasonable answer is: You can *do* anything you choose, and ponder the potential meaning of the results for your re-search. But keep in mind that the way you present the outcome(s) will affect the persuasiveness of the case you make. Usually it's not good to be too brash, but you don't want to be so pompous that you avoid the most cogent analysis. (At this point the student will probably say, "Yes, but can I *do* this?" whereupon you should send out for pizza and repeat your advice as many times as necessary.)

Liberal and Conservative Styles

The two extremes of unrestrained brashness and stultifying pomposity bracket a dimension along which styles of approach to statistics may vary. A *liberal* style emphasizes exploration of, and speculation about data. It is looser, more subjective, and more adventurous. A *conservative* style is tighter, more codified, and more cautious. In statistics as in politics, either style can be defended, and there are individual differences in preference. Also as in politics, the most successful arguments are those that satisfy both liberals and conservatives. This will happen when the investigator's substantive claims are backed by conservative procedures, because in that case the claims would also be warranted by liberal standards. Contrariwise, when a liberal approach produces null results, a conservative approach will, too.

Debatable cases arise when null hypotheses are rejected according to liberal test procedures, but accepted by conservative tests. In these circumstances, reasonable people may disagree. The investigator faces an apparent dilemma: "Should I pronounce my results significant according to liberal criteria, risking skepticism by critical readers, or should I play it safe with conservative procedures and have nothing much to say?" In the next few sections, we sketch some of the contextual features tilting the resolution one way or the other, keyed to our five rhetorical devices.

ONE-TAILED, TWO-TAILED, AND LOPSIDED TESTS

Consider the t test for the significance of the difference between the means (A and B) of two groups. This test is usually conducted on a two-tailed basis: If t has a large positive value (with A notably larger than B), or a large negative value (B larger than A), there are grounds for rejecting the null hypothesis. The rejection region—the set of outcomes that will count against the null hypothesis—is divided equally between the positive and negative tails of the t distribution. For the 5% level, each tail contains 2.5% of the total area under the t curve.

When there is a strong theoretical expectation that any group difference will be in a given direction (say, A > B), some investigators and textbook writers consider it permissible to use a one-tailed test, that is, to concentrate the rejection region all in the predicted tail (say, the upper 5% of the positive tail). The paradigmatic example of a one-tailed situation is the test of whether some new medical or psychological treatment, or educational improvement plan (A) produces results superior to the standard treatment or practice (B). Because only the outcome A > B is interesting, that is, will lead to a therapeutic or educational reform, it seems sensible to concentrate attention solely on the upper tail of the t distribution.

If the data do fall in the upper tail, the one-tailed test is more liberal than the two-tailed test. The one-tailed 5% level corresponds to the two-tailed 10% level; thus if $t = 1.80$, say, with 36 df, the result is significant by a one-tailed test (critical $t = 1.69$), but not with a two-tailed test (critical $t = 2.03$). Investigators with a generally liberal style are thus prone to view one-tailed tests permissively, whereas conservatives frown upon them.

The One-and-a-Half Tailed Test

Whatever one's general style, the critical question with a one-tailed test is what you would say if the results fell far out in the "wrong" tail. Suppose that in using a new therapeutic procedure, Group A, the experimental group, does far *worse* than the control Group B—so much worse, in fact, that using a two-tailed test, one would reject the null hypothesis and declare the new treatment significantly detrimental. If you start with the intention of using a one-tailed test, but switch to a two-tailed test when faced with a surprising data reversal, then your rejection region has 5% in the upper tail and 2.5% in the lower tail. With such a rejection region, the probability that a true null hypothesis will be rejected is .075, not the nominal .05. This is a bit too brash; the stated 5% level is misleading.

We wryly call this a "one-and-a-half tailed test," and note that it can also arise if you start with the intention of using a two-tailed test, but switch to a one-tailed test argument if the data show A > B, but not quite strongly enough to fall in the upper 2.5% tail. This happens not infrequently, because researchers often find particular directional expectations "obvious" (more stimulus rehearsal improves memory, e.g., or more highly educated citizens show greater political interest, etc.). The potential slipperiness of inducing arguments after the fact has to some extent given the one-tailed test a bad reputation.

What, then, distinguishes the defensible one-tailed test from the misleading one-and-a-half tailed test? Clearly, it is the totally blank lower tail of the former. That is to say, a one-tailed test is only well justified if in addition to the existence of a strong directional hypothesis, it can be convincingly argued that an outcome in the wrong tail is meaningless and might as well be dismissed as a chance occurrence.[1]

This condition is extremely difficult to meet, because researchers are very inventive at concocting potential explanations of wrong-tailed

---

[1]A different consideration applies to one-tailed tests in the application of meta-analysis (Rosenthal, 1991). This technique examines the strength and consistency of direction of a set of results from studies on the same topic. The meta-analyst must keep consistent track of the direction of each study. Therefore, in the amalgamation of p values, a one-tail orientation for the typical result is appropriate. A null result in any study is entered as $p = .50$, and a result at, say, the 5% value for the wrong tail is taken as $p = .95$.

results. Results in the wrong tail are rarely easy to simply ignore, as a pure one-tailed test would require.

The Lopsided Test

A compromise between the two brands of t test is possible. Consider a rejection region of 5% in the expected tail, and .5% in the supposedly wrong tail. Tests based on this region would be liberal in the expected direction, and conservative in the wrong tail. Such a test might be called a lopsided test. The rejection rule would be to declare the result statistically significant if it fell in the expected tail with two-sided $p < .10$, or in the unexpected tail with two-sided $p < .01$. This lopsided test entails a .055 probability that a true null hypothesis would be rejected, close to what the one- and two-tailed tests specify, but melding the virtues of those two alternatives.

ALTERNATIVE TESTS APPLIED TO THE SAME DATA SET

There are many other situations in which alternative test procedures can be applied to the same data set, to the potential confusion of the investigator. Nowadays, such confusion is amplified by the tendency for statistical analysis packages such as SAS (SAS Institute, 1985), to include the results of a plethora of alternative tests, some of which very few people ever heard of. How is one to cope with this unwelcome freedom of choice? To do different tests and pick the one that comes out best smacks of cheating, but if only a single test is to be done, which one should be preferred? We do not try to catalogue every such situation, but we broach the issues involved.

We distinguish three cases: one that involves different ways of expressing the data; the second, different calculation formulas applied to the same data; the third case, different philosophies for framing the analysis of the data configuration.

Different Modes of Data Expression

Parametric Versus Nonparametric Tests.   In the simple situation of two independent samples that could be t-tested for a difference between means, the argument could be made that because of the potential lack of fit of normal distributions to the data, it is preferable to use the Mann–Whitney (1947) or the (equivalent) Wilcoxon (1945) test—a "nonparametric" procedure that avoids the normality assumption by replacing the original quantitative measures with their rank orders. To make matters still more complicated, there are several other nonparametric tests applicable to the same simple data situation (e.g., the exceedance test [Tukey, 1955]; see also Cliff, 1993; Madansky, 1988).

The argument in favor of nonparametric tests as protection against non-normal distributions has been undercut by demonstrations (Sawilowsky & Blair, 1992) that the t test is fairly "robust" against (i.e., insensitive to) violations of the assumption of normal distributions. A similar statement can be made for F tests comparing the means of several groups. Besides the weakening of the original motivation for using them, non-parametric tests have also suffered from a lack of ability to articulate detail in presenting results (see chap. 6 on contrasts, comparisons, and beyond). Thus the general preference in the social sciences has been for parametric procedures.[2] A standard exception occurs when the data speak with overwhelming strength to a simple major point, and one merely wants to state an acceptably significant p value in the most straightforward way. In such cases, simple methods like the median test (see, e.g., Siegel, 1956) may be handy.

Original Versus Transformed Data (Between-Group Analyses).
For better articulation (chap. 6), or to repair heterogeneous variances among distributions, data are sometimes transformed to a different scale; for example, every score may be replaced by its logarithm. Significance tests performed both on the original data and on the transformed data typically yield very modest differences in p values, with the transformed version yielding a more conservative result. The safest procedure is to use the transformed scale if it homogenizes variance, although this creates a stylistic irony: The conservative analyst naturally prefers the more conservative significance test, but may be uncomfortable using a transformation, because the units of the new scale may not seem as "real" as those of the original scale. It is difficult to get a feel for the logarithm of the time taken to solve a problem, for example, or the square root of the number of errors on a task. By refraining from the transformation, however, the conservative researcher not only passes up the other advantages of the transformation, but is stuck with a generally more liberal significance test. Thus he is hoist with his own petard.[3]

Original Versus Transformed Data (Repeated Measures Analyses).
In repeated measures designs, that is, situations in which subjects are exposed to more than one experimental treatment or are observed for

---

[2]My brief discussion of this many-sided topic is oversimplified. It is possible that in the 1990s, there will be a resurgence of nonparametric procedures in the form of randomization tests (Edgington, 1987). These procedures are computer-intensive, but with recent increases of computer efficiency by orders of magnitude, formerly prohibitive calculations have become feasible. Another sign of the possible resurgence of nonparametric tests is the development of dominance statistics (Cliff, 1993).

[3]For a good exposition of how to choose a transformation, with commentary on the occasional awkwardness of doing so, see Emerson (1991b). Incidentally, if you think that a petard is a short flagstaff, you are wrong. The dictionary definition refers to an explosive device.

more than one trial, the usefulness of transformations is sharply increased. In contrast to the case of between-groups analyses, F tests in repeated measures designs are highly vulnerable to violations of underlying assumptions, and in cases with such violations, a transformation may be imperative. Here, unlike the simple between-groups case, the p values on the original and transformed data can be wildly discrepant. If one is unfamiliar with this pathology in repeated measures designs, such an outcome can seem bizarre. Here again, the transformed scale that roughly equalizes variances is to be preferred, more urgently than in the between-groups case.

Times Versus Speeds.   A prototypical case in which a transform is vital arises in experiments in which time to complete a simple, unfamiliar task is measured over a number of learning trials. Times tend to be highly variable from subject to subject in early trials, but become less variable as subjects learn the task. A transformation that often tends to equalize variances for different trials is the *reciprocal* transformation— which turns times into speeds. As a case in point, I have seen a data set of times for rats to run an alley for different sized rewards, in which the variances were quite heterogeneous (a ratio of 200 to 1 for the first trial vs. the last trial). When the null hypothesis of no reward effect was tested on the these data, the p value was > .90; when the times were transformed to speeds and the data reanalyzed, the p value was < .01! In this case, speed is the proper measure, and time is inappropriate. For designs involving replications of conditions within individuals who have different variances, see Bush, Hess, and Wohlford (1993).

Absolute Versus Relative Effects

Example: Negative Persuasion Using Insults.   A common type of conundrum arises when an effect can be regarded in either absolute or relative terms. This case gives rise to a difficult stylistic issue.

We begin with an example, a slightly simplified version of a field experiment conducted by Abelson and Miller (1967). Those investigators wanted to test for "boomerang effects" in persuasion, that is, circumstances in which a speaker not only fails to persuade his audience, but actually drives their attitudes further away from his position. This phenomenon almost never occurs in laboratory studies with captive, polite audiences. In the field experiment, the situation was engineered so that the speaker presented his arguments in an insulting fashion.[4] The hypothesis was that this would produce a boomerang effect.

---

[4]This experiment was performed during a period in which misgivings about the ethics of psychological experiments were not as widespread as they are nowadays.

The persuasion situation was prepared by having a confederate seat himself next to a potential subject on a park bench, whereupon the experimenter arrived as a roving reporter seeking the spontaneous opinions of ordinary citizens on a public issue. After obtaining agreement to participate, the experimenter invited the discussants to check their initial opinions on a 21-point rating scale and then to take turns offering arguments for their positions. In the Insult condition, the confederate ridiculed the subject's opinions before giving his own prepared views. In the Control condition, the insulting remarks were omitted. After six turns by each participant, ratings on the opinion scale were again solicited by the experimenter.

Table 4.1 presents the mean opinion scores before and after debate, and their differences, for each condition. A negative sign for the difference indicates a change *away* from the confederate's side of the issue, that is, a boomerang effect; a positive sign indicates change toward the confederate, an accommodation to his expressed views.

The Insult group indeed demonstrates a boomerang effect; a t test of the mean change score of -1.81 against the zero change null hypothesis yields the significant value $t_{23} = -2.16$. But what about the No Insult control group? The conventional wisdom is that when change is measured in an experimental group and a control group, one should test the experimental change *relative* to the control change. The difference between the mean change scores of the Insults and No Insults groups is -2.25, bigger than the mean change score of -1.81 for the Insults group alone. Yet the t test for this bigger difference is now smaller than the previous t, and not significant ($t_{46} = -1.90$)! For those who wish to verify this numerical result, we supply the additional fact that the pooled within group mean square was 16.86, which with $n = 24$ per group yields the standard error of each mean change as .838. The rest follows from standard t-test formulas.

What's going on here?? At first blush, an outcome like this appears to violate common sense, because a bigger difference yields a smaller t. The sophisticated reader who has seen this sort of thing before will realize that the paradox arises because the difference between two changes has a bigger standard error than either one alone. The relative effect is

TABLE 4.1
Opinion Scores Before and After Debate, With and Without Insults

	Before	After	Change	t	p
Insult Group	5.44	3.63	−1.81	−2.16	< .05
No Insult Group	5.09	5.53	+.44	.52	n.s.
Differential Change: Insult vs. No Insult			−2.25	−1.90	> .05

Note. Group means; $n = 24$.

statistically more unstable than the absolute effect, and therefore requires a stronger result to achieve the same level of significance.

The 42% Rule.   Let us examine this phenomenon in more detail, in a more general context. Consider a 2×2 design, with the columns representing some consequential comparison or difference, and the rows, the presence or absence of a key experimental condition. The investigator is interested primarily in the comparative difference (i.e., column effect) in the presence of the key condition (the first row); she has included the second row as a control, but expects it to show no column difference.

Now suppose that the experimenter t tests the comparison separately for the two rows and finds a significant effect for the first row, but no effect whatsoever for the second row. It is tempting to stop there, declare victory, and write it up for publication. But that would contradict the logic of including a control comparison in the first place. The point of running the control condition is to test the *relative* claim that the effect in the presence of the experimental factor exceeds the effect in its absence. The appropriate test seems to be a test of the *interaction* between the rows and the columns.

Imagine the two t tests, $t(1)$ and $t(2)$, performed respectively on the two rows. Suppose further that the interaction, conventionally reported with an F value, is converted to a t value, call it $t(*)$. [The square root of the F yields the $t(*)$.] Assuming that the same pooled error term is used for all t tests, it can be shown that:

$$t(*) = \frac{t(1) - t(2)}{\sqrt{2}} \tag{1}$$

This innocent equation produces the paradoxical type of result. The interaction test can lead to acceptance of the null hypothesis of no relative difference in the column comparisons for the two rows, even when the test for the first row, $t(1)$, comes out significant, and for the second row, $t(2)$, yields a flat zero. In this case, the equation tells us that $t(*)$, the interaction test statistic, is smaller than $t(1)$, the simple effect for the first row, by a factor of the square root of two. Further tinkering with the equation creates the 42% Rule:[5] When a mean difference in one

---

[5]The critical percentage is actually 41.4%, but I have rounded it up to 42%. Readers familiar with *A Hitchhiker's Guide to the Galaxy* (Adams, 1980) will recognize the cosmic status of the number 42. In Adams' futuristic spoof, the most powerful computer in the universe is set working on the question of the meaning of life, the universe, and everything. After millions of years of contemplation, the computer—to everyone's dismay—prints out, "42."

This interesting number was first noticed (Feynman, 1965) as the exponent of the ratio of certain fundamental physical quantities, and more recently ("Eggplant Flavor," 1992) has turned up in the vegetable garden. It was also Jackie Robinson's uniform number. (But don't take any of this too seriously.)

subsample is contrasted with a mean difference in a second, equally sized subsample, the t statistic for the interaction is larger than the t for the first difference if and only if the second difference is in the opposite direction, and is at least 42% as big as the first.

The Insult/No Insult data provide a pernicious example of the 42% rule. Look back at Table 4.1. The No Insult mean change score was in the opposite direction from the Insult mean change score, all right, but it was less than 42% as big[6] in absolute size [(.44/1.81) = .243], forcing $t(*)$ to be less than $t(1)$.

The Stylistic Conundrum.   I faced a stylistic conundrum when submitting this study for publication. Using the .05 level, the Insult group by itself showed a significant boomerang effect, but when the Insult group was compared to the No Insult group, the boomerang finding was not significant. This was despite the fact that the No Insult group, taken alone, demonstrated nothing that would weaken the claim of a boomerang effect from insults. It yielded a banal and nonsignificant tendency of moving toward the speaker's position. As we have seen, the villain of the piece is the statistical fact that every time you introduce new observations for purposes of comparison, the variability of the summary statistic (here, the mean difference) goes up, by a factor of the square root of 2 (if the n of additional cases = the n of old cases.)

Well, what did I do? I could have been brash and tried to argue that comparison with a No Insult control group was irrelevant. Editors and readers, however, don't generally like experiments with no control group. My eclectic solution was to give the comparisons of the Insult group mean change score with both the zero baseline ($t = 2.16, p < .03$), and the No Insult control group mean change score ($t = 1.90$, two-tailed $p < .07$; one-tailed $p < .04$). I argued for the one-tailed test on the Insult/No Insult difference, because the entire conception of the experiment revolved around the expectation of a boomerang effect under insult. (Had a positive mean change score been found in the Insult group, I would have gone back to the drawing board.) There are other choices here, such as being content with the two-tailed p of .07, or if you want to be really adventurous, claiming that the t of 1.90 is significant at the .05 level by the lopsided test (see the discussion of one-tailed tests, this chapter).

I have the sense that a compromise statistical test could be invented that would resolve the apparent paradox in this type of situation. In any

---

[6]Note that the difference scores indexing the experimental (Insult) and control (No Insult) effects are within-subject, not between-subject effects. This does not, however, affect the applicability of the equation. Another thing to note is that $t(*)$ has more degrees of freedom than do $t(1)$ or $t(2)$, which helps slightly in rejecting the null hypothesis for the relative difference—but with groups of reasonable size, this advantage is quite small.

case, it is important to understand the mischievous potential consequences of the 42% Rule.

Different Calculation Formulas

There are a number of pairs of significance tests with different formulas for achieving the same purpose. For some pairs it is mathematically guaranteed that they will yield the same p value when both are applied to the same data set. For other pairs, the two formulas are based on alternative conceptions, and the results may diverge.

Difference Between Two Means, t Test and F Test. When testing for a difference between the means of two independent groups, it is immaterial whether a (two-tailed) t test or an F test is used. Both are based on the same assumptions—homogeneous variances and normal distributions— and it would be dastardly if they came out different. Fortunately they don't, even though their formulas look rather dissimilar. Given k degrees of freedom for the t test (where k is the total number of cases in the two groups, minus 2), the corresponding F test will have 1 and k degrees of freedom. Given the well-known mathematical relationship $F_{1,k} = t_k2$, it will always be the case that the square of the calculated t value will equal the F value for the equivalent comparison on the same data. The tables of significant values reflect this, and therefore the two tests yield exactly the same p value. It is a simple matter to inspect t and F tables to see the equivalence between F (with 1 df in the numerator) and t-squared. A useful exercise for the student is to verify that the calculating formulas for F and t lead algebraically to the well-known relationship just described. Another simple case in which two formulas look different but yield the same result arises from the critical ratio test of a difference between proportions (say, the proportion of men who agree with an opinion item minus the proportion of women who agree), and the ordinary, uncorrected chi-square test of association in the 2 × 2 table (here, gender by agreement).

Sometimes, of course, when two significance tests have formulas that look different, they are different. There are several situations in which the different significance test formulas can yield somewhat different outcomes. Some may involve "pathology" in the data, that is, violation of some critical restriction.

Different Chi-Square Formulas in Log-Linear Analysis. We mention here an important case that is relatively unfamiliar to psychologists, but familiar to sociologists and others who deal with categorical data arranged as frequency counts in multiway cross-classification tables. (In two dimensions, this is the familiar contingency table.) The general method for analyzing associations among the ways of the table is log-linear analysis (Fienberg, 1980; Wickens, 1989). The standard significance test for goodness of fit of log-linear models is a chi-square test, a small chi-square indicating a good fit. But there are two different methods for calculating a chi-square: the familiar Pearson chi-square as used on simple two-way contingency tables, and the chi-square derived from the maximum likelihood method. These two methods usually yield only slightly different values.

There are two circumstances in which the difference between the two methods can be notable. One case is when both chi-squares are very large and highly significant, but they differ in size. This happens because the approximations to an exact chi-square gradually break down as the model being tested fits more and more badly. Here the discrepancy is rather harmless, because the conclusion is the same in both cases: The model being tested is resoundingly rejected.

A more interesting circumstance that may yield a large discrepancy is the presence in the contingency table of one or more cells with very small expected frequencies (less than 1.0 or even .5). Many elementary statistics texts warn of inexact p values when expected frequencies are small, but specification of what small means depends on when and by whom the text was written. The point of such warnings is that the calculated chi-square may not approximate well the exact distribution given in the chi-square tables. When the two distinct chi-square formulas —the Pearson and the maximum likelihood—give discrepant (but not huge) values, it is a sign that some of the expected values are indeed too small. In this event, one recourse is to recalculate a chi-square leaving out the cells with small expected frequencies. An interesting example of this device can be found in Duncan, Sloane, and Brody (1982). For an excellent discussion of small cell problems, see Wickens (1989).

Different Ways to Frame an Analysis

A rather different kind of case arises when alternative formulas signify differences in the guiding philosophy of the analysis.

Combining p Values from Multiple Experiments.   In the procedure of meta-analysis, discussed in chapter 7, it may be desired to combine p values from multiple, independent studies of the same null hypothesis, to create a single, omnibus test: for example, of departures of mental telepathy scores from chance baseline scores (Honorton et al., 1990). The most popular procedure for combining p values is the Stouffer test popularized by Mosteller and Bush (1954), but there are seven or eight alternative methods (Rosenthal, 1991). To make a point, we focus on one of these, a little-used alternative (Fisher, 1946) that involves adding logarithmically transformed p values. The Stouffer and Fisher tests yield predictably different results. The Stouffer test statistic is sensitive

TABLE 4.2
Results From Two Ways of Combining *p* Values: A Vexing Comparison

	p Values From Four Independent Studies	
Procedure	*All Four at p = .15*	*Three at .50, One at .001*
Stouffer test	$z = 2.07, p < .02$	$z = 1.54, p > .05$
Fisher test	$\chi^2 = 15.18, p > .05$	$\chi^2 = 18.71, p < .02$

to *consistent*, even if mild, departures from the null hypothesis in separate studies (say, four results at $p = .15$), whereas the Fisher procedure is most sensitive to *occasional*, *extreme* departures (say, three results at $p = .50$, and one at $p = .001$). Table 4.2 contrasts the results of the two tests for these two data situations. (The Stouffer test is based on critical ratios, the Fisher on a chi-square statistic with degrees of freedom = twice the number of p values.)

The table gives the p value attaching to the aggregate, that is, a significance test of the omnibus null hypothesis, for each of the two tests on each of the two sets of results. When all four studies yield $p < .15$, the Stouffer test rejects the omnibus (at .02), but the Fisher test does not. When three of the individual results produce $p < .50$, but one reaches $p < .001$, the tests reverse roles. The Fisher is significant (at $p < .02$), but the Stouffer is not. If one were always to choose the test yielding the most extreme p value, that would be too brash. The choice could be made resistant to criticism by using the conventional test (here, the Stouffer). However, there might be theoretical reasons to use the Fisher test for certain applications. For example, if one is to believe the rhetoric of proponents of ESP, success at mental telepathy comes and goes, but when present, is impressive. Multiple tests of mental telepathy therefore might be a rare candidate for p value aggregation by the Fisher test.

Summary of Alternative Test Procedures

A breezy summary of the various cases of alternative tests applied to the same data set might go something like this: Often the choice between alternatives makes no practical difference. Occasionally (as in the log-linear case discussed earlier) what is important is not so much the choice between alternative methods, as what their discrepancy signifies about the nature of the data. In the remaining cases, when different tests do come out somewhat differently, one of them is usually conventional. As in the situation with two-tailed tests versus one-tailed or lopsided tests, a prudent policy is to choose the more conventional approach, but remain willing to deviate from it when an intelligent rationale based on appropriate special conditions can be put forward.

DEFECTIVE OBSERVATIONS

"Klinkers"

Almost all data sets contain defective observations. Recording equipment may fail; respondents may blatantly misperceive, misunderstand, or misrespond; samples of subjects may include one or more obviously inappropriate people (such as those who don't understand English); experimenters may bollix the experimental procedure. The more obvious the circumstances producing klinkers, the less problematic it is for the investigator simply to eliminate these observations from the data set,[7] or to replace flawed subjects with new subjects.

Circumstances may not be obvious, however. The investigator may be unsure whether or not Subject 17 was drugged out, whether Subject 34 wrote his intended response on the wrong line of the questionnaire, and so on. The usual solution for ambiguous cases is to run data analysis both ways—that is, with and without inclusion of the questionable data points. The happiest outcome would be that it does not make (much of) a difference.[8] In marginal cases when it does make a difference, a conservative policy would dictate that possible klinkers helping you to reject the null hypothesis should be thrown out, but those that hurt your ability to reject the null hypothesis should be kept in. This is appropriately cautious advice, but there is a catch. The research audience cannot notice possible peculiarities of individual observations, because they are not available to public scrutiny. Thus it is left up to the investigator to notice oddities, take them seriously, and nobly throw away klinkers even when they help you. Consider the following legend, possibly apochryphal but instructive nonetheless.

An experienced experimenter, in carefully reviewing an experiment testing a hypothesis about overweight people, eliminated the data of one subject because it turned out that he was a wrestler, who should be

---

[7]The omission of observations from a carefully designed data structure may sometimes create awkwardness for the statistical analysis. Problems caused by missing data, and recommended solutions, are discussed by Cohen and Cohen (1983) and by Kirk (in press), among others.

[8]Typically, when "both ways" of analysis are run, one way is presented in the text of the research report, and the alternative way in a footnote. To the best of my recollection, such footnotes always say that the alternative choice made no difference. This, of course, is what the investigator would like to say, and I am made somewhat suspicious by the unanimity of happy accounts in these footnotes. The exact wording may be a tip-off to the convenient suppression of unpleasant details. Thus, when the footnote reads, "...inclusion [exclusion] of these observations did not affect the conclusions of the study...," it could be the case that inclusion (exclusion) changed a p value from $p < .05$ to $p < .15$, but that the investigator still drew the same *conclusions*. Stylistically, the conservative investigator—as opposed to the brash investigator—will use more precise wording of such footnotes (e.g., "...inclusion...did not weaken the p level[s] by more than such and such...").

considered not really overweight, merely "bulked up." The wrestler's data had gone strongly against the experimenter's prediction. Without faulting the experimenter for deliberate bias, one may nevertheless question whether the distinction between being overweight and being bulked up would have been constructed had the wrestler's data been supportive of the experimental hypothesis. The experimenter would probably not have been vigilant enough to scrutinize the details of favorable data, and might never even have discovered that one subject was a wrestler. The moral is as easy to preach as it is hard to carry out: Be your own toughest critic.

Outliers

We have labeled as klinkers those observations deemed inappropriate by external criteria such as failed equipment or errors in the selection or handling of subjects. Also vexing are *outliers* (Tukey, 1977)—observations obtained under seemingly normal circumstances, but that turn out to be extremely deviant from the main body of observations. To illustrate, consider a reaction time study in which almost all of the reaction times fall, say, between .6 and 1.2 seconds, but for no apparent reason there suddenly arises a time of 8.5 seconds. Was the subject daydreaming? Did he miss the ready signal? We will never know, but it is clear that such an outlier will distort the mean and standard deviation of any group of observations within which it is included.[9] This problem is so common in reaction time studies that cognitive psychologists have developed a variety of methods to handle it: for example, using "trimmed means" (Bush et al., 1993; Wilcox, 1992) instead of ordinary means, or simply eliminating outliers entirely from the data set. An authoritative treatment of the various possibilities was given by Ratcliff (1993).

General Advice

Discussion of these alternative fixes for the outlier problem would carry us too far afield. A key observation here is that except for those who study reaction times, most psychological and other social science researchers have not confronted the problem of what to do with outliers— but they should. A generalized conservative suspicion against doing anything, lest it seem brash, is not a good solution. Doing nothing is as much a choice as is doing something.

---

[9]The vulnerability of means and standard deviations to being overinfluenced by one or more wildly discrepant observations is a phenomenon much analyzed by statisticians under the heading of *robustness*. Measures of central tendency (or variability, etc.) that are not vulnerable to distortion by outliers are called robust statistics (Hoaglin et al., 1983; Tukey, 1962).

The general effect of doing nothing about outliers is to tolerate more noisiness in data, that is, to have lower power, rejecting null hypotheses less often. In any particular case, however, the do-nothing policy could either help or hurt the investigator wanting to reject the null, depending on the location of the outlier(s). Thus, what one wants to avoid is ad hoc treatment of outliers, differing by whim from one study to the next. Instead, one wants to develop a consistent policy applying to all studies of a given type. This advice gives rise to Abelson's Third Law: *Never flout a convention just once.*[10] In other words, either stick consistently to conventional procedures, or better, violate convention in a coherent way if informed consideration provides good reason for so doing. This advice in favor of stylistic consistency applies not only to treatment of outliers, but in general.

MULTIPLE TESTS WITHIN THE SAME DATA SET

When there are multiple tests within the same study or series of studies, a stylistic issue is unavoidable. As Diaconis (1985) put it, "Multiplicity is one of the most prominent difficulties with data-analytic procedures. Roughly speaking, if enough different statistics are computed, some of them will be sure to show structure" (p. 9). In other words, random patterns will seem to contain something systematic when scrutinized in many particular ways. If you look at enough boulders, there is bound to be one that looks like a sculpted human face. Knowing this, if you apply extremely strict criteria for what is to be recognized as an intentionally carved face, you might miss the whole show on Easter Island.

Setting the Error Rate

We discuss multiplicity issues from the standpoint of the Type I error rate, that is, the proportion of times that hypothetically true null hypotheses would be rejected. The conventional .05 level signifies that for every 100 tests of a true null hypothesis, false significance will be claimed for 5 of them—an error rate of 5 in 100. This sounds precise, but avoids the question of the scope of each null hypothesis. A null hypothesis could be specific to a test on a single mean, between a pair of means, or among several means—or it could apply to every test whatsoever within a study, or over a whole series of studies.

---

[10]Because there is a community of researchers in any given field, the development of a new statistical convention requires an authoritative explicit declaration, or the implicit negotiation of a consensus. The former usually comes about via methodological articles in prestige journals (e.g., Clark, 1973; Green & Tukey, 1960). The latter could arise from the gradual diffusion of illustrative applications of a given policy decision, perhaps marked by occasional public debates over the advantages and disadvantages of alternatives.

Manny Powers, the Psychic.   Suppose, for example, that an investigator interested in extrasensory perception comes across an individual with a reputation as a psychic (call him Manny Powers). The investigator carries out 40 studies on Powers, one study per day. Each day, Powers is tested on five different ESP tasks (telepathy, precognition, psychokinesis, etc.). The goal is to find the circumstances under which Powers is psychic, operationally defined as performing better than chance on a given task on a given day.

How should the investigator specify what is meant by the .05 significance level? A skeptic who doesn't believe in any manifestation of ESP whatsoever would point out that if a significance level of .05 is established for each task on each day, there would be 200 separate opportunities to reject a null hypothesis. Thus, assuming that the skeptic's nonbelief is warranted, nevertheless (.05 × 200) = 10 rejections of a null hypothesis will be expected on average. In other words, there will be about 10 occasions on which extrasensory skill will be claimed for Powers because he performed "better than chance" on some particular task. A cunning or self-deluded investigator might focus on these 10 or so successes, setting aside the approximately 190 failures—the *hocus focus* trick. (The lack of public knowledge of the number of failures is called the *file drawer problem*; Iyengar & Greenhouse, 1988; Rosenthal, 1979.)

Considering the whole series of studies and tasks as a single unit, the error rate is 200 times too high. To achieve an error rate of only 5 per 100 hypothetical repetitions of the whole series of studies, the investigator would have to set the significance level per individual significance test at .05/200, or .00025. This procedure of adjusting the significance level according to the number of tests is called the Bonferroni method (Emerson, 1991a; Miller, 1981). Obviously, it would make it much harder to claim ESP for any specific occasion.

However, a side effect of such a conservative procedure, as Duncan, 1955) and others have complained, is to penalize the investigator who is ambitious enough to have run so many repeated tests. A lazier investigator who ran Manny Powers on five tasks for only 1 day would by the same reasoning be able to set the significance level per task at .05/5, or .01. And the laziest investigator of all, using one task on 1 day, could simply use the .05 level without modification.

The Policy Dilemma.   The stylistic debate pitting stuffiness against brashness is very stark here. When contemplating a significance testing policy for a series of studies, with multiple tests to be performed within each study, the most stultifyingly conservative thing to do is to set the error rate at 5 potentially false claims per 100 *series*. This forces an extremely high threshold for making a claim of significance from any single test. At the other extreme, the most loosely liberal policy is to establish the error rate at 5 per 100 *tests*, allowing a multitude of potentially false claims to fall where they may. Neither extreme policy is particularly attractive; the best argument for each lies in the potential folly of the other.

There is no universal right answer to this policy dilemma, and different conventional answers have grown up around different types of analysis. In multiway analyses of variance designed to test two or more main effects and some number of interactions, for example, the standard thing to do has been to apply the same significance level, usually .05, to each effect, ignoring the proliferation of tests. This extremely liberal policy is inconsistent with more conservative practice in other cases, but most researchers follow this convention without second thoughts. If a defense for this policy had to be spelled out, it would make two points: First, multiway designs are generally only run after preliminary research has established that there is a phenomenon to be studied; thus, the overall null hypothesis of no real effects whatever is even less of a serious possibility than it typically is. Second, the investigator is usually interested in a small handful of particular effects; if the analysis of variance table has many lines to it, scattered effects besides the interesting ones might well beat the .05 level by chance, but the investigator should not go to great lengths trying to interpret them. A clear analytic focus, established prior to running the study, serves to diminish the vagaries of multiplicity.

Focused Tests in the Many-Group Study.   Conflicting standards also obtain for multiple tests applied to the several means of a many-group main effect. When there are several degrees of freedom for an effect, the ordinary F test is called an *omnibus* test. It tests the overall null hypothesis that none of the means truly differ, against the vague alternative hypothesis that some of them differ to some extent from some of the others. The null hypothesis might come to be rejected in many ways, none of which are specified in advance. Specification of particular alternatives to the null hypothesis may involve planned contrasts—*planned* because they should be specified before looking at the data, and *contrasts* because they involve patterns of differences among the means (e.g., the linear contrast, whereby the means of groups A, B, C, etc., increase from left to right in equal sized steps). Because planned contrasts are usually more powerful than omnibus tests, they tend to yield stronger p values for rejecting the null hypothesis. They are also better articulated (as is discussed in chap. 7).

An issue of style can nonetheless arise when an unusual contrast is chosen, because the stronger p value may come at a cost in rhetorical credibility—the critic may not be convinced that the quirky-looking contrast was really planned. Instead, it may seem like a brash attempt to make something out of whatever pattern happened to appear in the data. In line with our Third Law, then, the reasoning behind the choice of a contrast must be clear and used often to be convincing. As a fallback, there is also a significance test appropriate for *un*planned contrasts— the Scheffé (1959) test—but it is extremely conservative.

Moderately conservative orientations characterize some of the many methods of *multiple comparisons*, in which each of a set of means is compared with every other to determine which pairs of means should be declared significantly different. The bellwether of the family of possible multiple comparisons procedures is the Tukey (1953) test. If in a series of experiments, each with several groups, the overall null hypothesis were always true, the Tukey test would on average make five false declarations of significance per 100 experiments. The per-experiment error rate seems a reasonable compromise between per-comparison and per-series error rates.

The two most ultraliberal procedures—multiple *t* tests and Duncan's (1955) test—which base the error rate on the number of false claims per 100 *comparisons*, have very bad reputations among statisticians. Scheffé (1959), for example, in his authoritative book on the analysis of variance, had the scathing footnote, "I have not included the multiple comparison methods of D. B. Duncan because I am unable to understand their justification" (p. 78). Even the middle-of-the-road Newman–Keuls test (Keuls, 1952; Newman, 1937), which sets the error rate at five experiments out of 100, offends conservative sensibilities (Ramsey, 1981). A reason for this is that when the Newman–Keuls does produce false claims in a given experiment, it may tend to produce several of them—and thus a higher *total* number of errors in 100 experiments, compared to the Tukey test.

Different multiple comparison tests have proliferated like raspberry bushes (see Hochberg & Tamhane, 1987). Perhaps because of the confusion attaching to the steady introduction of new tests, different subfields in psychology differ in the degree of liberality they are willing to tolerate in multiple comparisons tests. Social psychologists in particular, for reasons that escape me, tend to be rather profligate in the use of multiple *t* tests.[11] My own view is that the decision to use multiple comparison procedures should bring with it a somewhat conservative attitude. That is the price of multiplicity. If the investigator finds the Tukey (1953) test, or something like it, too conservative, she should ponder whether complete testing of every mean against every other is really to the point. Perhaps she really only cares about a couple of particular differences. Or better, perhaps she could apply a meaningful contrast. Conceptual focusing not only helps ease the stylistic dilemma, it leads to cleaner studies and clearer theories.

---

[11]Some sociologist of knowledge should study this! Differences in conventions are diagnostic of boundaries between different research subcultures.

STATING AND INTERPRETING *p* VALUES

Word Play

The desperate investigator with an almost significant result, say *p* = .07, may try to talk the result across the conventional .05 boundary, or to rationalize the failure to reach the boundary.

Typical Rhetorical Flourishes.   Among the phrases used to attempt such rhetorical feats are these:

- The result was significant at the .07 level....
- The result was marginally significant (*p* = .07)....
- Although the result did not reach the conventional .05 level, it is nevertheless highly suggestive....
- Because of the limited number of subjects (or low power), the result just missed the .05 level. Nevertheless....

These verbal devices, though not entirely unreasonable, make for somewhat defensive rhetoric, suggesting a penchant for weaseling. (Note especially the gambit in the reference to the *conventional* .05 level, as though to blame the convention rather than the result.) On the other hand, the .05 level is admittedly an arbitrary standard, and there is not much real difference between results at the *p* = .07 and *p* = .05 levels. What is the author to do?

Common sense suggests being straightforward—not trying to make too much out of the situation. Give the test statistic and the *p* value of .07. Leave it to intelligent readers to appreciate for themselves that your result just missed.

Results That "Lean" and "Hint."   Interestingly, John Tukey, the developer of moderately conservative procedures for multiple comparisons, recently (Tukey, 1991) came out with what seems a shockingly radical proposal. He recommended coining new words for results at certain benchmark levels weaker than the .05. His starting point is the assertion that the null hypothesis is *never* literally true (see also Cohen, in press; Schmidt, 1992). Thus in testing the difference between two means, the so-called acceptance of the null hypothesis merely signifies a reluctance to bet on the direction of the true mean difference. If the two-tailed *p* were greater than .05, but less than, say .15, one might at least be tempted to bet that the observed direction of difference were the true one. Tukey suggested saying in this case that the difference between A and B *leans* in the positive direction. For .15 < *p* < .25, he proposed stating that there is a *hint* about the direction. Imagine using a level as scorned as .25 to enable a substantive statement about one's results! Will wonders never cease?

Let us take pause, however, before cheering that now we can publish all those lousy studies that couldn't beat the .05 level. In using a new term, Tukey (1991) was not authorizing the use of .25 as a new significance level for rejecting null hypotheses. A hint is just a hint is just a hint. There is nothing very definitive about it. Instead, what he was telling us is to stop treating statistical testing as a two-valued decision procedure, and instead to use shades of wording to indicate different degrees of uncertainty.

Replicability and Power: The Real Issues

One can also envisage a semantics of confidence rather than of doubt. In a challenging article by Greenwald, Gonzalez, Harris, and Guthrie (1993), the authors showed that if a two-group study achieves $p < .005$, the probability that an exact replication of the study will yield $p < .05$ is approximately .8. Greenwald et al. therefore suggested that the label *replicable* might be attached to a *p* level of .005. (This result is insensitive to the group *n*s, but does depend on the assumption that the effect size in the first study is the best estimate of the effect size in the replication.) Yes, I know that the whole thing sounds weird, because if the original study came out as strongly as $p < .005$, how could the chance of getting a replication to yield merely $p < .05$ be as modest as .8?

The Replication Fallacy.   Readers who are baffled by this assault on their intuitions are suffering from the *replication fallacy* (Gigerenzer, 1993), an overconfidence in the repeatability of statistically significant results. The following thought experiment may help to correct the fallacy. Imagine an experimenter who has run a two-group study, and has found by *t* test the result $p = .05$. What is the chance that if she exactly repeated the study with a new sample of subjects (and the same *n* per group) that she would again get a significant result at the .05 level? First give an intuitive answer, and then study the analysis that follows.

Half the time, the observed effect size from the second study ought to be bigger than that of the first study, and half the time, smaller. Because the first observed effect size was just big enough to obtain a *p* value of .05, anything smaller would yield a nonsignificant $p > .05$. This analysis thus yields an expected repeatability of 50-50, much lower than the usual intuition. Psychologically, overconfidence arises because once you find a significant result, you say to yourself, "Ah, now I've got it. The real thing is there. No more problems!" But this falls into the trap of thinking that just because you have made a categorical assertion about a significant result, the influence of chance has disappeared. Remember that when we discredit a chance explanation, we are merely saying that an *entirely* chance account is inadequate. We then claim a systematic effect *in addition to chance effects.*

Power and the Wishful Experimenter.   The probability that a significance test will reject the null hypothesis is called its *power* (Cohen, 1988). Power can be increased by running more subjects, or by increasing the effect size via an increase in the cause size (chap. 3) and/or by a decrease in the influence of chance factors. Long ago, Cohen (1962) criticized the psychological research community for running studies with much too little power (about .42, on the average), and the situation has not improved since (Cohen, 1990). This raises a stylistic issue different from liberal versus conservative result presentations. It concerns the style of *designing experiments,* and we might call the poles of this dimension *vigilant versus wishful.* The experimenter who estimates how many subjects are needed to ensure adequate power (Cohen, 1988) is vigilantly guarding against the worst-case scenario of indecisive results. The wishful experimenter, on the other hand, assumes that a divine hand is guiding his research, and plunges ahead to frequent disappointments and blind alleys.

Silly Significance Tests

The ethos of doing significance tests as the hallmark of an appropriately conservative style is now so deeply ingrained that tests are sometimes used even when they need not be. Indeed, there are several contexts in which it is really silly to carry out a significance test (Cohen, in press), much less to present its result. For example, if a sample is divided at the median into high scorers and low scorers, there is no point in showing by a *t* test that the high scorers differ significantly from the low scorers. A somewhat subtler case arises when a trustworthy procedure for random assignment of subjects to experimental conditions seems to go awry, yielding a cluster of smarter or faster (or whatever) subjects in one particular group. In this situation, students are prone to test the significance of the difference between the groups. But because the null hypothesis here is that the samples were randomly drawn from the same population, it is true by definition, and needs no data. What has happened is that one of those flukey outcomes that arise from time to time has arisen *this* time. As Abelson's First Law says, chance is lumpy. The investigator might want to adjust for the lucky advantage of the one group (say, by analysis of covariance), but a significance test has no relevance to this decision.

Needless Clutter with *p* Values

Meanwhile, there are some subfields of specialization within psychology (and other social and natural sciences) where the prevailing ethos is that experimental results should be so clear that statistical tests are totally unnecessary. The reader need only look at a graph of the results, and the pertinent trends or skips or blips will be obvious. As behaviorist B. F. Skinner (1963) wrote, "...in the experimental analysis of behavior... statistical methods are unnecessary.... When a variable is changed and the effect on performance observed, it is for most purposes idle to prove statistically that a change has occurred." (p. 508)

I have some sympathy for this position. Nothing is more tedious than a research report cluttered with obligatory $p < .001$s for every conceivable claim, including such blatantly obvious assertions as that performance improves with practice, or is correlated with ability. On the other hand, occasionally it happens that "obvious" conclusions are false. And it is easy to overreact to appearances in graphs. For example, there is a strong tendency to perceive approximately regular cycles in the ups and downs of a random time series (Abelson, 1953), or to find mysterious coordination between separate time series, as in the "Maharishi effect" (Orme-Johnson et al., 1988).

Research reports can in various ways avoid belaboring the obvious with p value clutter. The most suspect way is to give a couple of p values at the outset for major results, and then to focus on other data features merely with a look-and-see-the-graph approach. The perceptive reader will be wary of this potentially misleading practice. The prudent investigator can anticipate objections by asking the self-critical question, "How can I demonstrate the statistical significance, if I have to, of each assertion I want to make?" Even a rough-and-ready answer would be salutary, and there is almost always a way to choose an approximate significance test. The text of the report need not be littered with p values. Sections in which all claims are judged significant can be covered by an opening remark or footnote stating that every claim has $p < .05$, or better.

IN THE LAST ANALYSIS

Most of the noisy stylistic battles fought over the anxious pursuit of $p < .05$ are needless. Though contention over style will never completely disappear, a low level of stylistic disagreement between investigators is quite tolerable—perhaps even adaptive. Research conclusions arise not from single studies alone, but from cumulative replication. In this cumulative process (which we discuss in chaps. 7 and 9), liberal versus conservative stylistic differences will tend to cancel out, and if the community learns to be selective in its research designs and focused in its statistical tests, cumulation will be more rapid.

5 On Suspecting Fishiness

Sometimes, statistical evidence that looks good on the face of it nevertheless turns out to be flawed. Broadly speaking, there are two ways in which an argument based on apparently persuasive evidence might lose its impact after further inspection. One possibility is that the data were mishandled or the statistical analysis misapplied. A second possibility is the discovery of some artifact in the research procedure, such that the substantive conclusions drawn by the investigator may not logically be warranted by the observational comparisons made. In this chapter we emphasize the first class of cases—mangled statistics—and save the treatment of artifacts until we come to counterarguments in chapter 9.

An experienced data handler develops a nose for strange features of data and statistical summaries. An odd pattern, irregularity, or coincidence is often a clue that something fishy may be going on—a mistake in recording the data, a statistical miscalculation, a departure from the assumptions and conventions of a particular type of analysis, or in unusual cases even downright fraud. In this chapter, we present a catalog of some common types of statistical strangeness, hoping by examples to sharpen the reader's skill in finding and analyzing fishiness. The categorization of errors is arranged according to types of clues a data snooper can look for. These clues can be used both to check one's own results, or to prowl through other people's.

Our diagnostics pertain mainly to scholarly research reports giving more details than usually appear in sketchy news stories. For detecting common statistical errors or deceptions in the media, the reader is referred to other sources (e.g., Huff, 1954; Maier, 1991; Tufte, 1983).

STRANGE DISTRIBUTIONS OF OBSERVATIONS

A powerful and simple way to snoop for peculiarities in data sets is to plot the distributions of observations—that is, the frequencies of occurrence of each score. One can use histograms, or Tukey's (1977) stem-and-leaf procedure.

Looking for Outliers, Gaps, and Dips

Repeated runs of most random processes produce smooth, single-peaked distributions of outcomes. Typically, strange-looking distributions arise because of an irregular process intruding into the production of an ordinary-looking distribution, as if a nonconformist leprechaun had joined the data generation process. The term *compound distribution*, or *contaminated distribution* (Hoaglin et al., 1983), refers to a distribution arising from a mixture of random processes—a *regular* process producing most of the observations, mixed with a *deviant* process that contributes the rest. Consider the likely appearance of a compound distribution, depending on the relation between the regular process and the deviant process. If the deviant process has a much larger variance than the regular process, one or more observations separated from the main body of the distribution will tend to appear. Such sports are called *outliers*. If there are a sufficient number of observations from a deviant process with a distinctly higher or lower mean than the regular process, the resulting compound will have two peaks, separated by a *gap* or a *dip*.[1]

The appearance of outliers, gaps, or dips signals the presence of a deviant process, wanting explanation. Many deviant processes arise benignly, as when subjects become fatigued or distracted amidst a series of otherwise regular responses. Others suggest more mischievous causes, as we illustrate with the following examples. The first example happens not to come from an experiment, but from a naturally occurring set of voting data.

Example: Suspicious Vote Totals.   In the 1969 and 1971 Democratic mayoral primaries in New Haven, Connecticut, the opponents were the same: a reform-minded candidate versus the incumbent mayor. More people voted in the 1971 primary than the 1969 primary, reflecting a more intense, bitter campaign, marked by allegations of cheating and mistallying of votes in particular wards. There was a rumor that party regulars were submitting absentee ballots in the names of dead voters. There was contention over voting machine tallies as well, having to do with whether some wards tallied all three of their voting machines.

---

[1]Another general phenomenon besides mixing can produce gaps or dips in distributions. The impish leprechaun, instead of mixing deviant observations in with regular ones, could remove or inhibit a selected subset of the regular data. This produces so-called *censored* distributions. For example, the distribution of the dates on old pennies has a substantial dip from 1941 to 1945—because of the military use of copper during World War II.

Table 5.1a gives the ratio of total vote reported on the night of the election in 1971 to total vote in 1969, for each of 30 wards. These ratios are arrayed in a stem-and-leaf plot (Tukey, 1977), shown in Table 5.1b. Each *leaf* to the right of the vertical line represents the last digit of a particular ratio, with the prior digit(s) given by the *stem* to its left. Each

TABLE 5.1a
Ratio of Total 1971 Vote to Total 1969 Vote in Each of 30 Wards

Ward	Ratio	Ward	Ratio	Ward	Ratio
1	1.11	2	1.18	3	1.04
4	1.59	5	1.15	6	1.23
7	1.35	8	1.00	9	1.27
10	1.15	11	1.20	12	1.20
13	1.22	14	1.26	15	1.24
16	1.28	17	1.03	18	1.08
19	1.11	20	1.04	21	1.09
22	.70	23	1.10	24	1.09
25	1.20	26	1.05	27	1.12
28	1.11	29	1.17	30	1.09

TABLE 5.1b
Stem-and-Leaf Display of the Ratios in Table 5.1a

```
                                    Outer fence = 1.61
        1.5 | 9
        1.5 |
        1.4 |
        1.4 |                       Inner fence = 1.415
        1.3 | 5
        1.3 |
        1.2 | 678
        1.2 | 000234                 Upper hinge = 1.22
        1.1 | 5578
        1.1 | 01112
        1.0 | 58999                  Median = 1.135
        1.0 | 0344                   Lower hinge = 1.09
         .9 |
         .9 |
         .8 |                        Inner fence = .895
         .8 |
         .7 |
         .7 | 0                      Outer fence = .70
```

Note. Tukey's term *hinges* is closely related to *quartiles*, but may differ for small *ns*. In Tukey, Mosteller, and Youtz (1991), the term *fourths* is used. The *step size* is 1.5 times the difference between the hinges. This step is marked off once, then twice, beyond each hinge. This locates the inner and outer *fences* or cutoffs. Data beyond the fences are outliers or extreme outliers. See Tukey (1977), or Hoaglin, Iglwicz and Tukey (1986).

stem occurs twice, so as to sort the accompanying leaves of 0–4 from those of 5–9. This better articulates some distributions, such as this one. The display is akin to a histogram for showing the distribution, but it is vertical rather than horizontal, and preserves the information from the final digit rather than lumping data within class intervals.

We note by eye that there is one case of an unusually high ratio, and one case of an unusually low ratio. The upper case, from Ward 4, shows a fishily large increase in 1971 vote over the 1969 vote. The lower one, from Ward 22, represents a substantial decrease in the 1971 vote. Both are suspicious because votes were fairly homogeneously increasing in all the other wards, and there were no major population shifts or redrawn ward boundaries.

Of course, every distribution has highest and lowest observations. We need some orderly procedure for deciding whether extreme cases are so separated from the body of the distribution as to warrant concluding that they have come from a deviant process different from the regular process that generated the rest of the distribution. Tukey's (1977) method for identifying such outliers is indicated in the notes beneath the table. Here, one suspicious data point lies on the "outer fence" at the bottom of the distribution, and the other one lies very close to the outer fence at the top of the distribution. Both may be considered so deviant as to need special explanation.

Indeed, as it turned out, there were very concrete explanations for both of these aberrations. In Ward 22, with the low ratio, it was discovered the morning after the election that the count from one of the three machines had been omitted. With correction, the ratio became 1.05. A year later, a scandal broke, having to do with false absentee ballots made out in the names of dead people. This chicanery was heavily concentrated in one vulnerable ward, where the ratio was 1.59—Ward 4!

The striking thing about this example is that a data analyst knowing nothing about the political foibles of New Haven, Connecticut, could be cued to the strong possibility that strange things were going on in two wards, just by following the straightforward procedure for identifying outliers in the distribution in Table 5.1b.

Example: Tests of Clairvoyance.   A different sort of peculiar data distribution arises from the Pearce–Pratt ESP study referred to in chapter 2. Pratt, the experimenter, turned over decks of symbol cards one by one. Pearce, the reputed clairvoyant, sat in a building 100 yards away (or on one series, 250 yards away). After completing his decks, Pratt wrote down the succession of symbols. The distant Pearce had recorded his impressions of what the symbols had been, and the two lists were later compared by a third party for symbol matches. Each symbol was one of five possibilities, so that the chance level of successful matching was 20%. The reported overall success rate, with 50 trials on each of 35 days, was 30.1%, significant at $p < .000000001$. However—and this is what makes the example pertinent here—the success rate was highly variable, giving rise to what critic Morris Hansel (1980) characterized as a bimodal distribution.

Hansel (1980) found the situation suspicious. Some days yielded upwards of 40% correct, but other days only 15% correct. Why? Inspecting the site on the Duke University campus, he constructed an elaborate hypothesis of fraud. According to Hansel, the receiver Pearce, motivated by notoriety as a presumed psychic, cheated. On many of the days, he slipped out of the other building as the trials began, hid across the hall from Pratt's office, and stood on a table from which he could see Pratt's symbols through a pair of open transoms. With time enough to copy some or all of them, he left his hiding place and simulated an arrival from the other building. On his symbol sheet, he made sure not to look too perfect, but otherwise produced strong "data." Pratt, his back to the transoms, was an innocent party to the deception.

The distribution, given by stem-and-leaf in Table 5.2, is even more peculiar than Hansel (1980) thought. Note that there is an apparent gap in the distribution at 10 correct answers; scores of 10, 11, and 12 never occurred. If the process generating the distribution were a binomial with $p = .2$, then 10 would be the most likely outcome, with 11 and 12 not far behind. There is an apparent separation of the data into two distinct clusters, one for successful days and one for days of negative success. Defenders of ESP typically account for two-mode distributions by arguing that extrasensory perception is a delicate process often disrupted by fatigue, distraction, or skepticism, producing performance at or below chance level (e.g., Bem & Honorton, 1994). This argument is not very compelling as a post hoc explanation of a given data set for which there is no independent evidence that such unfavorable conditions were

TABLE 5.2
Stem-and-Leaf of the Pratt–Pearce ESP Data: Successful Hits Per 50 Trials

2	4	
2	333	
2	0000001	
1	89	
1	677	
1	445	
1	3333	
1		←—— Note the strange gap!
0	8889999	
0	6	
0	55	
0	3	

present. In any case, it is very odd that if some of the days' performances were attributable to chance, there would be seven scores of 8 or 9, but none of 10, 11, or 12. And if some days were systematically worse than chance, why weren't they more strikingly worse? The lower tail of the distribution is about what one would expect from a binomial process.

If Hansel (1980) is right that cheating occurred, a speculative account of the strange distribution might go like this: Pearce wrote down his sincere guesses of the cards, hoping that he would spontaneously do better than chance. Upon getting a peek at Pratt's decks, he quickly added up his score. If it was average or better—10 or more—he altered somewhere between three and eight responses to juice up his score. If it was 9 or worse, he left it alone, figuring that too many changes would be needed, and doing always better than chance would look suspicious.

I should note that before constructing this elaborate speculation, I considered the possibility that the gap in the distribution in Table 5.2 was merely a fluke departure from a smooth unimodal distribution. After all, chance is lumpy. We need a significance test for the presence of gaps in distributions. In fact, at least one such test exists (Wainer & Schacht, 1978). The details are not necessary for us here, but when the gap test is applied to the present data, the test statistic is the critical ratio $z = 5.81$, which is extraordinarily highly significant. In other words, even allowing for the fact that the gap was noticed post hoc, we can be highly confident that the gap was not a chance fluke.

Sometimes gaps are incomplete; the number of cases in the underpopulated portion of the distribution may be small rather than zero. There exists a "dip test," too, for assessing whether a dip is reasonably attributable to chance (Hartigan & Hartigan, 1985). If a significant dip is found, it is evidence for the mixture of two separate generating processes.

This test is rather complex, however. The whole area of distribution snooping is a candidate for the development of new statistical techniques, to solidify the inferences we make by eyeballing distributions. Reliance on appearance alone risks underappreciation of the lumpiness of chance. These remarks apply also to two other distributional anomalies, *cliffs* and *peaks*, discussed later.

When Gaps or Dips Are Hypothesized

Fishiness aside, the search for gaps and dips can also be performed as a test of theoretical expectations. I have run across two examples of this, and there are undoubtedly many more.

Example: Bimodal Distribution of a Trait.   Gangestad and Snyder (1991) hypothesized that a subgroup of the general population is genetically constituted so as to be distinctly high on the personality trait of "self-monitoring" (Snyder, 1974). They argued that were it not for environmental influences and measurement errors tending to blur the manifestation of this trait, its distribution in the population would be discontinuous. Even at that, the observed distribution on a scale assessing self-monitoring should be bimodal. Their article presents an analysis like a dip test, and concludes in favor of their hypothesis.

Example: Is Dyslexia a Distinct Entity?   The second example is of considerable consequence for educational policy toward children with learning disabilities, estimated to constitute about 15% of the school-age population. There is an ongoing debate (Rosenberger, 1992) as to whether or not children diagnosed as "dyslexic" constitute a discrete group, potentially distinguishable from other children by some particular brain defect, as yet undiscovered.

Shaywitz, Escobar, Shaywitz, Fletcher, and Makuch (1992) accumulated the test scores used in dyslexia diagnosis on several hundred school children, and looked for a dip in the distribution. The reasoning was that if indeed dyslexia were a discrete condition (either you have it or you don't), a clear dip would separate dyslexics from normals. The investigators found a smooth distribution with no discernible dip, and concluded that dyslexia cannot be characterized as discrete. Rather, it must be a condition that can vary in degree, some people being more dyslexic than others.

This analysis might conceivably be misleading. A hidden problem of interpretation arises from measurement errors. The widely accepted diagnostic score for dyslexia, used in the Shaywitz et al. (1992) research, consists of the *difference* between an overall IQ score and the score on a particular reading test. Errors of measurement are especially pronounced for difference scores between two related ability measures (Cohen & Cohen, 1983). To understand the effect of measurement error, picture an underlying distribution of "true" scores on a scale of dyslexia proneness, with a dip in it. Now turn loose a bunch of measurement-error leprechauns who play horseshoes with the scores, tossing each of them haphazardly to the left or right along the scale. If the variability of the lengths of the tosses were great enough, the result would be that the dip in the distribution would be concealed (covered by sand from the horseshoe game, one might say).

The lesson in this is that although a gap or dip in an observed distribution implies a mixture of underlying processes, the converse does not necessarily hold. The failure to find a gap or dip could occasionally be because due to the obscuring effects of measurement error.

Cliffs

Some frequency distributions pile up as one or the other tail is approached, and then abruptly drop off entirely. The type of distribution confusingly named the J-shaped distribution is of this character. There are very few observations in the upper tail. As we move leftward from the upper tail, the frequencies increase until we reach a mode at a score of zero. There are no scores below zero, so we might say that there is a *cliff* at zero.

Distributions of Looking Time.   As an illustration of a legitimate cliff, consider a study of the smiling responses of infants when they are presented with adult faces, real or simulated. Each face is shown for, say, 2 minutes, and the amount of time the infant stares at the face is recorded. When distributions of looking time are tallied across infants, times of zero (i.e., no looking) can occur often. Because negative times are impossible, this creates a cliff.

A Disclaimer.   The next two examples are undocumented, as my only exposure to them was through anonymous public statements. Nevertheless, they are sufficiently interesting to warrant inclusion.

Example: Differences Between Ratings of Ingroup and Outgroup. In the previous example, the striking occurrence of a cliff at zero has an obvious explanation: negative looking times are meaningless. Thus the cliff, although visually arresting, is not fishy. In some other cases, negative scores are possible but never (or hardly ever) occur, even though scores of zero are quite frequent. This is cause for detective work.

Consider the bellwether finding of "social identity theory" (Tajfel & Turner, 1986) that most members of racial and ethnic groups judge their own group to possess favorable characteristics in greater degree than opposing groups. This provides a useful way to diagnose racial or other prejudices, as asking directly about *negative* characteristics of out-groups arouses resistance in the many respondents who are averse to blatant expression of stereotypes.

When Whites are asked to rate on a 7-point scale various groups on such positive traits as "industriousness," for example, it is typical that Whites are rated higher than African Americans, consistent with a stereotype. There is a curious property of these ratings, however. If one takes for each respondent the difference between his ratings of indus-triousness for Whites and African Americans, the left-hand tail of the distribution of differences contains a number of respondents for whom the difference is as small as zero, yet there are virtually no negative differences! That is, there is a cliff at zero: Some Whites are willing to grant that African Americans are as industrious as Whites, but not that they are more industrious. If the ratings were made without self-con-sciousness, measurement error alone would produce a smooth tail containing some negative differences. The cliff suggests that, collectively, racially tolerant Whites are expressing their egalitarianism by highly self-conscious design.

Peaks

Another distributional property suggesting that something odd may be going on is a high peak at a central mode. Smooth distributions such as the normal distribution are usually referred to as "bell-shaped." An important characteristic of this shape is that the central region of the distribution is rounded off, like the profiles of small mountains in the eastern United States, such as the Adirondacks. Contrast this with the geologically newer Rockies, which have sharp, nearly conical peaks. When a distribution has this shape, a possible explanation is a compound distribution in which a deviant process contributes extra observations at the mode of the regular process (rather than outliers in the tails). It is also possible that the distribution is really bell-shaped, but has a very small standard deviation.

To distinguish between these two possibilities, we need to consider the *slope* of the frequency distribution as we move away from a central peak. Like a smooth ski slope, the top is steep, but at a critical point—the "point of inflection"—there begins a gradual leveling off. In a (nearly) normal distribution, the point of inflection is (approximately) 1 *SD* (standard deviation) from the peak. If one has some estimate of the appropriate size for the standard deviation, one can assess whether the peak is too steep and narrow, thereby suggesting a deviant process. This becomes clearer from the example.

Example: The Blackout and the Baby Boom.   Shortly after 5 p.m. on November 10, 1965, a huge blackout struck parts of Canada and New England and most of the New York metropolitan area. Elevator service was knocked out in offices and apartment buildings; subways didn't run; dark streets and inoperative traffic lights discouraged automobile travel. People who somehow managed to get home, or were already there, spent the evening in darkness, without the diversion of television. The event much impressed itself on the collective consciousness of New Yorkers, who told stories about that night for a long time to come.

The following August, a newspaper reporter happened to be in Bellevue Hospital in the maternity ward, where he noticed an unusual amount of activity. Curious, he inquired of a nurse whether there seemed to be a larger than usual number of babies being born. She agreed that there were. In discussing this fact, the reporter recalled that the blackout had been exactly 9 months before. Sensing a human interest story, the reporter contacted several other New York hospitals, and all confirmed high numbers of births.

It was a Monday. On Tuesday, birth rates were still high in New York hospitals. The newspapers published figures showing that the number of babies born on those 2 days were far in excess of what would be expected from the annual birth rate, and any statistically trained reader who cared to apply a statistical significance test would have confirmed that the excess was statistically reliable. The news media circulated a story concluding that New Yorkers had found a productive way to use the darkness thrust upon them by the blackout.

By Wednesday of the critical week the number of births fell substantially, and on Thursday and Friday, births leveled off. Follow-up stories took this downtrend as confirmation of a blackout sex spree, as the time gap now surpassed 9 months.

I know of no systematic survey of belief in this charming hypothesis, but my recollection of informal conversations at the time the news broke is that the phenomenon was widely accepted. (A few years later, I asked an undergraduate class how many of them believed that there was an excess of births 9 months after the New York blackout, and about three-fourths raised their hands. The others weren't disbelievers—they simply hadn't heard about the blackout.)

A thoughtful statistician (anonymous) was suspicious of the matter, however, because the drop-off of births seemed too sudden to him. The point of inflection of the slope occurred on Wednesday, 2 days after the critical Monday, implying a standard deviation of 2 days for human gestation times. The statistician knew, however, that the time from conception to birth has a standard deviation of about a week.

To explore the cause of the strange peak in the distribution, the statistician sought comparison data. He assembled birth records from the major maternity wards in New York over a time period stretching from many weeks before the critical 9-month target date to many weeks after, and a remarkably consistent pattern emerged. On *every* Monday and Tuesday, births exceeded the weekly average, and on every Friday, Saturday, and Sunday, births were lower than average. The pattern for the week on which the reporter had focused was not significantly different from the general pattern, and there was no reliable evidence for an excess number of births in the target week. The newspaper reporter had simply stumbled upon the usual within-week trend, and had fallaciously associated the birth data with the blackout. (Note that his error falls into the general category of insufficient comparison, discussed in chap. 1.)

But why, you may wonder, should there be a within-week trend? Why should women be differentially likely to go into labor on different days of the week? Upon discussion with obstetricians, a perfectly plausible explanation emerged. In the not inconsiderable number of cases requiring induced labor or Caesarean operations, doctors tend to schedule the procedure for the beginning of the week, rather than for a weekend. The excess births reported at the beginning of the critical week had to do with doctors' needs for rest and recreation rather than with the aphrodisiac properties of blackouts.

THE OCCURRENCE OF IMPOSSIBLE SCORES

We now shift gears to consider an oddity that arises from errors of coding of raw scores. It is frequently the case that data sets with many measures on many subjects have holes in them, that is, missing observations for particular scores of a few subjects. Computer data analysis packages such as SAS promise the user that missing data will be properly handled (either by dropping some cases or by estimation of the missing data points). The user's part of the bargain is to denote by a given code which observations are missing. In SAS, a period (.) is the proper code, but for one reason or another, missing data indicators may not find their way into the input file in the right places.

One common error is to put blanks where periods should be. These will ordinarily be converted to data points with a score of zero. If zero is a possible score on the measure in use, these phonies are likely to go undetected. If, luckily, zero is an impossible score, a simple inspection of the distribution in the computer file will reveal the mistake. This is something you cannot usually do with other people's data, but should get in the habit of doing with your own.

Another variant of this situation arises often in dealing with survey data files obtained from established survey organizations such as the General Social Survey (Davis & Smith, 1991). Missing data are typically indicated by out-of-range response codes. For example, the respondent's education is coded as number of years of school completed: 08 for completing grade school, 12 for completing high school, 16 for a college graduate, 20 for a PhD, and intermediate numbers for partial completions. If a respondent fails to answer the education question (or the interviewer to recode it), this is coded as 99. Obviously, all statistical analysis programs should be told in one way or another to treat 99s as missing observations. Imagine the chaos caused by averaging 99s with 12s and 16s to obtain mean numbers of school years completed; or the deformed correlations of education with other variables such as income, each variable contaminated with its bogus sets of 99s.

The obvious prophylactic against such arithmetical butchery is to inspect the distributions of codes after the files have been edited. If 99s remain, fix them! If the 99 virus somehow survives in your data, you may have later chances to detect this through the occurrence of strange means, strange variances, or strange test statistics—but it is risky to let matters get that far.

STRANGE TEST STATISTICS

Fishy things turn up not only in raw data, but also commonly in summary statistics or in the results of statistical tests. We cover several diagnostics that can be applied to these quantities. First we deal with null hypothesis tests, in which test statistics such as t or F that are much too large—or much too small—are cause for raised eyebrows.

A Huge Test Statistic

When hoping to reject a null hypothesis, the investigator welcomes large values of F, or chi-square, or whatever the test statistic happens to be. Fs of 10 or 20 are thus cause for celebration. But when the computer printout tells you that you have an F of 500, hold the champagne. It is quite rare in psychological research for Fs to be that huge, except for crushingly obvious relationships (such as the average height of men in a large sample differing from the average height of women), or for routine checks of strong experimental manipulations.

To give the reader some feeling for big F values, we first note that larger samples tend to produce larger Fs. For any given effect magnitude, the average value of F is approximately proportional to the n of cases per group. A useful way to interpret the ratio of F to n is in terms of the standardized effect size (chap. 3). It is easy to show (e.g., from Rosenthal, 1991, Equation 2.14) that the (F/n) ratio is approximately equal to one half the squared standardized effect size.

Distributions of standardized effect sizes arising in meta-analyses show that in domains of substantive research interest, it is unusual for this magnitude measure to be as big as 1.0, quite rare for it to be as big as 1.4, and extraordinary[2] for it to be as big as 2.0. These statements of rarity can be translated into, "It is unusual for F/n to be as big as .5, quite rare for it to be 1.0 or larger, and extraordinary for it to exceed 2.0." In other words, if you've got a typically modest n, say 25, an F of 25 would border on being amazing, and an F of 50 would represent either a mistake or a result so obvious that any child would have anticipated it in advance. To check the possibility of a mistake, the investigator could

---

[2]The reader might try the following exercise. Find three or four meta-analyses in the journal of your choice, and for each one using the standardized effect size as their measure, tabulate the percentages of occurrence of values numerically greater than 1.0, 1.4, and 2.0. I did this with the first three *Psychological Bulletin* articles I happened to pick up: Oliver and Hyde (1993), on gender differences in sexual attitudes and practices; Roese and Jamieson (1993) on the *bogus pipeline* technique for eliciting honest responses from subjects; and Polich, Pollock, and Bloom (1994), on the P300 brain wave in relation to alcoholism. In the first article, 8% of the effect sizes had absolute values above 1.0, only 2% above 1.4, and .2% above 2.0. The second article contained 13% with values beyond 1.0, and none at the higher levels. The third analysis had 7% above 1.0, and 3% above 1.4.

boxplot (Hoaglin et al., 1991; Tukey, 1977) the distributions of the observations to be assured that the separate groups look grossly different from one another, as implied by the humongous F.

There is a subtle alternative explanation of many overplump Fs. This has to do with *positive bias* in F tests, arising when extra variables beyond those being tested contribute more variance to the numerator than to the denominator of the F test. A paradigmatic case is the following scenario: Two different educational programs are compared, by administering Program A to a number of randomly selected children in a few randomly selected schools, and Program B in similar fashion to other children in other schools. Suppose that the statistical analysis is conducted by comparing all the Program A children en masse with all the Program B children, without taking schools into account. If scores for different schools differ systematically from each other for reasons having nothing to do with the tested programs (as they usually will), then the F ratio will be artificially inflated, possibly by a considerable amount.

Such cases occur in many guises, having in common that the observations are not all independent (Kenny & Judd, 1986) of each other, as required by the statistical model for the F test. The clumping of similar cases (e.g., children in the same school) must be dealt with in the statistical analysis (see Kirk, in press).

Parallel explanations occur for chi-squares or other test statistics that come out astonishingly large: Either the test was extremely uninteresting, or a numerical error occurred, or the test was conceptually faulty. The general moral is, don't be overjoyed when your test statistics come out whopping. Be suspicious.

A Test Statistic That Seems Too Good for the Data It Came From

Example: Power to the Students (and to the t Test).   Sometimes a test statistic that is not enormous in absolute terms nevertheless seems larger than it deserves to be. Consider the example used in Table 2.1, showing the mean self-ratings on a liberalism–conservatism scale for participants and nonparticipants in a campus demonstration. We did not say so in chapter 2, but those figures came from a *revised* calculation. The table originally developed by the student contained the figures in Table 5.3. The mean difference is the same as in the previous table, but the t value is much larger here.

When I originally saw this result in a larger table, I did a double take. The difference between the means is said to be .02. As noted in chapter 2, if 1 of the 29 people in the participant group had given himself a rating of 2 rather than 3, say, the mean rating would have been lower by $\frac{1}{29}$,

TABLE 5.3
Mean Self-Ratings of Liberalism by Participants and Nonparticipants in a
Campus Demonstration

Participants (N = 29)	Nonparticipants (N = 23)
2.72	2.70

Note. On a 7-point scale, 1 = very liberal, 7 = very conservative.
$t(50) = 5.56, p < .0001$.

or .034, reversing the direction of the difference between participants and nonparticipants. Yet the t value is given as 5.56, with $p < .0001$. Think! Could the formula for t possibly be so vulnerable to a minimal change in a single score as to drop from 5.56 to a negative value?

When told that the means and the t value could not possibly be consistent, the student who generated the table said, "Well, maybe the assumptions of the t test were violated." This superficially plausible response gets a flunking mark on that week's test in Statistics 101. Satisfaction of the assumptions of the t test (normal distributions, homogeneous variances) guarantees the relationship between t and its tabled p value. If the assumptions are violated, the p value could be somewhat distorted. But here the t itself is arithmetically suspect, and the laws of arithmetic do not depend on homogeneous variances. There is no way a t ratio with a numerator of .02 can come out as big as 5.56 in this situation.[3] Sure enough, the student eventually discovered a data entry problem, and recalculated the t to be .07.

The error here was large in absolute terms. In other cases, a large relative increase in a test statistic from analysis to reanalysis provides the clue. I call this "the Amazing Grace effect."

A Sharp Increase in the Test Statistic on Reanalysis

The lovely gospel song, "Amazing Grace," expresses the feelings of a sinner who has miraculously found salvation. The thematic line is, "I once was lost, but now I'm found." I am reminded of this theme when I see an incredible transformation of a dreadful statistical situation into a triumphant one.

Here is how it goes: The investigator, desperately seeking a finding significant at the .05 level, is wracked with despair that tests of all the interesting effects yield nothing even remotely approaching significance. But then he rearranges the numbers, or reconceptualizes a comparison,

---

[3]One might try to argue that the t ratio can have any large value at all, even with a numerator as small as .02, simply by virtue of an even smaller denominator. Here, however, the ratings were whole numbers on a 7-point scale, and the means came out in between. Given these means, there must necessarily be variability within each group. In fact, the denominator cannot be less than .129, and the t ratio cannot exceed .22.

or does an F test in some other way, and suddenly and miraculously, he is saved by a rejection of the null hypothesis. Redemption is at hand, as the born-again investigator can now claim a substantive result.

Example: Does a Good Mood Dull the Mind?   A case of an amazing rescue of a null result occurred in the following example from the initial draft of a Yale dissertation, designed to test the joint effects of mood and motivation on sensitivity of judgment.

Prior investigators (Worth & Mackie, 1987) had found that people in a good mood tend to be less discriminating in making stimulus judgments, as though lulled into an inattentive state of mind. The dissertation student noted that in those prior studies, however, subjects' motivations for performing well in the experimental task were probably quite low. He set out to explore the possibility that the relative cognitive sluggishness of good mood would disappear if the motivation for doing the experimental task were at a higher level.

Accordingly, he evoked either neutral or good moods under either poorly or highly motivating circumstances, with subjects randomly assigned to the four possible groups. Mood was manipulated with film and music, and motivation by varying the apparent importance of the results for the student community. The experimental task involved rating the quality of arguments in a speech that had been designed by the experimenter to contain some strong and some weak arguments. The measure of each subject's sensitivity was the difference between his mean quality ratings of the good and the bad arguments. Table 5.4 shows the means of these measures for each of the four groups.

The student investigator presenting these results saw a hint of support for his hypothesis. Under low motivation, the good-mood group displayed less sensitivity than did the neutral-mood group, whereas under high motivation, the good-mood group was more sensitive than the neutrals. Of course, these mood effects look small, as the student noted, so that a significance test is called for. The standard null hypothesis here would be that the superiority of the neutral- over the good-mood condition is the same under high and low motivation, that is, that there is no interaction between mood and motivation. The student hoped to reject this null hypothesis, but alas, the appropriate F ratio came out

TABLE 5.4
Mean Sensitivity Scores in Rating the Quality of Arguments

Mood	Motivation	
	Low	*High*
Neutral	1.00	3.05
Good	.50	3.10

Note. $N = 20$ per cell. Within-group mean square = 10.83.

$F(1,76) = .14$, a trifling value nowhere near the 3.96 needed to reach the 5% rejection region. It would be extraordinarily brash to claim a systematic interaction on the basis of these data; one can have virtually no confidence that the directions of difference between good mood and neutral mood in the two columns would hold up if a new sample of subjects were run. (Even taking just the low-motivation groups, a t test of the difference between the means of 1.00 and .50 yields a skimpy t of .48.)

Dejected but prayerful, the student came up with a new way to look at the matter. What he was really claiming, he said, was that sensitivity of judgment was at its lowest when subjects had a good mood and low motivation, and any change in these conditions would produce an improvement. Accordingly, he calculated the *contrast* (Rosenthal & Rosnow, 1985) between the good-mood, low-motivation cell mean and the average of the three other cell means. Miraculously, the F test of this contrast yielded $F(1,76) = 4.91$, $p < .05$, and the student regarded his claim as supported. Amazing grace!

What's going on here? How did an F ratio of .14 increase 35-fold to 4.91 with an apparently minor shift in emphasis in the statement of the investigator's substantive hypothesis? Exploration of the concrete numerical effect of the investigator's rescue procedure is needed.

Looking back at Table 5.4, we see that what his procedure did was to compare .50 with the average of 1.00, 3.05, and 3.10, that is, .50 versus 2.38. The difference of 1.88 was significant at the 5% level. But the 2.38 figure was clearly pulled up by the two high-motivation means of 3.05 and 3.10. Despite the statistical sleight of hand here, common sense should tell us that what the student has done is to take advantage of the main effect of motivation to make an unwarranted claim concerning the mood variable.

I hasten to add that not every statistical salvation is illusory. In chapter 4, we referred to the sometimes amazing but justifiable effects of transformations of the response scale, and in chapter 6, we give an example applauding the use of a contrast of one cell against the mean of the other three cells of a 2×2 table. What we can say for sure, though, is that enough miracles are fraudulent to suggest very close examination of fantastic statistical redemptions.

Statistics That Come Out Too Small

Also diagnostic of potential fishiness, but less obvious, are cases when the test statistic comes out too small, rather than too large. Suppose, for example, that with four groups of 10 subjects each, the test of between-group differences yields the value $F_{3,36} = .005$. Such a minuscule F is extraordinary, if you stop to think about it. It is easy to pass it by without notice, perhaps mistaking it for a p value instead of an F, or categorizing it simply as < 1, thus nonsignificant. However, it indicates that the four group means are almost exactly identical, as though someone were naively trying to cook the data to support the null hypothesis.

How can we test whether an F is too small, and what would such a result suggest? An F can be judged significantly too small by seeing if the associated p value on the computer printout is above .95—or more stringently, above .99. When you do this, you are using the lower, rather than the upper tail of the F distribution. If you are not using a computer, or the program doesn't print exact p values for the lower tail, then what you can do is to reverse the degrees of freedom and refer the *reciprocal* of F to the usual F tables. In our example, you would get reciprocal $F_{36,3}$ = 200. This value exceeds the tabled 1% value of 26.45 with 36 and 3 degrees of freedom. Because the reciprocal F is significantly too big, the original F was significantly too small. (With very few degrees of freedom in the denominator, the critical tabled values of F run rather large; thus the reciprocal F has to be quite sizable to achieve significance.)

There are two main interpretations of an overly tiny F in one's data. It could be a fluke, or (the more interesting alternative) a characteristic aberration in the experimental design. Not much can be said about flukes (chance results). An F can every once in a while come out too small when the null hypothesis is approximately true, just as an F can occasionally come out too large by chance. An isolated case of a tiny F can readily be dismissed as a fluke, but a consistent pattern of too-small Fs very likely indicates a design flaw.

Clusters of small Fs suggest the presence of negative bias, that is, a systematic tendency for the mean squares in the numerators of the F ratios to be smaller than the error mean squares. Such negative bias occurs when some systematic factor contributes a lot of variance to the error term, but not to the numerator(s) of the F test(s).

Example: Rats!   My cousin Robert M. Abelson has suggested the following example, based loosely on a dissertation at the University of Maine: An experiment with rats is designed to compare the effects of three different reinforcement schedules on a bar-pressing response. For this study, the experimenter has available five litters of six rats each. Aware that rats from different litters vary a great deal, he seeks to balance out from the three conditions any bias due to litters: He randomly assigns two rats from each litter to each of the three conditions. The response data are analyzed by F test, with the three conditions as the between-groups factor, and subjects (10 per condition) as the within-groups factor. Litters are ignored in the analysis, because the experimenter feels he has balanced them out. In fact, he is so confident that litter bias has been eliminated that he keeps no records of which rats came from which litter.

When he performs his F test, however, he discovers that the F for conditions is nowhere near significant; in fact it is considerably below 1.

He analyzes several different variants of the response measure, with the same outcome. In desperation, he revises the experimental manipulations to try to make them stronger, and repeats the entire study with rats from five new litters. The same type of analysis again yields Fs the size of pinheads.

What's the catch? Evidently, litters make a huge contribution to variation in the response measure. This variation enters the within-condition sum of squares (because the various litters are each represented within each condition), but does not enter the between-condition sum of squares, as the experimenter so carefully equated their representation across conditions. The result is a large negative bias in the F ratio, swamping the opportunity for a systematic between-condition effect to manifest itself. The cure that suggests itself is to calculate and set aside between-litter effects by treating the design as a two-way factorial, Conditions by Litters, with two subjects in each cell. Alas, the experimenter could not do this because he no longer knew which rats were from which litter. Ironically, had the experimenter randomly assigned rats to conditions without balancing for litters—causing the litters component of variation to inflate the between-conditions sum of squares as well as the within-conditions—he would have been better off than he was in the actual circumstances. This seems paradoxical, as it releases control over a known source of variance. Indeed, the resulting F test lacks power—but at least it is not negatively biased.

A conceptually similar case occurs when subjects of varying skill or ability levels are carefully matched across experimental conditions, and then the data are analyzed by an ordinary t or F test. In these examples, the extraneous balancing factor is explicitly recognized (albeit mishandled) by the experimenter. More insidious are cases with an important but unknown source of variation unwittingly balanced across experimental conditions. This is especially likely to occur when, for convenience, subjects are run in small groups of equal size, with random assignment of whole groups to experimental conditions. Some unsuspected factor, like seating position, or particular computer terminal, might contribute to response variation within each group. (Say, people seated nearer the window consistently score worse because of distractions outside.)

The inadvertent balancing of this factor across experimental conditions introduces a bias tending to make the F test for conditions come out too small. Such a factor could be subtle enough to escape notice in the design of the experiment, but small Fs should cue the investigator to look for this phenomenon. The corrective actions are comparable to those for the rat litter example. If the perfectly balanced factor can be identified, include it explicitly in the analysis. A second choice would be to randomize the factor among conditions in future studies rather than balancing it.

A Model That Fits Too Well

Thus far in this book, we have dealt with statistical tests of a null hypothesis that the investigator hopes to discredit in favor of her statistical alternative. There is another whole class of applications of statistical tests in which the investigator tries to fit her data with a substantive quantitative model. The F or chi-square statistic indexes the *degree of departure* of the data from the model.[4] Here the researcher likes to see a small value of the test statistic.

If the statistic is not merely small, but is very small, there may occasionally be cause for suspicion. It is fine for a model to fit well, but it is too much to expect that it will fit *perfectly*.[5] "Cooking" or selectively biasing the data so as to make the theory look good can be entertained as a possible explanation of one or more oversmall test statistics.

> *Example. Mendel's Pea Plants.*   One of the most shocking accusations of data cooking concerns the pioneer geneticist Gregor Mendel, whose experiments with pea plants are credited with establishing the hereditary roles of dominant and recessive genes.
>
> In cross-breeding a tall plant with a short plant, for example, every descendant is a hybrid, having one gene for tallness and one for shortness; because tallness is dominant, the plants will all be tall. Crossing a pair of these hybrid plants with each other gives rise to four equiprobable genotypic possibilities—tall/tall, tall/short, short/tall, and short/short—of which only the last yields a visibly short plant. This simple model thus predicts a 3:1 ratio favoring the dominant feature among offspring of hybrid parents. Observed relative frequencies from such breeding can be compared with the expected 3:1 ratio by a simple chi-square test.
>
> Mendel's published data proposed in support of this analysis were critically scrutinized by the renowned, but crusty statistician Sir Ronald Fisher (1936). He noted a large number of outcomes for which the chi-square was too small (i.e., $p > .90$). A typical instance was from a study predicting a 3:1 ratio of plants with yellow versus green seeds. The data presented were: (Yellow, 6,022; Green, 2,001). The chi-square on these frequencies is .015 with 1 df (degree of freedom), corresponding to $p > .90$. Altogether, the evidence presented in support of the theory looked to Fisher too good to be believed, leading him to suggest that Mendel or his assistants may have falsified something when presenting his data.
>
> A more benign explanation was given by Olby (1985). He noted that the frequency counts were tallied cumulatively over time, as different

---

[4]A systematic treatment of this strategy is given by Judd and McClelland (1989).

[5]My Aunt Sara tells the story of *her* aunt, who had a foolproof method of dismissing criticism. Great-aunt would draw herself up to her full 4'11". *"Poifeck?!"* she would snort, "You want I should be *poifeck?!*"

batches of plants were processed. The stopping points were variable, and this led Olby to conjecture that Mendel quit each study when satisfied that sufficient numbers of cases had been accumulated. This procedure, although apparently innocently done, of course is subject to the bias that you can wait until things look really good for the model before you stop.

Because Mendel's theory turns out to be true despite this transgression, he can be forgiven his bias. At the time Mendel performed his experiments, statistical sophistication was low, and chi-square tests were not available. Imagine the dilemma, then, when an experiment with 120 offspring predicted to divide 90:30 came out, say, 98:22, a ratio well over 4:1 instead of the predicted 3:1. Nowadays we might run the chi-square test, get a value of 2.84 with 1 df, insignificant at the .05 level, and move on happily to the next data set. But Mendel and/or his assistants did not appreciate exactly how large the effects of chance were as a function of sample size. He knew enough to distrust small samples, but not enough to distrust the strategy of "quit when you're ahead."

INCONSISTENCIES BETWEEN PARALLEL STATISTICS

With considerable frequency, research reports include batches of significance tests: ts and Fs, usually, on different dependent variables, or on different subgroups of subjects. A few simple consistency checks in this situation often provide clues to fishiness.

Explicit statements of consistency principles will help in this detective process:

Principle 1: With degrees of freedom held constant, the bigger the absolute size of t (or F), the lower the p value. This principle is self-evident. All it says is that there is less area in the tails of a distribution, the farther out you go. Yet it is surprising that one can readily find research reports in which this principle is violated.

A manuscript[6] I reviewed in 1992 for a leading social psychological journal contained the following bizarre statement: "...Reliable interactions emerged for [Measure 1], $F_{1,66} = 5.25$, $p < .001$, and for [Measure 2], $F_{1,66} = 5.75$, $p < .05$..." Clearly there is a mistake. An F of 5.75 can't yield a weaker p level than an F of 5.25, when both are based on the same degrees of freedom. The first statement should say $p < .05$, not $< .001$.

Our second principle is slightly less obvious.

Principle 2: When two or more separate mean differences based on the same number of observations and the same standard error are t tested, the absolute sizes of the t ratios should be proportional to the absolute sizes of the mean differences. This principle follows from the

---

[6]The identity of the authors will be suppressed upon request.

TABLE 5.5
Stated Results of a Three-Group Experiment: Mean Ratings of Task Enjoyment

	Group		
	Control	$1	$20
Mean Ratings	−.45	+1.35	−.05
Differences	(1.80)		(1.40)
Stated t Ratios	2.48		2.22

concept of (and formula for) a t test as the ratio of a mean difference to its standard error.[7]

Example: That $1/$20 Study Again. For an example in which this principle appears to have been violated, let us consider again the classic Festinger and Carlsmith (1959) experiment discussed in chapter 2. Recall the dissonance theory prediction: Subjects paid $1, rather than $20, to tell someone that the dull experimental task had been fun would later agree more that the task indeed had been enjoyable. The mean ratings of the task as "interesting and enjoyable," on a scale from −3 to +3, were +1.35 by the $1 group, and −.05 by the $20 group. The authors gave the value $t = 2.22$ (with $p < .03$), for the test of the theoretically predicted difference between the $1 and $20 groups. The experimenters also ran a control group, whose subjects were asked about the enjoyability of the task without previously having told anybody anything about it. The control group mean was given as −.45, and the test of the difference between the $1 group and the control group as $t = 2.48, p < .02$. (At the time the article was written, multiple comparison procedures had not been developed, and the liberal procedure of multiple t testing among a group of means was widely practiced.)

In Table 5.5, the essential quantitative statements are organized for comparison. By Principle 2, the t values, 2.48 and 2.22, should be in the same ratio as the mean differences, 1.80 and 1.40. But $(2.48/2.22) = 1.12$, whereas $(1.80/1.40) = 1.29$. Is there statistical skullduggery going on here?

The authors did not provide within-group variances, so we cannot simply recompute everything. We must use Principle 2 as our basis for reinterpreting the numbers. If we accept the mean differences as accurate, and direct our scrutiny at the t tests, we conclude that either the $t = 2.48$ between the $1 group and the control group should be bigger, or the $t = 2.22$ between the $1 group and the $20 group should be smaller. Because it is hard to imagine investigators erring by underclaiming a desirable and legitimate result, our best bet is the latter conclusion—the 2.22 should be smaller. A simple fix for this would be to lower this t by

---

[7]When F ratios instead of t ratios are used, the principle is that two F ratios with the same error terms should be proportional to the *squares* of the respective mean differences.

just enough to satisfy Principle 2. This yields a corrected $t = 2.48 \times (1.40/1.80) = 1.93$, which is not significant at the (two-tailed) .05 level for any number of degrees of freedom. Because this t pertains to the key theoretical difference between the $1 and $20 conditions, a nonsignificant t would have been a rhetorical annoyance or worse for these researchers, and one could imagine them somehow inflating the 1.93 to 2.22.

Before we jump to skullduggery as the explanation, however, a more benign account should be considered. Examining the fine print, as it were, of Principle 2, we note the presupposition that the two t ratios are based on the same standard error. It is conventional practice nowadays, when calculating more than one t value (or when performing a multiple comparison test) in a multiple group study, to use the *pooled within-group mean square* as the basis for standard errors of all means and mean differences. This practice guarantees the presupposition needed for Principle 2. However, when the Festinger and Carlsmith (1959) article was written, the use of a pooled error term was sometimes advocated, but was not yet conventional. What they must have done[8] was to use the variability of ratings within the $1 and $20 groups for the t test of that group difference, and the variability within the $1 and control groups for the other t test. For the former t (2.22) to come out larger than Principle 2 requires, implies that the variability of scores within the $20 group was smaller than that within the control group.

What message should one carry away from this supersleuthing job? One might fault the authors for the somewhat brash choice of the more favorable of two analytic options, though the practical difference between a t of 1.93, with $p < .06$ and a t of 2.22, with $p < .03$, is not huge if one is not obsessed with the literal .05 level. The investigators are lucky that the crucial t, when "corrected," had not shrunk to say, $t = 1.00$, with $p = .32$. Then the dramatic, evocative result of this classic experiment could have been reduced to mush by a critic sharp-eyed enough to notice the violation of Principle 2.

But is the convention of using the single pooled error term "right"? The investigators might have made the reasonable argument that the variability of scores within the control group should have no bearing on the $1 versus $20 comparison. Statistics texts tend to tell readers (if they say anything at all) that the reason for pooling error is to increase degrees of freedom (e.g., Keppel, 1991; Kirk, in press). There is a better reason, however, which can best be understood in terms of:

Principle 3: When two or more separate mean differences based on the same number of observations and the same standard error are t tested, the bigger the mean difference, the smaller the p value.

This principle follows immediately from the conjunction of Principles 1 and 2. Note the qualifying phrase, "the same standard error." Omit this, and Principle 3 need not hold in a given case. And what a fine

---

[8]No one connected with the analysis of the original data is still alive.

how-de-do *that* would be! You could have a bigger mean difference in a given data set declared less significant (i.e., having a larger p value) than the smaller mean difference. Such an outcome would yield different orderings on the two magnitude measures—raw effect size and p value (see chap. 3). When mean differences (or sums of squares) are tested with different standard errors (or mean squares) in a complex design, this awkward state of affairs may be unavoidable.

In a simple, one-way analysis, the practice of using a pooled error guarantees against the occurrence of such embarrassing inversions. In the vast majority of specific cases (including the Festinger and Carlsmith, 1959, example), larger mean differences would be more significant even without pooling error; but the *possibility* of inversions argues for the adoption of the pooled error convention. There is a trade-off here between the long-run coherence of a practice and its convincingness in any particular case. The convention of pooled error would seem ill-advised if the within-group variances were wildly different, but otherwise is quite sensible.

TOO MUCH CONSISTENCY IN PARALLEL STATISTICS

Just as one ought to be suspicious of inconsistencies between related statistics, one should do a double-take when parallel sets of statistical conclusions are too consistent. For example, there would be grounds for skepticism if 20 independent tests of a mean difference or correlation all came out in the same direction, even though the overall effect size was small. (The distribution of the test statistics would be strange: The zero value would provide a cliff, with no cases on the negative side, but a pileup on the positive side.) A common cause of this symptom is a failure by the investigator to retain negative signs in data presentations.

Cloning

The most extreme case of too much consistency lies in results identical to several digits. Occasionally one sees a data table with two perfectly identical means or totals in different places. We refer to such a situation as cloning.

The odds that cloning is due to chance are ordinarily very small,[9] and one should look for some other explanation. A common reason is that a

---

[9]The odds against numerical coincidences, however, are usually not as small as one might think. In the classic birthday problem (Diaconis & Mosteller, 1989), a bet is offered to a naive subject, who is told to imagine a group of 25 randomly selected people. The subject wins if no two of those people have the same birthday, and loses if there is at least

copying error occurred—the investigator absent-mindedly entered the same numbers twice, once in the right place, and once in a wrong place.

Example: The Cyril Burt Affair.   Cloning was noticed in the celebrated case of Sir Cyril Burt, who published copious research on the role of genetic factors in intelligence. Suspicion centered on a comparison of two data tables. Table 1 in Burt (1955) and Table 2 in Burt (1966) both give intraclass correlation coefficients on six mental tests and five physical measurements for six different categories of paired children: identical twins reared together, identical twins reared apart, nonidentical twins reared together, and so on.

The later table, as far as one can figure out from the rather confusing presentation, includes the cases from the earlier table, aggregated with new cases collected between 1955 and 1966. In comparing early and late correlations for each of the 11 measures on children within a given category, curious patterns emerge. A prototypic example, abstracted from Burt's two tables, is given in Table 5.6. Comparing correlation coefficients for pairs of siblings reared apart—131 such pairs in the early report and 151 in the later—one finds that on 5 of the 11 measures, the coefficients are identical to three decimals, whereas on the other 6 measures, changes from early to late data occur in amounts ranging from −.079 to +.020.

Burt's views on intelligence had long been controversial, and his work had been criticized on several grounds. The strange numerical identities of these correlations became part of the bill of particulars in a general charge of fraud against Sir Cyril, a charge most forcefully stated by Dorfman (1978).

Burt had since died, and was unable to defend himself. The assistants who had worked on the data were nowhere to be found. Defenders of Burt conjectured variously about the cloned correlations, some saying that maybe there really were no extra cases between 1955 and 1966, others that maybe a portion of the new data was overlooked, and still others that this was just an isolated instance of sloppiness.

---

one birthday in common within the group. Most people think this bet favors the subject, but in fact the odds are approximately 6:5 he will lose. Diaconis and Mosteller gave several applications of this problem to other real-world coincidences.

Here is a different case of numerical identity: Years ago at Yale, a campus-wide vote on permitting ROTC recruiting on campus came out 1,208 yes, 1,208 no. "A million to one shot," was a comment often heard the next day. Actually, with 2,416 voters, there were only 2,417 possible numbers of yes votes (counting zero). Of these, the close ones were much more likely. If one takes the probability that a random Yaleperson would vote yes as .5, independent of other voters, then a binomial generating process can be invoked, and the probability of 1,208 heads in 2,416 flips estimated. This yields odds of roughly 60:1 against a tie, not 1,000,000:1. The chance of a tie was indeed small, but not *that* small. Incidentally, the tie vote was such a conversation piece that debate over the ROTC issue itself faded in campus interest.

TABLE 5.6
Evidence in the Cyril Burt Case: Intraclass Correlation Coefficients—
Burt (1955) Versus Burt (1966)

Year of Publication	1955	1966
Number of Cases	131	151 (the 131, plus 20 new?)
Group	Siblings reared apart	
Correlations on Measures of:		
Intelligence—		
Group Test	.441	.412
Individual Test	.463	.423
Final Assessment	.517	.438
Scholastic Achievement—		(Clones in boldface)
General Attainments	**.526**	**.526**
Reading and Spelling	**.490**	**.490**
Arithmetic	**.563**	**.563**
Physical Attributes—		
Height	**.536**	**.536**
Weight	**.427**	**.427**
Head Length	.536	.506
Head Breadth	.472	.492
Eye Color	.504	.524

Green (1992), in even-handedly reviewing the Burt affair, concluded that Sir Cyril had been treated unfairly. I agree, at least with respect to the infamous cloned coefficients. There is a benign explanation of the identity between early and late results, despite added cases. A reasonable conjecture is that not all of the measures were administered to the new cases. Because cases were hard to find, it is not unlikely that some compromises were made in the interest of fattening the total N. One such compromise might have been to omit some of the measures on some batches of cases; for siblings reared apart the omitted measures would have been height, weight, and the three achievement scores listed in Table 5.6. This would explain identity of results from early to late summaries. On the omitted tests, the 20 new siblings-reared-apart did not contribute any data. On tests administered to new cases, the new data shifted the overall correlations slightly.

This speculation is, well, speculative. It leaves unexplained the omission of height and weight, the easiest physical measurement to obtain, but the inclusion of head length and head breadth. But this case makes the point that something that looks fishy might be okay (albeit poorly set forth by an author who did not make clear what was going on). Thus one should not be too quick to cry fraud. This brings me to a final caveat.

A CAUTIONARY NOTE ON THE DETECTION OF FISHINESS

We have reviewed a number of clues to possible fishiness in data presentations: outliers, gaps, dips, cliffs, and peaks in distributions; test statistics that are too large, too small, or too good to be true; and pairs of observations or test statistics that are too inconsistent, or too consistent. There are still other types of error we have not had the space to discuss—the regression artifact (see Crano & Brewer, 1986), which because of measurement errors produces the appearance of dramatic improvements over time in the health, performance, or good behavior of the worst cases in a population. Or the apparent result that ratings of opposites (such as feeling good and feeling bad) seem to constitute two independent scales rather than a single, bipolar scale. This is often artifactual, resulting from correlated errors in respondents' use of the scales (Green, Goldman, & Salovey, 1993).

Therein lies a negative side effect of exercising expertise in spotting statistical boo-boos. There is undeniably a certain entertainment value in the detection of potential fishiness (and I confess that I probably have been too free in this chapter with some of my speculations). There is also a self-righteous aspect to whistle blowing, so that some people—even whole university departments or academic subfields—seem to relish challenging the integrity of the procedures and conclusions of others. Most people in the course of heated theoretical debates find data on their own side wonderfully convincing, and the other side's data miserably flawed (Lord, Ross, & Lepper, 1979)

One recommendation to counteract overpermissiveness toward one's own research products is to internalize a kindly but insistent critic (Lord, Lepper, & Preston, 1984) who brings to one's awareness all the suspicions that are likely to be raised by others later on. A second useful inner voice would be a public defender of the integrity of the works of other investigators. With experience and effort, one perhaps may learn to calibrate the volume of these inner voices so that they are neither too soft to be heeded nor so loud as to be numbing.

6 Articulation of Results: Ticks and Buts

In the first five chapters of this book, we have discussed the role of statistical argument in making simple claims. Here we broach cases where multiple claims may be involved.

Students and young investigators often have trouble sorting out what to convey in their research reports. They may get lost in a welter of irrelevant detail, or suffer confusion about which results to emphasize and which to send to footnote Siberia. These are matters of *articulation*, the topic of this chapter. My presentation is not meant to be the last word on articulation, but it offers a meaty introduction on which readers may chew. (Apologies to vegetarians.)

A well-articulated research presentation tells readers concisely what they ought to know to understand the point of a given study and to tell the results to others. It conveys the important information in the clearest, simplest form.

Putting good articulation into practice is not nearly as easy as trumpeting its virtues, however. Articulation depends both on thoughtful research planning and on felicitous outcomes, presented with a clear focus. Beyond a few simple principles, it requires judgment and wisdom. This should not surprise us, of course, as this is characteristic of the whole enterprise of statistics as principled argument.

TICKS AND BUTS

We discuss two concepts associated with the articulation of research narratives: *ticks,* the detailed statements of distinct research results, and *buts*, statements that qualify or constrain ticks. These concepts are my inventions, not to be found as such in the statistical literature. The term tick reflects the second syllable of articulation and the use of tick marks for each separate point in a summary. It is related to the concept of a degree of freedom, but is differently applied. The term but was chosen to express reservation. A third term, *blob,* is used to characterize a cluster of undifferentiated research results.

Defining Characteristics

A tick is a claim of a specific comparative difference, typically stemming from the rejection of a focused null hypothesis, such as a comparison of a designated pair of means, a test of a main effect in a 2×2 design, or (much more controversially) a significant correlation coefficient. In other words, a tick specifies a relationship between a causal factor and a response variable. Empirical findings of relationships always occur in specific contexts, and thus every tick should be accompanied by a context *specifier.* (The generalization of a relationship over many contexts is an issue discussed in chap. 7.)

A tick claim may be distinguished from other, weaker, assertions: If a null hypothesis survives a significance test, it is not usually clear what can be said. As we have noted repeatedly, this outcome does not mean that a value of zero can be assigned to the true comparative difference; it merely signifies that we are not confident of the direction of the (somewhat small) true difference. Thus we will ordinarily not credit a tick for this outcome. Exceptions occur when null results are inconsistent with strong expectations of a clear effect, as in our examples in chapter 1.

A second type of result that does not lead to an articulated claim is the rejection of an *omnibus* null hypothesis that several means are all equal. The test result does not specify which means are different from which, and therefore is a mere blob. Omnibus testing is like playing the guitar with mittens on.

There is one further case in which a tick is available to be claimed, but the investigator refrains from doing so because it is vacuous. For example, in a study on adults and children of their relative understanding of differing types of family budgeting and spending problems, the incidental result that the average adult did better overall than the average child would not be worth mentioning.

TICKS AND THE EVOLUTION OF KNOWLEDGE

The Lore

When a well-articulated research claim that also satisfies the other MAGIC criteria is put forward in public, either by lecture or in print, it is likely to be absorbed and repeated by other investigators in the same field. When there is general acceptance by the research community of claims in a subfield, ticks are added to the *lore* of that field. This is not a formal process with an award ceremony, of course. Psychologists win neither Nobel Prizes nor Oscars. Tick acceptance begins implicitly when other investigators quote the finding without challenge, and is even more firmly established when it is quoted in review chapters and textbooks on the subject matter.

The Lore is Not Perfect.   Lore is expertise, much of it qualitative and informal in the social sciences. It is mainly shared but sometimes idiosyncratic. As with any individual or communal mental product, lore is vulnerable to error. One source of distortion comes from the strained reinterpretation of results so as to fit a particular investigator's theory. Occasionally, a *collective* misunderstanding occurs, whereby a result based on belief rather than evidence sneaks into the lore as something that everybody accepts, but that has never actually been demonstrated. Unless its phantom quality is discovered and the relationship skeptically examined, for all intents and purposes it functions in the lore as though it were a genuine tick. Contrariwise, there may be generally accepted ticks that a particular investigator or subcommunity is unfamiliar with, or regards as invalid. Thus the lore based on ticks will be to some extent different for different investigators.

The Role of Buts.   Some ticks enter the lore with doubt or contingency attached to them. A clear relationship may have been obtained in a well publicized experiment, but never replicated.[1] Or for reasons that are not understood, a result may hold under one condition, but not under another. These buts—for that is the name we are attaching to such reservations—play a part in the lore as well. They prod the research community to explain them. They also act as warning signals accompanying particular ticks, telling researchers to be careful in accepting them too readily. (Occasionally these warnings fade from collective memory over time, often because the corresponding ticks make intriguing stories that are spoiled by the cautious addition of buts.)[2]

Buts are related to the specifiers on ticks, in ways to be indicated. Sometimes, buts are removed by new research or new ways of construing the available evidence. Either there are successful replications of the

---

[1]One striking example was the demonstration by Miller and Banuazizi (1968) that it is possible to obtain changes in heart rate in laboratory animals by operant conditioning. The mere possibility of autonomic conditioning would have profound consequences for psychology, biology, and medicine. However, the result could not be clearly repeated by anybody, and the claim was later accorded considerable skepticism by the original investigator (Miller, 1972).

[2]An apt example here is the experiment by Schachter and Singer (1962) supporting Schachter's radical theory of emotion. In truth, the support from the data was quite weak, with some inconsistencies and anomalies (Marshall & Zimbardo, 1979).

original tick, or a reframing of results that parsimoniously explains why there was variation over conditions. Likewise, ticks may undergo some revision over time. New buts may be attached to them, as qualifications are discovered. Or a clever conceptual stroke may replace several old ticks with fewer new ones. Overall, the lore shifts and settles, with new research and conceptualization sometimes adding confusion, sometimes greater clarity.

Despite its vicissitudes, the existence of a body of lore provides common ground that enhances communication in a field, and helps guide research. Investigators have some sense of which issues are currently interesting, and where the knowledge gaps lie. The formulation of ticks and buts should be responsive to the current and potential future states of the lore. The investigator should ask herself, "Where does my result fit?" "Why is it important?" "What do I want people to remember about it?"

The Record

Summaries of research results in the social sciences, whether we call them ticks and buts or something else, accentuate some outcomes at the expense of others. This is inevitable. The cognitive capacity of researchers to absorb every possibly systematic signal is swamped by the noisy uncertainties we face.

Therefore, every field needs the capacity to reexamine old claims, or recombine data from various sources, in order to facilitate challenges and reconceptualizations. Ideally, it should be possible to access every investigator's raw data, or at a minimum, the important summary information (research design, means, ns, variances, and statistical tests). The *record* is the name we give to the potential data bank from all high-quality studies of a given type, or in a given field. The record is typically more reliable than the lore, but it sometimes requires effort and ingenuity to reconstruct.

Ambiguity or inconsistency on an interesting particular point (e.g., "Is psychoanalysis really effective?") often motivates close examination of the record. The technique of meta-analysis (to which we return in chap. 7) is designed for precisely this purpose. Effect size measures and other details of all high-quality studies on the point at issue are summarized and compared. If a meta-analysis (or any other type of careful data review) is successful and is noticed, it usually will have the consequence that the lore will be updated, with ticks being expressed at a higher level of generality.

The information revolution of the 1990s may well increase practical access to the records in various fields. Now that virtually every investigator can e-mail her data files to virtually everyone else, the possibilities of centralized data banking and of a norm of data-files-on-request are both enhanced.

COMPARISONS OF PAIRS OF MEANS

After this brief glimpse of research heaven, let us return to the earth of the individual study, and to the simplest cases of ticks and buts. In so doing, we refer often to the outcomes of significance tests. Despite their considerable limitations, such tests provide a familiar language for introducing the ideas of ticks and buts.

Illustration: The Effect of an Audience on Task Performance

The Simple One-Tick Claim.   The simplest claims involve the comparison of the mean score in an experimental group with either a baseline expectation or the mean of a control group (see chap. 2). For illustration of the latter, let us consider the old question in social psychology of whether the presence of an audience tends to improve or to damage an individual's task performance.

Suppose that an experiment obtains a positive effect of a student audience on subjects' rate of correct completion of easy numerical tasks involving elementary numerical reasoning and calculation. On average in this hypothetical experiment, subjects watched by an audience score higher on a composite index of task success than do subjects working alone. (Suppose $t = 3.50$, $p < .001$, with a standardized effect size of .58, a fairly strong value.) The claim of a beneficial audience effect is made, and gets a name: the "social facilitation effect." Score one tick.

The Next Level of Complication: A 2 × 2 Design.   Let's alter this example. Imagine that the first study of audience effects uses both simple numerical tasks, as previously described, and also simple verbal tasks (say, easy anagrams and vocabulary items). A student sample is scored for rate of successful completion of tasks. Suppose the experimenter runs four conditions in a 2 × 2 factorial design. In two of the conditions, subjects work on numerical tasks, with or without an audience, respectively. Subjects in the two other conditions do verbal tasks, with or without an audience. The *point* of the study is to test for the direction of an audience effect, if any, and to explore whether and how such an effect depends on type of task.

Main Effect of Audience Conditions: One Tick.   One pattern of hypothetical results is shown in Table 6.1. We suppose that the scores on

TABLE 6.1
Test Scores, With or Without an Audience (Easy Numerical and Verbal Tasks)

(Cell n = 36)	Audience	No Audience	Social Facilitation	t
Numerical	108.5	101.5	+7.0	+3.50
Verbal	104.3	99.3	+5.0	+2.50
Mean	(106.4)	(100.4)	(+6.0)	+4.24

Note. Standard error of mean social facilitation = 2.00.

the two types of tasks have been referred to national norms, with means of the college age population at 100 for both types.

There is a significant audience effect for numerical tasks: The audience group's average score was 108.5, compared to 101.5 for the no-audience group, a difference of 7 points. Let us suppose that in this study, the standard error of the difference is 2.00, so that the t ratio is 3.50, with $p < .001$ and a standardized effect size of .58. If we focus only on this one comparative difference—a so-called "simple effect" to distinguish it from comparisons involving more than two cells—we would declare one tick, as in the simpler design outlined earlier. But there is more to summarize in the table.

The second row in the table, for verbal tasks, also shows a simple effect of the audience, consistent in direction with the numerical task result, albeit the comparative difference is a bit smaller—5.0 instead of 7.0. If we consider the second row in isolation, we find $t = 2.50, p < .05$. We have the option at this point of a separate claim, namely that there is a social facilitation effect for verbal tasks. Should Table 6.1 thus yield two ticks, one for numerical and one for verbal problems?

If separate claims were made for the two simple effects, the outcome statement would be a bit klutzy: "There was a social facilitation effect for numerical tasks. There was also a social facilitation effect for verbal tasks." It is usually preferable to combine two such results into a single statement, "There was a social facilitation effect for basic skills." This more general claim is readily conceptualized as a reference to the *main effect* in the factorial design of Table 6.1. The means for the audience and no audience conditions can be each averaged over the two row variations, and these summary means then compared. They differ by 6.0, which yields $t = 4.24$ (or $F = 17.98$), for a summary claim with one tick.

(Note that the number of problems solved in both audience and no-audience conditions is somewhat higher for the numerical than for the verbal problems, and would be significant if t-tested. But this effect has to do with the skills of the sample of subjects, and has no relevance to audience effects. It should not be given a tick, as it adds nothing to the lore.)

Choosing Between a One-Tick and a Two-Tick Summary.
When two parallel simple effects are both significant, the goal of parsimony generally leads to a preference for a one-tick, main effect summary over a two-tick, simple effect summary. Other considerations may be involved, however.

Imagine that the rows specify two types of animals as subjects, say, giraffes and cockroaches, each tested for the effect of an audience on the rate of learning to run an appropriately designed maze. It would not be reasonable to refer to an audience main effect defined by averaging over giraffes and cockroaches.[3] Presumably one would state the two simple effects.

The decision between one overall tick and two particularized ticks occurs also in the circumstance of Investigator B replicating a comparative difference found by Investigator A. Each researcher tends to feel possessive about his or her obviously brilliant research findings, and reluctant to pool the results with those from lesser mortals. There is thus the habit of summarizing the pair of parallel positive outcomes with something like, "He/she got it, and I got it too, better."

A disinterested observer, beyond the resistance to treating significant results like communicable diseases, would be likely instead to conceptualize the two studies as a package, perhaps even visualizing the two data sets in a single array, with columns representing the experimental variable, and rows identifying investigators. The summary from this perspective would be, "They got it." More formally, the statement would be of the form, "Over a pair of studies of the social facilitation effect, a significant positive influence of audience on simple task performance was shown. The average effect size was such and such." The packaging of results, whether in twos or larger bundles, is an important aid in reducing the cognitive overload of the lore.

One-Tick Main Effect, Despite a Nonsignificant Simple Effect.
Let us now consider other possible patterns of results for the two simple *t* values in the final column of Table 6.1. (We need consider only *t*s, not individual cell means, as this is the payoff column, and we could always reconstruct what mean differences would have been required to achieve the particular pair of *t* values.) We denote the *t* for the first row (numerical problems) with $t(1)$, and for the second row (verbal problems), $t(2)$.

---

[3]Lest the reader think that the author had gone bananas when writing this section, I hasten to add this note: In fact there was a successful test of social facilitation for cockroaches learning to run a T-maze, using an "audience" of cockroaches (Zajonc, 1965). The author's point was to show that audience effects do not necessarily require much in the way of brain work. (To my knowledge, giraffes have never been tested. And don't hold your breath.)

Suppose that with numerical materials, the audience effect were significant, $t(1) = 3.50$, although with verbal materials, the presence of an audience yielded only the nonsignificant value $t(2) = 1.50$. Is a one-tick claim of an audience main effect still appropriate, when the simple effect of audience is not significant for verbal problems?

If you think the answer is no, you are suffering from *categoritis*, the tendency to think too categorically about the results of significance tests. The audience effect for verbal materials is not sharply different from the effect for numerical materials. An exaggerated impression of difference is due to categoritis. That one result is significant, and the other not significant, makes the two results seem inconsistent. But it is readily imaginable that the t value for the true audience effect falls in the general vicinity of 2.0, or 2.5, or 3.0, and the apparent discrepancy reflects chance variation introducing a somewhat bigger effect for numerical problems, and a somewhat smaller effect for verbal problems.

In order to make a sensible claim of a larger audience effect for numerical than verbal problems, what ought to be tested is the *interaction* between the row (task type) factor and the column (audience) factor. Though interactions are ordinarily tested with the F ratio, a t value can be calculated in the 2×2 case. For $t(1) = 3.50$, and $t(2) = 1.50$, the interaction t would be $1.41, p = .16$, not a very strong basis for a confident directional claim.[4] Thus our attitude toward this outcome ought to be similar to that toward the previous case with $t(1)$ and $t(2)$ both significant. As with the previous case, the single main effect tick is to be preferred. In the present case, the main effect t would be $3.53, p < .001$.

There is a general prescription that helps cure categoritis. *Do as much numerical comparison as you can before categorizing.* The difference between two numerical differences is a number that can be used as the basis for a categorical statement. But the difference between two categorical statements does not yield a meaningful categorical statement (much less a number).

Other Possible Outcomes in the 2×2.   Let us lay out some other possible tick and but statements for our 2×2 example in terms of the t values. In Table 6.2, we list t values for the simple effects, the interaction, and the column (audience) main effect for a series of hypothetical

---

[4]The t values for the interaction, $t(I)$, and the column main effect, $t(M)$, are simple functions of the t's for the simple effects, $t(1)$ and $t(2)$:

$$t(I) = \frac{t(1) - t(2)}{\sqrt{2}}$$

$$t(M) = \frac{t(1) + t(2)}{\sqrt{2}}$$

The first formula was introduced in chapter 4, leading up to the 42% rule. The second formula is a simple variant of the first.

TABLE 6.2
Ticks and Buts for Several Sets of t Values

| | Audience Effects | | | | | |
| Case | Simple Effects | | Overall Effects | | Suggested Ticks and Buts | |
	Numerical	Verbal	Main	Interaction	Ticks	Buts
A	$t = 3.50$	2.50	4.24	.71	Main	—
B	$t = 3.50$	1.50	3.53	1.41	Main	—
C	$t = 3.50$	.50	2.83	2.12	Main	Interaction
D	$t = 3.50$	−.50	2.12	2.83	Numerical	Verbal
E	$t = 3.50$	−1.50	1.41	3.53	Interaction	—
F	$t = 3.50$	−2.50	.71	4.24	Interaction	—

Note. Significant ts at the 5% level are in boldface.

cases. We limit the set of possibilities by fixing t for the simple effect on numerical tasks at 3.50, and we make the interaction more and more prominent as we go down the table. (Significant ts at the 5% level are in boldface.) By way of comparison, we repeat our first two cases, for which the single main effect tick would usually be the preferred summary.

In Case C, we have supposed that the simple effect for verbal problems is almost nil, whereas the effect for numerical problems remains strong. The audience main effect is still significant, but the interaction is now big enough to yield a significant t also. This is a case of *quantitative interaction*—two simple effects in the same direction, but differing in magnitude. The main effect still deserves to be cited as a tick, now qualified by a but. The summary statement might be, "There is a significant audience main effect, but its magnitude is significantly greater for numerical problems."

A reasonable alternative here is to say, "There is a significant audience effect for numerical problems, but its magnitude is significantly smaller for verbal problems." These two alternatives have different initial emphasis (main effect vs. simple effect,) but both contain essentially the same but.

Case D presents the same two tick-and-a-but alternatives. Here the choice between them shifts toward ticking the simple effect rather than the main effect statement, as there is a (small) reversal of direction of the observed audience effect for the verbal problems ($t = −.50$), tarnishing the generality of the main effect. An interaction arising from simple effects in opposing directions is called a *qualitative interaction* (Schaffer, 1991).[5]

Here the reversal is small, so that we are not sure the interaction is qualitative. Still, we can safely say, "There is a significant audience

---

[5]The term *cross-over interaction* is often used for the subclass of qualitative interactions for which the effects "cross over" on a graphical display of the four means.

effect for numerical problems, but the effect is significantly less for verbal problems, and it may even reverse direction." Were the reversal stronger, as in Case E, one might amend the last part to say something like, "...but the effect is significantly less for verbal problems, and there is a clear hint of a reversal in direction."

When Buts Become Ticks.   At some point in our hypothetical series with the interaction becoming stronger and stronger, the focus of the summary statement ought to shift to the interaction itself. Case E might fit this description, and Case F, with the two simple effects both significant and in opposite directions, clearly does. The interaction that in the previous cases was a but, now becomes a tick. Rather than being a qualification on some other result, it becomes the dominant finding. Though more complicated than a simple effect or main effect tick, it is a tick nonetheless.

The summary statement of results might be, "There was a significant, strong qualitative interaction between the presence of an audience and the type of task, with numerical tasks yielding the positive audience effect." If both simple effects are significant in opposite directions, the summary might break out as two ticks: "On the numerical tasks, the audience had a positive effect, and on the verbal tasks, a negative effect."

The Love–Hate Orientation Toward Interactions

Subfields of psychology (and other social sciences) differ in their receptivity to interactions. Some researchers prefer to book simple effects or main effects. For them, the complications come from continually purifying their experimental (or observational) techniques so as to reveal the effects most clearly. For others, interactions are intrinsically interesting, and their elucidation is a central concern.

Social psychologists love 2 × 2 interactions. This is particularly so when the reversal of direction of an effect seems paradoxical, as in the Festinger and Carlsmith (1959) example we have discussed. In fact, Festinger's influence is probably largely responsible for the focus in social psychology on surprising interactions. McGuire (1983) starkly stated the essence of an approach that seeks interactions when he said, "...all theories are right...empirical confrontation is a discovery process...clarifying circumstances under which a hypothesis is true and those under which it is false" (p. 7). In any event, if it is the habit in one's field to cherish interactions, it becomes easier to talk about them, and see them as gestalts much like main effects.

In fact, there is a general condition under which the presence of an audience facilitates performance, and an alternative condition under which an audience is inhibitory. If we change the row factor in our example to be the *difficulty* of the task, then a qualitative interaction occurs (Zajonc, 1965). Happily, there is a unifying concept that predicts and explains such an interaction. What the audience does is to produce general arousal in the subjects, which strengthens already dominant response tendencies. For easy tasks, the dominant responses are usually the correct ones, whereas for difficult tasks, incorrect responses are often stronger. Thus the audience makes easy tasks easier, and hard tasks harder.

The habit-strengthening explanation provides a packaging for the social facilitation interaction, which makes that interaction easier to remember (or reconstruct). In the history of research on the audience phenomenon, the facilitative results came first. When inhibitory results first appeared, they were buts. They were exceptions that were hard to explain. With Zajonc's (1965) neat synthesis, however, the but disappeared, as both directions of result were included in a new tick.[6]

REFRAMING RESULTS FOR BETTER ARTICULATION

We have seen that the packaging or "framing" of pairs of results across studies affects their articulation, which in turn may influence the impact they have on the lore of a field.

The possibility of reframing research results to eliminate buts and reduce the number of ticks is also available *within* single data sets. We first give a simple and noncontroversial illustration of this idea.

Relational Relabeling

In certain cases the columns of a 2 × 2 table can be relabeled in a way that turns an interaction into a main effect and vice versa. Consider the case where rows represent male and female subjects, and columns male and female conversational partners, or male and female characters in hypothetical situations presented to the subjects. Table 6.3 depicts this situation, denoting the column variable as the gender of the "stimulus person."

Suppose that there were a large qualitative interaction in the original gender × gender table on the left side of Table 6.3, whereby the cells male/male and female/female on one diagonal (**T** and **W**, in boldface) were much larger than the cells male/female and female/male (U and V) on the other.

We have seen that direction-reversing interactions in the 2 × 2 can be a source of annoying buts. Here, however, the interaction can be reframed as a main effect by using the *relationship* of the stimulus person's

---

[6]When a former but becomes a tick, there is a tendency for its statement to change: The linking but can be replaced by an and. Thus, "...the audience makes easy tasks easier, and hard tasks harder."

TABLE 6.3
The General Idea of Relabeling in a 2 × 2 Table

Gender of Subject	Gender of Stimulus Person		Gender of Stimulus Person Relative to Subject	
	Male	Female	Same	Opposite
Male	T	U	T	U
Female	V	W	W	V

gender to the subject's gender as an alternative column variable. The new columns, replacing the old as shown on the right side of Table 6.3, are same gender and opposite gender. The cells in the first row remain as they were, but the cells in the second row switch places. (The female/male cell becomes female/opposite in the new table, and female/female becomes female/same.) The values V and W are flipped, and correspondingly, the interaction becomes a column main effect. This is the simplest variety of tick, because it is the easiest to communicate. Thus the switch helps articulate the results when cells T and W are relatively large.

This switching trick will not always help. If the original data showed a column main effect, reframing would turn it into an interaction. One must be selective in using this device. In this connection, note that relational switching in the 2 × 2 does not change the set of p values for the collection of significance tests; it merely reallocates two of them between a main effect and the interaction. This is important because of the habitual resistance to changing the arrangement (or any other aspect) of data. Reluctance to tamper with data arises from anxiety about "capitalizing on chance," conveying a very loose style (chap. 4). With the relabeling device, this misgiving is inappropriate, as there is no change in p values.

Example: Gender and Emotional Expressiveness.   A real research example illustrating relabeling is given in Table 6.4. The researcher (Beall, 1994) was investigating the stereotype of women as more emotionally expressive than men. To explore the basic phenomenon under controlled conditions, she presented male and female subjects with many short paragraphs depicting simple social behaviors (e.g., touching someone's arm and saying, "Good luck with everything.") The person engaging in the behavior was either a hypothetical man (John) or woman (Jean), and the behaviors were identical in these two versions of each paragraph. The experimental design was such that each subject got only one of the two versions of each vignette.

Subjects were asked to rate the intensity of emotional expression by the person in each paragraph. The left side of Table 6.4 gives the mean ratings

TABLE 6.4
A Research Example of Relabeling (Ratings of Intensity of Emotion on a 7-Point Scale)

Gender of Subject	Gender of Story Character		Gender of Story Character Relative to Subject	
	Male	Female	Same	Opposite
Male	**4.52**	4.20	**4.52**	4.20
Female	4.46	**4.66** ⟵⟶	**4.66**	4.46
Column Means	(4.49)	(4.43)	(4.59)	(4.33)

by male and female subjects of the intensity of emotional expression by the male and female characters, averaged over paragraphs.

In the data table on the left, the two biggest of the four means lie on the main diagonal (indicated in boldface). This implies an interaction between the gender of the subject and the gender of the character. Indeed, this interaction was significant at $p < .01$. The analysis of variance also yielded a significant row effect at $p < .01$, but no significant column effect. The lack of a column effect warns us that the data are not in conformance with initial expectations—the female story characters are not seen as more emotional than the male characters when the content of the behaviors is held constant.

Well, what then is the summary of these results? The row effect says that on average, female subjects impute more emotional intensity to the behaviors of the characters than do male subjects. However, the inter-action is pesky here, as it qualifies (buts) the row effect: Female subjects do not impute more emotionality when the character is male.

Spelling out the nature of the interaction in terms of the original labeling of the rows and columns is confusing. The relabeling trick, however, comes to our aid. The right side of Table 6.4 shows what happens when the data are arranged according to whether the character is of the same gender as the subject, or the opposite gender. Now the two significant effects are main effects, and the interaction is not significant. The summary is straightforward: (a) Female subjects attribute more emotionality both to same-gender characters and opposite-gender char-acters than do male subjects; and (b) subjects of both genders attribute more emotionality to characters of their own gender.[7]

The reframing strategy can be used in any 2×2 case for which there is a *matching* relation between the row and column factors. For example, if subjects trained on either Task A or Task B are then tested on a task

---

[7]The astute reader will have noted that the effect sizes seem quite small—fractions of a point on a 7-point scale. This affects the impact of the results, but not the wisdom of the relabeling device. A summary of the reframed results would be that both men and women view their own gender as the one with relatively deeper feelings, albeit women give generally higher absolute ratings.

similar to A or similar to B, the original design— training (A vs. B) × test (A′ vs. B′)—can be repackaged as training (A vs. B) × test (similar vs. dissimilar).

A general treatment of relabeling, for larger designs, was given by Schaffer (1977). Potential improvement of data descriptions can also be achieved by devices other than reframing, as demonstrated in the next section.

Data Re-expression Via Transformation

Another useful method of re-expression is the transformation of the response scale, say, by taking logarithms of the original observations (See chap. 4). Without going into much detail (for which consult Emerson, 1991b), we simply illustrate the idea, using the hypothetical 2 × 2 example shown in Table 6.5.

The table shows a bigger column difference, 8, in the first row than in the second row, 4, and thus a putative interaction. Let us suppose that the standard error of the means is 1.00. The t value for the simple column effect in the first row is therefore $t(1) = 8.00$, and for the second row, $t(2) = 4.00$. Using the quick and dirty formulas in footnote 4, we calculate $t(M) = 8.49$, and $t(I) = 2.83$. Thus we have a column effect tick, and a significant interaction.

Should we call the latter a but? It wouldn't seem so, because the column effect is strong, and not called into question by the interaction. The interaction is just another tick. In addition, if the row main effect had any conceptual integrity, it too would constitute a tick. Thus this simple arrangement can have three ticks: both main effects and a

TABLE 6.5
Reducing the Tick Count by a Transformation

	Column 1	Column 2	Row Mean	Simple Column Difference	Ticks and Buts
Original Table					
Row 1	12	4	(8)	(8)	Column & row means & inter-
Row 2	6	2	(4)	(4)	action. Three ticks, no buts.
Means	(9)	(3)			
Taking Logarithms of the Original Entries					
Row 1	1.08	.60	(.84)	(.48)	Column & row means; no
Row 2	.78	.30	(.54)	(.48)	interaction. Two ticks, no buts.
Means	(.93)	(.45)			

quantitative interaction. The latter can be worded, "The column difference is larger in the first row than in the second row."

Now suppose we take logarithms[8] of each of the four entries. The second table shows what happens. All the entries get squeezed down, with the entry 12 in the upper left-hand corner getting squeezed into greater proximity with the other transformed entries. The smaller entries get squeezed less, and the net result is that the interaction disappears. On the logarithmic scale we end up with two ticks rather than three. By a parsimony criterion, the transformation produces a preferable description.

Readers with legal minds may protest that an unparsimonious detail in the table has been eliminated only by introducing a new unparsimonious detail *under* the table, so to speak. In order to communicate the results, the investigator must supply the information that a particular transformation was applied. With a single data set, the point is well taken. However, with repeated studies using given procedures and response measures, a particular transformation of scale (such as the logarithmic) may become a standard feature requiring no special mention. (See Abelson's Third Law, chap. 4.)

This particular tick-saving scheme works only when the effects of the column factor are in the same direction for each row, but differ in degree so as to form a fan pattern. A general treatment of transformations that tend to eliminate interactions in two-way tables is given by Emerson (1991b).

We now consider tick and but counts for other types of data arrangements than factorial designs.

MULTIPLE COMPARISONS

Suppose we have a number of means requiring statistical comparison. Multiple comparison methods make declarations about every pair of means, claiming in each case that one mean is significantly larger than the other, or that the two are not reliably separated (i.e., that the direction of the true difference between them is not known with confidence). There are many multiple comparison methods, differing somewhat in their details (Kirk, in press). The general preference in psychological research seems to be for the Tukey test (1953), but the particular choice is not germane to our discussion of ticks and buts.

---

[8]Common logs rather than natural logs are used because the rounded entries are more convenient for the example. In practice it makes no difference. In application to real two-way layouts instead of an oversimplified example, the logarithmic transformation would actually not be applied directly to the cell means. Rather, the transformation would be applied to every individual observation within each cell, and new means would be calculated on these transformed observations. The net result is qualitatively similar, though not numerically equivalent.

Counting Ticks and Buts for Multiple Comparisons

Typically, a comparison procedure is organized by arranging the means in rank order from smallest to largest, and systematically applying a criterion of statistical significance to the several observed differences between them. The criterial difference for claiming significance depends on the standard error of the means and (most commonly) an appropriate tabled value of the "Studentized range." Braces of two or more adjacent means all lacking significant separation are indicated by underlining, as illustrated by the hypothetical displays in Table 6.6. (For these displays, we take the criterial difference to be 10.)

In the first display the brace of means [A,B,C] is significantly separated from the D mean, and that's the whole story, as there is no articulation within the brace. In the second display, the set [P,Q,R] is separated from the S mean; further, there is a significant difference between the P and R means, but the intermediate Q mean is distinguishable neither from P nor from R. The second display thus makes one more significant distinction than does the first display, but also contains a but—the final clause of the previous sentence. The first display is coded as having one tick and the second display, two ticks and a but. The additional detail of the second display attaches to the seemingly paradoxical conclusion that P is not statistically differentiable from Q, nor Q from R, though P and R can confidently be declared different. (This is not a real paradox—it only seems like one to those who think too categorically about nonsignificant differences.)

TABLE 6.6
Two Multiple Comparisons Displays

	I. Criterial difference = 10			
Group	A	B	C	D
Mean	30	35	39	55

	II. Criterial difference = 10			
Group	P	Q	R	S
Mean	58	65	71	87

Note. The means for Groups A, B, and C all differ by less than the significant separation of 10. The underline indicates no significant differences among these three group means. Once it is determined that the A and C means are insignificantly separated, the B mean lying between them necessarily belongs to their brace. The D mean significantly separates from all others.

Means P and Q differ by less than 10, so the brace consisting of P and Q is underlined. A similar statement applies to the Q and R brace, but P and R differ by more than 10, so there is no single brace connecting P, Q, and R. The mean for Group S is significantly separated from all others.

TABLE 6.7
Ticks and Buts for Selected Multiple Comparisons of Four Means

Structure	Ticks	Buts	Structure	Ticks	Buts
A B C D	3	0	A B C D (underline A B)	2	1
A B C D (underline A B)	2	0	A B C D (underline B C)	1	1
A B C D (underline A B C)	1	0	A B C D (underline A B, underline C D)	2	2
A B C D (underline A B, underline C D)	1	0			

Note. Means sharing an underline are not significantly different.

Table 6.7 gives some of the possible outcomes of the multiple comparison of four means, and their associated counts of ticks and buts. The table only classifies the *structure* of an outcome, not its content. The lettering of the means is always given as A, B, C, D, from lowest to highest, without regard to which mean represents what level or version of the independent variable.

The maximum number of ticks for four means is three, which occurs when all the means are significantly separated. It might be argued that there are six ticks in this case, because there are six possible comparisons among four means. However, this argument is flawed, as there are redundancies among the comparisons. When the means are arranged from lowest to highest, as is implicit in Table 6.7, a declaration that B is significantly higher than A implies that C and D must also be significantly higher than A because they are at least as far from A as B is. Similarly, if C is declared significantly above B, so too must D significantly exceed B. Thus we should be concerned only with the number of nonredundant significances between means (which cannot exceed the number of degrees of freedom between groups)—here, 3.

In the three patterns in the left half of Table 6.7, the number of ticks is found by counting how many of the adjacent pairs (AB), (BC), (CD) are declared significantly different. There are no buts, as none of the nonsignificant braces overlap. In the right half of the figure are listed patterns with two (or three) nonsignificant braces, some of which overlap. Each such overlap implies that a seemingly paradoxical sentence is needed to describe the result —a but. The last pattern in the column has two regions of overlap, and therefore has two buts. Meanwhile, counting the number of ticks for each pattern requires examination of some nonadjacent means, though the count still equals the minimum number of nonredundant claims of statistical inequality. For example, in the last pattern, C significantly exceeds A, and D significantly exceeds B; thus, we count 2 ticks.

These schemes for counting ticks and buts generalize readily to cases involving more means. For k independent groups, the maximum number of ticks is $(k - 1)$, the number of degrees of freedom between groups. The maximum number of buts is $(k - 2)$, and the number of buts can never exceed the number of ticks.

Decomposition Versus Multiple Comparison

An interesting data situation involving alternative descriptions is the case in which one of the means in a 2×2 table comes out sharply different from the other three, which are all about the same. This case has been much debated (e.g., Myer, 1991, vs. Rosnow & Rosenthal, 1991). We illustrate with the data in Table 6.8 from a study by Langer and Abelson (1974).

Example: A Labeling Effect in Clinical Judgment   In this study, a videotaped interview was shown to various clinicians, 19 of whom had been trained with a classical psychoanalytic orientation, and 21 as behavior therapists. Each viewer was asked to write a short statement about the personality traits of the person being interviewed. The interview featured a somewhat rambling and ambiguous account by the interviewee of the reasons he had left his job. In half the viewings, the tape was introduced by the experimenter as "an interview with a job applicant," and in half as "an interview with a patient." This created the 2×2 design pictured in Table 6.8, with (approximately) 10 clinician viewers per cell.

The 40 personality sketches were randomly shuffled and given (source unspecified) to graduate students to rate the emotional maladjustment implied by each description, on a scale from 1 to 10. The hypothesis of the study was that for the analytic clinicians, the interviewee labeled a patient would be seen as much more deeply disturbed than the same interviewee labeled a job applicant, whereas for the behavior therapists, the label would make little or no difference.

The pattern of means in Table 6.8 (with higher numbers denoting more maladjustment) appears to support the investigators' hypothesis,

TABLE 6.8
Mean Ratings of Emotional Maladjustment of a Stimulus Person

	Person is Labeled	
Viewer's Training	A Patient	A Job Applicant
Psychoanalytic	7.40	4.80
Behavior Therapy	5.02	4.74

Note. $n = 10$ per cell; the mean square within cells is 2.81.

resoundingly. But what form of statistical analysis should be used for testing and framing the results? There are different choices. The straightforward, naive approach is to test the significance of the difference the label makes, separately for the two clinician types. This would come down to two t tests of simple effects, one for each row of the table. This procedure has the defects we noted earlier in the chapter—it risks categoritis, whereby we would grossly overinterpret the comparison of the categorical outcomes for the two simple effects.

The standard advice in a case like this, therefore, is to test the interaction in the 2×2 table. Because the habitual decomposition of the 2×2 includes this interaction, the stock advice is to run the usual analysis of variance and test the two main effects and the interaction all in one package.

A funny thing happens on the way to the conclusions when this conventional advice is applied to the data in Table 6.8, however. Not only does the interaction come out significant, but both main effects do also. The conventional research report for these results would go something like this: "The main effect for label is significant ($F_{1,36} = 7.38; p = .01$), as is the main effect for clinician type ($F_{1,36} = 5.30; p < .05$). Most important, there is a significant interaction between clinician type and label ($F_{1,36} = 4.79; p < .05$) in the predicted direction. For the analytic clinicians, labeling the stimulus person a patient rather than a job applicant raises the mean maladjustment rating from 4.80 to 7.40, whereas for the behavior therapists, the difference in rated maladjustment due to the labeling manipulation is much less (4.74 vs. 5.02)."

The major disadvantage of this conventional summary is that it contains uninteresting statements about the main effects, before we get to the crucial interaction. The suggestion of putting the main effect statements after the interaction does not really solve anything. The basic problem is that commitment to the conventional 2×2 analysis obliges you to say something about all significant effects—there are, after all, three potential *ticks* from the standard decomposition. The verbal statement of the results is correspondingly bulky, and would be even more so if some verbal elaboration of the main effects—including the fact that the interaction buts them—had been given.

There is an alternative set of significance tests that can be applied to Table 6.8, yielding fewer ticks and no buts. Even a statistically untutored person looking at the table would notice that the mean in the upper left-hand corner differs markedly from the other three means. Why then should we not test this appearance directly?! A Tukey multiple comparisons test on the four means yields the result that the (analytic clinician; patient) group provides the only significant differences. On average, members of this group perceive the interviewee as significantly more maladjusted than in any other group, and there are no reliable differences between the other three groups. Referring to Table 6.7, we find this case at the bottom of the left-hand panel, having one tick and no buts. The parsimony principle tells us that a summary with one tick is preferable to a three-tick summary. Thus, this criterion provides grounds for preferring the multiple comparisons procedure to the standard 2×2 decomposition. The substantive conclusion is that conjunction of an analytic orientation and the patient label is necessary to produce a sharp increase in the perception of maladjustment.

The habit of doing the standard decomposition is so overlearned by most students of analysis of variance[9] that it has become virtually automatic: The stimulus of a 2×2 table elicits the response of calculating two main effects and an interaction. Here, as we have seen, this habitual response entails a loss of parsimony in the results, and therefore it seems advantageous to abandon it in favor of the Tukey test. Habits, after all, are mindless. They should be canceled if there is a sufficiently good reason. My advice of analyzing the three-the-same, one-different pattern of means via multiple comparisons rather than the standard decomposition, by the way, has been advocated by others (e.g., Schmid, 1991), but the tick/but approach provides a rationale that heretofore has been lacking.

Example: Group Conflict in South Korea.   At the risk of running our point into the ground, consider the $2 \times 2 \times 2$ data in Table 6.9, from a Yale dissertation (Na, 1992).

Half of the subjects were from a low-status group of South Koreans, half from a high-status group. All subjects read a news story about the political relations between the groups. For half of each group, the story reported developments favoring the low-status group, and for the other half, the high-status group. Each of these four subgroups was further subdivided by whether previous subjects from the two groups were said to have been in conflict with each other about the issue in the story, or not. The dependent measure was agreement with the main point of the story, on a 9-point scale from 1 (absolutely disagree) to 9 (absolutely agree).

There were 20 subjects per cell, and the within-cell mean square was 2.43. The standard analysis of variance of this $2 \times 2 \times 2$ design produced mean squares for three main effects, three two-way interactions, and one three-way interaction. Six of these seven effects are significant at $p < .05$. Each is a tick. Four of these ticks are butted by qualitative interactions, undercutting their interpretation. Six ticks and four buts! A real mess.[10]

---

[9]It has also been a habitual response by many journal editors. For a particularly egregious example in which the authors were compelled to present a totally unintelligible traditional analysis to legitimize a very clear nontraditional summary, see Salovey and Rodin (1984).

[10]The mess can be cleaned slightly by the matching trick from an earlier section. We do not present either the original mess or its reframing here. The ambitious reader can try developing the analysis of variance tables from the information given.

TABLE 6.9
Group Ratings of Agreement with a Story Favoring the High- or Low-Status Group Under
Conditions of Perceived Conflict or Nonconflict

Group	Story Favoritism	Conflict	Nonconflict
Low-Status	Pro High-Status	1.05 (a)	1.40 (a)
	Pro Low-Status	7.75 (d)	5.35 (c)
High-Status	Pro High-Status	3.20 (b)	3.05 (b)
	Pro Low-Status	2.95 (b)	2.95 (b)

Note. Any two means marked by the same letter are not significantly different.

An alternative try is simply to apply the Tukey Test to the set of eight means, ignoring the $2 \times 2 \times 2$ structure. The results are indicated by the marker letters beside the means in the table. Any two means marked by the same letter are not significantly different.[11] We see that four distinct letters are needed, and none of the means requires multiple letters, that is, there are four nonoverlapping regions of nonsignificance. Thus there are three ticks and no buts. The significant results can be described concisely, as follows:

The high-status group shows roughly the same moderate level of disagreement with the stories in all cases. By contrast, the low-status group is very sensitive to story favoritism, absolutely disagreeing with stories slanted against them, and tending to agree with stories in their favor. Such agreement by them is greater under the condition of perceived intergroup conflict.

The general theoretical point is that a low-status group can be highly responsive to potential slights at the hands of a high-status group, all the while the high-status group is oblivious to the conflict. This point is brought out clearly in the three-tick summary, but would be totally obscured by the welter of ticks and buts in the standard decomposition.

"Can I Do That?"

When presented with unconventional approaches to conventional research designs, students often say, "Can I do that?" "What do you mean, Can I do that?," I reply. "Well, you know, is it...all right?" they say, looking at the floor. The conversation has become clinical.

Because of such student anxieties, it is useful to broach once again the stylistic problems accompanying unconventionality. We are not arguing that a multiple-comparisons procedure on the four means of a 2×2, or the eight means of a $2 \times 2 \times 2$, always provides better articulation than the standard decomposition. Indeed, examples can readily be given

---

[11]This notation is an alternative to the use of underlines in expressing the results of a multiple comparisons test. It is more flexible for tabular presentations. Each letter is equivalent to a separate underline.

in which the articulatory advantage lies very much with the decomposition. And therein lies a rub. If two (or more) statistically different procedures are tried with any given data set, there is always a suspicion that the investigator ended up choosing the one that yielded the statistically significant appearance, thereby capitalizing on chance. A conservative critic might go so far as to dismiss articulatory advantage as a rationalization, not a reason, for the choice of analysis.

In the examples in this chapter, the fussy issue of capitalizing on chance did not arise—both statistical procedures yielded highly significant results. In such a happy circumstance, the investigator(s) can highlight the more well-articulated procedure, and provide a footnote saying that some other procedure also yielded convincing p values. In the example of the clinicians watching the videotape of the person labeled either a patient or a job applicant, the text would feature the Tukey test, and the footnote would follow convention by giving the significant F for the interaction. (This stroke nicely avoids the burden of commenting on the uninteresting main effects.)

A crunch comes in 2×2 examples if the Tukey test yields one cell significantly different from the other three cells, but the interaction F based on $[(T - U) - (V - W)]$ comes out nonsignificant. Then, even though the unconventional analysis is better articulated, presenting it in lieu of the conventional procedure might seem too brash. A timorous investigator would feature the conventional analysis and footnote the unconventional one. However, I think a good case can be made that better articulation is usually worth a modest increase in the Type I error rate. I myself would therefore be willing to emphasize the well articulated alternative in the text, footnote the conventional analysis, and argue the point with a squeamish editor, if necessary.

CONTRASTS

A third method of articulation involves the calculation and F-testing of *contrasts* between means (Rosenthal & Rosnow, 1985; Kirk, in press), as opposed to an omnibus one-way F test on the whole set of means. The particular case of linear trend testing is fairly common, and as a method of articulation it presents new problems and opportunities. In this section, we use the linear contrast on four means to illustrate tick and but counts.

A contrast is specified by a set of weights [w(j)] to be applied to the respective group means [M(j)]. Simple formulas involving the sum over the group index j of the products w(j) • M(j) produce a mean square and an F test associated with the contrast. Relative to the omnibus F ratio, the contrast F ratio is potentially $(g - 1)$ times as large (where g is the number of groups). This potential for a stronger result tends to be realized to the degree that the pattern of weights captures the pattern of means.

There is a metaphor that I find helpful in comparing a contrast test with an omnibus test. At the beginning of this chapter I used the metaphor of guitar playing with or without mittens, and I risk mixing metaphors—nevertheless, let's go full hog ahead. Picture a sentry perched in a castle tower, scanning the nearby countryside for violations of the null hypothesis. If the sentry walks slowly around the tower, spreading his limited attention over the full 360°, that's like the omnibus test. If, however, he looks only in a single direction, he will be more sensitive to occurrences close to his line of vision, and totally oblivious to those at right angles. This represents the contrast test.

The contrast [−3, −1, +1, +3], for example, is "looking" for a pattern of steady increase from the first mean to the second mean to the third mean to the fourth mean; that is, a linear pattern or trend. If the data show such a steady increase, the contrast F will be at its relative maximum. If there is a pattern of irregular increase, however, or a pattern of successively diminishing increase (or no net increase at all), the contrast F will be less than maximum. Note that in the case of steady and sizable increases, a multiple comparisons test such as the Tukey may well yield a significant difference between every adjacent pair of means. This would produce three ticks in the case of four groups, and even more ticks with more groups.

How many ticks should we assign to a significant linear contrast? To answer this, we note that certain sets of contrast weights yield significance tests conceptually identical to the decomposition procedures discussed earlier. The main effect of columns in a 2×2, for example, can be tested with the one degree of freedom contrast [+1, −1, +1, −1], which looks at the difference between the means in the first and second columns, aggregated over rows. Because a significant column main effect counted as one tick in that case, it is reasonable to accord one tick to any significant contrast. Typically, therefore, well-fitting contrasts give a more parsimonious description than multiple comparisons (fewer ticks), and a more informative description than an omnibus test, which at best gives a blob. (An additional articulatory advantage of some contrasts is that their ticks contain specific quantitative information, e.g., that a pattern of means can be roughly characterized as linear. We do not pursue the quantitative aspects of ticks here, however.)

Albeit the linear (or any other precisely specified) contrast counts as one tick, possible departures from trend raise the question of the number of buts. If there is a clearly nonsignificant residual sum of squares after extracting the linear trend sum of squares, then the linear trend is an adequate description of the data, and we have an ideally parsimonious one-tick, no-but summary. If, however, the residual is significant, then the trend's tick is butted (so to speak). A strong residual says that the linear description may be misleading—something else is going on, and this case deserves a but. (The significant residual does not earn a tick

TABLE 6.10
Ticks, Buts, and Blobs for Contrasts Among Four Group Means

Source of Variation	df	Outcome	Ticks	Buts	Blobs
Omnibus between	3	significant	0	0	1
Linear contrast	1	significant	1	0	0
Residual	2	nonsignificant	0	0	0
Linear contrast	1	significant	1	0	0
Residual	2	significant	0	1	1
Linear contrast	1	significant	1	0	0
Quadratic contrast	1	significant	1	1	0
Residual (cubic)	1	nonsignificant	0	0	0
Linear contrast	1	significant	1	0	0
Quadratic contrast	1	significant	1	1	0
Residual (cubic)	1	significant	1	1	0

of its own, because with four or more groups, the test of the residual is an undiscriminating omnibus test that can only yield a blob.) If the residual sum of squares can be fitted by a second contrast, say, a quadratic trend, then that adds another tick. Whether or not a third tick and second but are added depends on whether or nor the final residual is significant. The possible cases for four means are listed in Table 6.10.

The message here is this: Application of a patterned contrast such as a linear trend potentially provides good articulation of results, but the articulatory advantage of the contrast is undercut when the residual is significant. Research reports frequently give significant trends without comment about residual variation, and this is very careless.

MORE THAN ONE DEPENDENT VARIABLE

Beyond the various ways of detailing differences or patterns among means, the need for articulation also arises when there are two or more dependent variables. This situation occurs very often in psychological research. In studies using questionnaire measures of attitude, more than one question may index the attitude. In studies of memory, different memory tasks can be employed. And so on.

Alternative Methods of Dealing With Multiple Dependent Variables

In such cases, the investigator faces a choice of whether to present the results for each variable separately, to aggregate them in some way before analysis, or to use multivariate analysis of variance (MANOVA). If the variables all refer to the same response scale, there is also the alternative of doing a standard "repeated measures" analysis of variance.

One of these alternatives—MANOVA—stands at the bottom of my list of options. Imagine a 2×2 design, say, with four response variables. Many an intimidated student will be led by the formal structure of the design to seize upon MANOVA as the "appropriate" analysis.

Technical discussion of MANOVA would carry us too far afield, but my experience with the method is that it is effortful to articulate its results. The output tables from a MANOVA are replete with omnibus tests, and unless the investigator is sophisticated enough to penetrate beyond this level, the results remain unarticulated blobs. Furthermore, when MANOVA comes out with simple results, there is almost always a way to present the same outcome with one of the simpler analytical alternatives. *Manova mania* is my name for the urge to use this technique. The risk from indulging this compulsion is that one may not fully digest the output, and end up by presenting the results with a murky profusion of p values. I hasten to add, however, that if used deftly and in moderation, MANOVAs can occasionally be helpful. Perhaps the matter can best be captured by Abelson's Fourth Law: *Don't talk Greek if you don't know the English translation.* A wise general practice in the statistical treatment of complex data arrays is first to display them graphically, and do rough, simple quantitative analyses. These will give a feel for the potential meaning of the results; only then should you resort to complex refinements.

Articulation When Each Variable Is Analyzed Separately

Returning to our discussion of ticks and buts, let us consider the simplest multivariate case: two dependent variables. We further simplify by supposing that the influence of the independent variables (in a 2×2 design, for example) is examined for each dependent variable separately.

We distinguish two possible situations, each with three types of outcome. The two dependent variables might be alternative measures of the same construct (e.g., two measures of the same attitude) or of different constructs (e.g., a belief and a behavior). In turn, the pattern of results (whether tested by decomposition, comparisons, or contrasts) may yield the same outcomes for both variables, a single difference between the outcomes for the two variables, or many differences. These six cases are shown[12] in Table 6.11. In the simplest case, when two measures of the same construct yield the same patterns of significant

---

[12]Cases with two or three differences in outcome could be treated like one-difference cases or many-difference cases, at the judgment of the investigator.

TABLE 6.11
Changes in Ticks and Buts When Using a Second Dependent Variable

| | Results Are | | |
Variables Are	All the Same	One Different	Many Different
Measures of the same construct	No change	Add one but	Reckon for the second variable separately
Measures of different constructs	Add one tick	Add a tick and a but	Reckon for the second variable separately

results, separate presentations would be redundant. The tick and but counts for one variable would be the same as for the other—and the same as the counts for a two-variable aggregate. The most streamlined presentation would simply use the aggregated data (as in fact we recommended for the case of significant social facilitation on both numerical and verbal tasks).

If measures presumed to represent the same construct yield the same results save for a single difference, that exception costs a single but. If there are many differences, then the measures are apparently behaving differently despite a presumption of similarity, and the investigator had better consider separately the ticks and buts attaching to each measure.

The case with conceptually distinct dependent variables is different. Consider, for example, the speed and the accuracy of response in low-level, repetitive decisions. Each subject is shown a succession of, say, short strings of letters, and for each string must decide whether it represents an English word or not (the "lexical decision task," Meyer & Schvaneveldt, 1971). There is some reason to suppose that fast responses would be more accurate—(subjects are more confident on some trials than others)—and some reason to suppose that fast responses would be less accurate—(subjects are more impulsive on some trials than others). These competing reasons imply that speed and accuracy might in principle have any net relationship whatever. If some experimental treatment produces the same pattern of significant results for the two measures, that is nonredundant and worth noting. The investigator might say, "These results hold not only for speed, but also for accuracy." A "not only" statement represents one tick.

If the pattern of results on two conceptually distinct measures is almost the same, with only a single exception, then an additional but is counted along with the additional tick. Finally, if the results for the two measures differ in several respects, it behooves the investigator to examine the patterns separately.

FURTHER REMARKS

We have set forth a scheme for choosing between alternative descriptions, based on clarity—for which buts should be minimized—and parsimony—for which ticks should be minimized.

Articulating Research Plans

We have not yet mentioned the questions that typically arise at the stage of designing an experiment. The investigator might ask what tick and but counts she would like the outcome to have. Is she concerned only with a single claim (one tick), or two claims, or more? What about buts? Buts in general are bad news for the investigator, but in some cases the researcher might want a but, principally to challenge the ticks set forth by someone else, or to demonstrate that the phenomenon in question is conditional on certain factors that should not be overlooked. This line of thought leads to consideration of *interestingness*, the topic of chapter 8.

Uncooperative Data

In our discussion and our examples, we have presumed tidy data, but a note of realism should be injected in the discussion. Sometimes real data allow parsimonious description, with few ticks and even fewer buts. On other occasions, however, real data are uncooperative. Either there are no ticks at all (because there are no significant effects), or a single omnibus blob, or an incoherent profusion of ticks and buts, with no apparent redescription trick available to simplify the mess. There is not too much that can be said about such cases. When nothing works, nothing works. The investigator should consider the possibility, however, that it was not bad luck that did him in, but a vague, messy research conception. If this is true, then it is better to return to the drawing board to design a cleaner study than to pile statistics higgledy-piggledy before befuddled readers. This caution leads to Abelson's Fifth Law: *If you have nothing to say, don't say anything.*

Staying Loose

From John Tukey I have learned the old Scotch proverb, "A man may ha' a gay, foine hoose, but he maun sit loose t' it." He means that we should not be so enamored of our rules and procedures that we stick with them under all conceivable circumstances. There comes a time when it is wise to abandon the house.

This brings us back to significance tests. Several times throughout this book, I have inveighed against the usual emphasis on significance testing as too categorical and hidebound a way of thinking. Now I come along in this chapter to discuss the concept of articulation, and my analysis of ticks and buts relies on categorical claims of significance. Categorization of results obviously brings some clarity to the analysis of articulation, and was advantageous to use in this chapter. One should still, however, allow for flexibility in significance statements. It might be, for example, that a pattern of results that is messy using the .05 level becomes neat using the .01 level. Or perhaps everything would be fine at the .05 level except for one result at .06, and there would be considerable narrative advantage to relaxing the significance level to .06. Thus, though one cannot avoid a categorical view of articulation, at least one can try to employ it with less than total rigidity.

7 Generality of Effects

As we have noted before, it is always appropriate to question the generality of effects found in any one study. The investigator and the critic alike wonder whether the results would come out the same if the study were replicated.

Unfortunately, the admonition to replicate does not come equipped with instructions. What contexts should be varied to try to establish generality? What aspects of the original study should be kept the same, in order to be sure that each new replication is testing for the "same" result? How shall we express different degrees of generality?

We first discuss the concept of generality, and then relate our discussion to the statistical issues involved.

THE NATURE OF GENERALITY

Any given experimental study[1] is conducted by a research team at a particular place and time, running groups of subjects through a carefully designed procedure to test the effects of some experimental treatments. Everything about the experiment beyond the critical manipulation of the treatment—research team, time, place, subjects, and ancillary aspects of the procedure and materials—becomes context.

The Variety of Contextual Features

There are so many aspects of context that the investigation of generality of treatment effects spawns many questions. If a study provides strong evidence that Treatment A differs from Treatment B in its effect on variable X, we can ask if this would remain the case if the study were run by a different research team at a different time and place, with different subjects, procedures, materials, and so on. The list of questions generated

---

[1]The points to be made in this chapter apply in essence also to observational studies. For conciseness, however, we use the terminology of the experimental approach throughout.

132

by enumerating contextual features of a study gives us some guidance on how to run replications to probe for generality, but unfortunately it is quite vague. What do we mean, "at a different time"? Time of day? Time of the year? Time in history? How should we interpret "in a different place"? On the next floor? At a different university? In a different country?

The narrower the interpretation of generality, the more similar a replication would be to the original study, and the more likely (one would guess) to support the original claim. The narrowest possible replication of a study occurs when the same experimenters run it again in the same place with the same procedures, materials, measures, and pool of available subjects, changing only the date and the particular subjects.[2]

Exact Replication. The term *exact replication* refers to the strategy of repeating a study in as nearly identical a form as can be managed. One cannot safely assume that a putatively exact replication will produce the same experimental result. The research literature in psychology—as well as in the physical sciences—is sprinkled with results failing the test of exact replication (e.g., Dworkin & Miller, 1986; Mayer & Bower, 1985; Pool, 1988; Pratkanis, Greenwald, Leippe, & Baumgartner, 1988). Therefore, it is a good idea for researchers themselves to conduct one or two replications before getting too carried away by the force of their initial claims. Indeed, it is a standard journal editorial policy to require of authors that they report experiments in clusters of three or more interrelated studies, serving (among other things) to provide a modicum of replication. Clusters of totally exact replications are usually felt to be on the overcautious side, however. Thus the usual practice is to provide modest breadth in initial replications, for example, by changing one or two aspects, such as the response measures and the procedures embodying the treatments.

The Influences of History, Culture, and the Laboratory. The other extreme on the range of generality, where the context varies a great deal from one study to another, raises a different set of questions. If the time of two studies is separated by decades rather than weeks, one may find in some research areas that societal developments can change the results. A case in point is given by Eagly (1978) in reviewing laboratory studies of gender differences in susceptibility to social conformity pressures. The author categorized each of a number of conformity studies as to whether women conformed *more* than men, or whether the genders conformed *equally*. (In two cases, men conformed more; these studies were grouped into the "equally" category.) Eagly conjectured that with the historical

---

[2]For a few phenomena, particular individuals with spectacular abilities or unusual defects are retained as subjects worthy of repeated study. This category would include idiots savants, reputed psychics, eidetic imagers, and people with unusual amnesias caused by brain injury.

growth of the women's rights movement, women have become generally more resistant to social pressures. Since 1970 or so, then, gender differences in observed conformity should tend to diminish, disappear, or conceivably even reverse. Sure enough, of 59 conformity studies run before 1970, women conformed more than men in 23 of them; of 64 studies run after 1970, women conformed more in only 8.

Some commentators (e.g., Gergen, 1973) have argued that if research results are particular to historical eras, and also to the language and culture of the research location, then it may be virtually impossible to establish a body of social science knowledge with any assurance of validity and permanence. The only stable findings, the argument goes, would be a small corpus of results with complete generality—so-called cultural universals (see, e.g., Jaynes & Bressler, 1971).

Anthropology and cultural psychology (Price-Williams, 1985) have struggled for many years with the question of what types of human behavior might be universal. Some universals have been claimed: for example, the sameness of the emotional responses of infants to the tone and inflectional pattern of maternal vocalizations, irrespective of particular language (Fernald, 1993); the emotional meaning of prototypic facial expressions, such as the furrowed brow of anger (Ekman, 1980; Mesquita & Frijda, 1992); and certain general value orientations (Schwartz, 1992). However, universals are rare, and notoriously debatable (Ekman, 1994; Russell, 1994).

Another possible constraint on generality is raised by the argument that research conducted in the laboratory does not generalize to the "real world." It is frequently asserted that laboratory settings are artificial—subjects are placed in an isolated environment, possibly with strange recording instruments, or computer displays; an experimenter instructs them to perform an unfamiliar task with unfamiliar stimuli, and keeps track of how they do it; subjects are concerned about the impression they will make; and so on. Will not subjects respond differently in these situations from the way they would in daily life (cf. Neisser & Winograd, 1988)?

There are several counterarguments to this thesis, among them the staunch endorsement of experimental control and inference (Banaji & Crowder, 1989) combined with a skepticism that there is any consequential loss of generality in using a laboratory environment. A milder, more eclectic reply is to urge the use of a mixture of techniques, inside and outside the laboratory (Jones, 1985).

Another counterargument to the assertion that laboratories are strange places is that real life often involves artificialities, too. Doctors and dentists use forbidding instruments and issue authoritative instructions. (Ever had a CAT scan?) Teachers give unintelligible assignments to students, and monitor their performance. And we are often mindful of the impression we will make on authority figures, not to mention co-workers and friends. Thus in several respects, life imitates science.

Aronson et al. (1985) distinguished between the *mundane realism* and the *experimental realism* of an experimental study. Mundane realism involves making the environment of the study more representative of the outside world in its surface features. By contrast, Aronson et al. emphasized experimental realism, by which they meant making the laboratory situation psychologically realistic and compelling for the subjects, regardless of the unfamiliarity of its surface features.

That the generality of research findings in the social sciences may well be constrained by history, culture, and the sometime leap between laboratory and life does not inexorably support the pessimistic conclusion that a psychological science is impossible. The appropriate reaction is not despair, but humility. True, we should often expect interactions between effects and contexts, and this should temper the grandiosity of our claims. But the interactions we encounter (e.g., the diminished gender difference in conformity after 1970) are more often lawful than capricious. In initial research in an area, unexplained interactions of effects with contexts are nuisances. They may cloud the articulation of results by introducing new buts (chap. 6), and they may even kill off our ability to establish significant main effects in the first place. But as we slowly develop sophistication in an area, we should begin to focus on the interactions rather than the main effects as the ticks of interest.

TREATMENT-BY-CONTEXT INTERACTIONS
WITHIN STUDIES

Interactions of effects with contexts are by no means limited to sweeping historical or cultural factors. The size and direction of experimental effects can be influenced by modest experimental variables, ranging from the general intelligence of the subjects to minute details of the instructions or stimulus materials. We now turn to the statistical analysis of these narrow, frequently encountered contextual influences.

Manageable Contextual Influences

Contextual influences may be investigated within studies, or across studies. The former application is related to what has been called "generalizability theory" (Shavelson & Webb, 1991),[3] and the latter to

---

[3]Generalizability theory arose in the field of mental testing, where one desires to generalize observed ability differences between people, over test items, occasions, raters, and other context factors or "facets." In the present discussion, the aim is to generalize experimental treatment differences over subjects and contexts. There is a formal analogy between the two situations, but translating from one to the other requires alertness to the switch in focus of the target of generalization.

meta-analysis. In our treatment, we attempt to exploit the similarities between the two.

Example: The Persuasive Influence of Expert Communicators.
Consider a research project on the relative persuasive influence of communicators with different degrees of expertise. The typical research finding is that expert communicators are more influential than nonexperts (Hovland, Janis, & Kelley, 1953). However, the magnitude of this expertness effect can be somewhat variable, depending among other things on the topic of the communication.[4] Imagine an exploratory study of the generality of the expertness effect across opinion topics. (The design we present is not the same as that of the actual early studies, but is more suitable for the present discussion.)

Four disparate controversial opinion topics are selected as vehicles for persuasive messages. On each topic, the consensus of opinion has been investigated in advance for the target audience, and an essay disagreeing with that consensus is written. For example, there might be one essay advocating that there be no regulation of genetic engineering whatever, one endorsing a comprehensive exam for college seniors, one arguing for a constitutional amendment denying statehood for Puerto Rico, and one urging mandatory parental consent for teenage abortion. There are two versions of each essay, identical except for attributed authorship: One author is described with authoritative credentials in the topic area, (say, genetic engineering) "Dr. X.Q., Professor of Genetics," and the other is said to be "X.Q., a local high school student." In a class of 80 students, 20 receive an essay on each topic, half of them attributed to the expert, half to the nonexpert. The students are then asked their opinions on the essay topics. Degree of agreement with the communicator's (previously unpopular) position is noted. The experimenter tabulates the difference between the mean agreement with the "expert"[5] and the "nonexpert" versions for each of the four topics. Consider these raw mean differences as measures of the effect sizes for expertness on each of the four topics.

---

[4]Some variability of expertness effects was in fact found across topics by Hovland and Weiss (1951), but not much commented upon. The raw effect sizes, assessed by the difference in net proportions changing opinions to agree with the communicator, were −.04, .09, .27., and .36 for their four particular topics.

[5]When we title a treatment factor, there is always a danger that we will proceed to use that label in our thinking and ignore the idiosyncratic nature of the actual treatment manipulation. I call this conflation of the title with its object the "knighthood fallacy." Here, we extend our conceptual sword, and vest the professor with expertness in public issues, and the student with nonexpertness, ignoring the fact that professors and high school students differ not only in expertness, but also in age, absent-mindedness, typical interests, and so forth. The professor–student manipulation, therefore, is not merely a variation in expertness. For that matter, the choice of essay topics carries with it variability in writing style, in importance, and so on, as well as in sheer topic content.

In the illustrative outcome given in the first part of Table 7.1, three of the four effects are in the direction of greater persuasiveness for the expert than the nonexpert. Two of these three effects are large, and one is small. The effect in the opposite direction is also small. The second part of Table 7.1 gives the analysis of variance, treating these data as a two-way factorial (Expertness × Communication Topic), with 10 subjects per cell.

What can we say from these results about the generality over topics of the expertness effect? First of all, based on the illustrative value of 2.50 for the pooled within-cell mean square, there seems to be a significant main effect for expertness. The F ratio for Expertness, using the within-cell MS as error term, is $F_{1,72} = 8.60, p < .01$. Following through on the standard two-way analysis, the Topic effect is also significant, with $F_{3,72} = 9.73, p < .01$, but this is not interesting (and would earn no ticks in a summary)—it simply indicates that some opinion statements housed in particular communications elicit more agreement than others. The Expertness by Communication Topic interaction is barely significant: $F_{3,72} = 2.81, p < .05$. The analysis gives no further details localizing this interaction.

Thus a mechanical application of statistical procedure to these illustrative data would lead to the conclusion that the expertness effect is significant, and appears to be somewhat variable across topics. This description has one tick (the main effect of expertness), and one blob (the undifferentiated interaction of expertness and topic). We cannot

TABLE 7.1
Analysis of Mean Agreements With Writer's Opinion

Part 1: Mean Agreement With Writer's Opinion			
Communication Topic	Expert	Nonexpert	Effect Size
Genetic	.20	−2.25	2.45
Senior Exam	.75	.30	.45
Puerto Rico	3.00	1.50	1.50
Abortion	−.90	−.65	−.25
Mean	(.76)	(−.28)	(1.04)

Part 2: Analysis of Variance					
Source	SS	df	MS	F	p
E: Expertness	21.53	1	21.53	8.60[a]	< .01
C: Communication Topic	72.96	3	24.32	9.73	< .01
E × C	21.10	3	7.03	2.81	< .05
Within cell (illustrative)		72	2.50	—	

Note. In Part 1, $n = 10$ per cell; scale of agreement runs from −5 to +5.
[a]With an alternative analysis, this would be $F = 3.06$. See text.

definitely say in what way the interaction buts the main effect, because the interaction has not been articulated.

The Fixed Effects Model and the Embarrassing Footnote

There is a huge catch to this analysis. The underlying assumption of the usual two-way factorial analysis of variance is that the levels of the two factors are fixed. The fundamental statistical model specifying the main effect and interaction parameters (the equation with all those Greek letters and subscripts; see e.g., Blackwell, Brown, & Mosteller, 1991; Winer, 1971) limits statistical inferences about the factors to the particular levels that the investigator specifies in advance. Thus, the significant main effect of Expertness strictly applies only to the particular versions of high expertness (a professor) and low expertness (a high school student) used here. (See footnote 5.) All statements about Topics, including the Expertness × Topics interaction—which speaks to the generality of the Expertness effect—apply only to the set of topics actually used.

If the investigator desires broad generality, such a limitation is painful. Its full impact can be appreciated from the feeble disclaimer that one ought to state for the analysis of Table 7.1:

"We can say with confidence only that the main effect of expertness is general over our particular set of communication topics—Genetic Engineering, Senior Exam, Puerto Rico, and Abortion. The effect seems to be somewhat variable in degree for these four topics. No statement can be made about its generality across other topics, nor other essays on the same topics."

Imagine a parallel disclaimer for generalizations of a main effect across the set of individual research subjects: "This main effect is general for the set of individuals [Tom Smith, Alice Johnson, Flavius Dibble, Mary Green, and...]. No statement can be made about its generality across other individuals." This type of disclaimer I call the "embarrassing footnote." It flatly states that the purported main effect has no generality beyond Tom, Alice, Flavius, Mary, and so forth. If another investigator wanted to replicate the study exactly, she would have to ask the original researcher to send Tom, Alice, et al. for use as subjects.

This embarrassment does not occur in practice with research subjects because subjects are not treated as fixed effects, that is, as particular "levels" of a factor in a factorial design. Rather, individual subjects are treated as nameless versions of a random factor, that is, as random effects.

The Random Effects Model and the Weak Test of Generality

If we want to avoid a similar embarrassment for generalizations across topics, we must consider treating topics as a random factor. This would mean withdrawing our focus from the particularities of individual topics, regarding them merely as tokens sampled from an infinite collection of appropriate topics. As Shavelson and Webb (1991) put it, one would have to be willing to exchange the communication topics in the sample for any other same-size set in an appropriate universe. Generalization to other, untried topics would thereby be encouraged—but a price would have to be paid for this generalization.

Look back at Table 7.1. The designation of topics as a random effect entails using F = MS(Expertness)/MS(Expertness × Communication Topic) as a test of the expertness main effect (Blackwell et al., 1991). The reason for this is that random sampling of topics might well introduce E × C interactions that, on average over repetitions of the random selection process, would inflate the size of the expertness mean square. The MS(Within) contains no information about this noising influence of interactions, and therefore will tend to be too small, biasing the F test upward. Here, instead of the F of 8.60 in the second part of Table 7.1, using the MS(Within) as the error term, the value F = 3.06 with (1,3) degrees of freedomis obtained when the MS(Expertness × Communication Topic) is the error term—clearly a nonsignificant value, as the critical $F_{1,3}$ at the .05 level is 10.13. This threshold value of F is unusually high because there are merely 3 df for the interaction mean square.

The reason there are only 3 df here is that only four topics were used. When we want to generalize over topics, the "N" is the N of topics, not the N of subjects. Think of it this way: The expertness effect has been tested four times, giving the raw effect size estimates 2.45, .45, 1.50, and −.25. These are rather different from one another. The mean of the four, 1.04, does not correspond closely with any of them. What, then, is the conceptual status of this mean, purported to indicate the general effect of expertness? If we regard topics as fixed—thereby abandoning license to generalize beyond the four topics used—the mean represents an arithmetic compromise, a single summary value for the four effects. On the other hand, if we treat Communication Topics as a random factor, the observed mean effect of expertness is an estimate of what the average effect would be if tested across an indefinitely large number of topics. This latter concept is what we ideally intend when investigating the true generality of an effect across a contextual factor.

Note, however, that with a small set of exemplars of that factor—here, only four topics—the estimate of the average effect of Expertness (1.04) is bound to be quite fuzzy. In our example, the great uncertainty of the estimated mean Expertness effect can be appreciated by establishing confidence limits on the true value. We use the square root of the Expertness × Communication Topic mean square as a basis for the standard error, along with the two-tailed .05 level for t with 3 degrees of freedom. We obtain the 95% confidence limits: −2.74 < Expertness main effect < 4.82. That the possible null value 0.00 is within these confidence limits is another way of indicating that when the data are interpreted by the random effects model, the evidence is insufficient even to claim a direction of the Expertness effect! Thus the investigator ends up without a satisfying story about generality over topics. The fixed effects model entails the embarrassing footnote, and the random effects model fatally weakens the claim of a general main effect of Expertness.

Minimizing the Dilemma

The serious dilemma we have illustrated here often occurs, but need not always. There are five circumstances that could help the investigator avoid getting stuck between the rock of the fixed model and the hard place of the random model. The first three apply to the random effects model, the last two to the fixed effects model.

1. *Huge main effect:* The main effect of the experimental treatment factor, call it E, might be of such great relative magnitude that it is significant even when the mean square for E is tested against the interaction of E with the context factor, C, despite the small number of degrees of freedom. This outcome would provide support for a claim of generality for the main effect of E over the universe of contexts from which the particular versions of C were drawn.

2. *Small interaction of effects with contexts:* Additionally or alternatively, the mean square for Effects × Contexts might be minimal, ideally no bigger than would arise from the variable samples of subjects contributing to the different cell means. This would legitimize the use of the MS(Within) as the error term, as in the fixed model.

3. *Many levels of the context factor:* If the effect of interest were studied in more contexts (e.g., if there were more topics for testing the expertness effect), the degrees of freedom for interaction would be larger, and the test would be more sensitive. This is the technical side of the commonsense idea that you get a better test of generality by trying more contexts. Of course, it takes more resources of one kind or another to run a larger study.

4. *Ordered context variables:* Sometimes a context factor varies along a continuum, in which case it can be well mapped with a few strategically placed levels, and be treated as a fixed factor that nevertheless allows sensible generalization. For example, in studies of the comparative performances of different groups of elementary school children (say, male vs. female, or standard educational program vs. experimental program), the age variable may be considered a context factor. That is, any between-group assertion such as, "Girls perform better than boys on tests of verbal ability" might have to be qualified by age. Suppose that tests were conducted at ages 7, 10, 13, and 17, and that boys showed

a trivial advantage at age 7, girls a small advantage at age 10, a moderate advantage at age 13, and a notable advantage at age 17. What general statement would be warranted? Presumably it would go something like this: "Girls outperformed boys on tests of verbal ability. No gender difference was evident at age 7, but a gap opened by age 10, and increased steadily throughout the school years."

Note that this statement implicitly generalizes to other, untested ages. No tests were conducted at ages 8, 9, 11, 12, 14, 15, and 16. Yet it does not seem unreasonable to assume that if a graph were drawn by connecting data points for the tested ages, it would not seriously misrepresent the situation at the intermediate ages. We expect age-related functions to be smooth, not to go jumping about from one year to the next. Given this expectation, we can treat the age levels as fixed, yet still be able to generalize over other ages.

5. *Exhaustive levels of the context factor:* When all possible levels of a fixed context factor are represented in the design, then there is no generalization problem. (There are no other levels to which to generalize.) Gender is an obvious example. If a given treatment effect is found equally for both men and women, then one can cross gender off the list of contextual factors likely to interact with treatments.

Caveat

In toting up the advantages and disadvantages of treating contexts as random effects, there is one further consideration. Herbert Clark's (1973) seminal article recommending much more frequent use of the random effects model brought forth braces of hecklers (Forster & Dickinson, 1976; Wike & Church, 1976) with a mutual complaint. The problem, they said, was that merely declaring a set of variations to be random does not make it so. The levels of contextual variables (in Clark's case, linguistic stimuli) are rarely chosen by an explicitly random process; rather, they are strategically selected to meet certain criteria, with an attempt to choose a variety of exemplars. How then can one have warrant to generalize to a population?

Essentially, Clark's reply (Clark, Cohen, Smith, & Keppel, 1976) was that the main function of the random effects model is to restrain investigators from easy generalization. The type of experimental layouts he analyzed were different from our experimental treatments × contexts design, but in both designs, random effects models create very high thresholds for rejecting the null hypothesis of no treatment effects. In other words, generalization does not come cheaply. But making the attempt to generalize is better than accepting the embarrassing footnote of the fixed effects model. To be sure, if the generalization test succeeds, one should carefully define the characteristics of the population of contexts to which generalization is claimed. For example, with our communication topics in Table 7.1, we can hardly pretend that we have a random sample of all possible topics, but we might plausibly argue that we have a quasi-random sample of mildly controversial, impersonal, relatively undiscussed issues on which undergraduates generally agree, but are influenceable.

In sum, it is fundamental to specify the boundaries of generalization of one's claims. At one extreme, (the fixed effects model), these boundaries are usually painfully narrow. At the other extreme (the random effects model), the price of trying to broaden the boundaries is either to make them somewhat vague—or worse, to lose warrant to claim any generality at all. This is simply the way the research life is. One does not deserve a general result by wishing it. This leads us to coin Abelson's Sixth Law: *There is no free hunch.*

Consistency of Effect Direction Across Contexts

In chapter 6, we introduced the distinction between quantitative and qualitative interaction. In terms of the present discussion, purely quantitative interaction corresponds to the situation of consistent direction of the main effect across contexts, and qualitative interaction to demonstrable inconsistency in direction.

Inconsistency of Directions of Results: Systematic, or Chance?
Although multicontext results entirely consistent in direction would support a claim of qualitative generality, it is not true that one or two results in the opposite direction would necessarily rule out such a claim. Because there is sampling variability affecting every cell of a design such as that of Table 7.1, a wrong-way effect might be produced by chance. Looking again at Table 7.1, the results come out in the negative direction for the abortion topic, but it is easy to imagine that the raw effect for this topic might have come out positive, consistent with the other three topics. A simple t test for the departure from zero of this single wrong-way result yields $t = -.36$, hardly a convincing demonstration that we really know the true direction of the effect for the abortion topic. If we had some theoretical reason to believe that the expertness by topic interaction were quantitative but not qualitative, the given data would not provide strong contrary evidence.

In one-tailed situations (see chap. 3), where one direction of effect is much more sensible than the other direction, the investigator might require strong evidence before accepting the reality of an apparent qualitative interaction. Ciminera, Heyse, Nguyen, and Tukey (1992) discussed this issue for medical experiments run concurrently at a number of medical centers. In this treatment-by-center design, each center has an experimental group and a control group for testing the efficacy of a new drug or other therapeutic intervention. Center is taken to be a random factor. Suppose there is a significant treatment effect despite a significant treatment by center interaction. Suppose further that the research team has the initial supposition that any such interaction will be quantitative and not qualitative. (If the treated subjects at any center do not show a better result than the controls, so be it, but there is no reason to expect them to be significantly worse.)

If the research yields no centers with the wrong directionality, everything is fine. The treatment generally works, though in varying degree from center to center. If in one or more centers, the experimental group does worse than the control group, a correction for random variability (called the *pushback procedure*) is applied. If these reversals are eliminated by the pushback, then the same conclusions as in the previous case apply. However, if any reversed results remain after the pushback,[6] then systematic qualitative interaction is indicated, contradicting the initial optimism that the treatment could never be more damaging than doing nothing.

Direction Reversal Can Be Interesting

Although qualitative generality across a context variable is desirable on grounds of parsimony and simplicity of application, the occurrence of systematic qualitative interactions is more interesting and theoretically informative. The famous mathematical sociologist Paul Lazarsfeld once said, "You never understand a phenomenon unless you can make it go away."[7] We might add, "or unless you can reverse its direction."

Psychologist William McGuire (1983, 1989) suggested as one of many ways to develop new hypotheses that you take some seemingly obvious relationship and imagine conditions where its opposite would hold.

Example: The "Risky Shift" in Group Decision Making. Often the crucial properties of direction-reversing contexts are discovered by flashes of insight, after a long period of inconclusive research. A celebrated and instructive example of this in social psychology stems from the so-called "risky shift effect" (Bem, Wallach, & Kogan, 1965; Wallach & Kogan, 1965), which was concerned with differences between individuals and groups in attitudes toward risk. For 12 different decision scenarios pitting the status quo against a promising but risky alternative, individuals were asked what advice they would give. For example, a writer unhappy at turning out popular pulp fiction considers abandon-

---

[6]An additional way to test the interpretation of results in the wrong direction is to apply the procedures for diagnosing outliers given in Table 1.1. The pushback approach is distinct, however, because it assumes a smooth-tailed distribution of treatment effects over contexts. For a third approach to directional errors, see Schaffer (1991).

[7]I cannot find a written citation for this profound remark. I am quoting from memory of a seminar Lazarsfeld gave in 1962.

ing his steady income to spend all his time on an epic novel. Should he attempt this if the probability of success is only 1 in 10?; 2 in 10?; (etc.). (Being willing to accept a lower probability is taken as more risky.) After making their ratings, business school students were gathered into discussion groups, with instructions to reach consensus on the best rating. The research question was whether the advice for the protagonists became more conservative or more risky after group discussion.

In their study, Wallach and Kogan (1965) averaged the shifts over the 12 scenarios, and made the striking claim that group discussion encourages riskier decisions—the risky shift effect. This contradicted the lore on group behavior in business contexts.

However, if the investigators had jumped into a time machine and traveled forward far enough, they would have realized the great importance of a qualitative interaction of the shift effect with scenarios. This interaction was clearly present in their data, but its implications were not appreciated. Ten of the original scenarios demonstrated a reliable risky shift, but two showed a reliable cautious shift. According to the Lazarsfeld dictum, the two scenarios that make the risky shift go away are the clue to understanding the nature of that shift. For many years, insufficient heed was paid to the importance of scenario differences. Finally, several people realized that the two examples yielding a cautious shift had the distinct property that the risky behavior was socially undesirable (e.g., the protagonist investing his family's life savings in a highly speculative South Seas stock), whereas in the 10 examples that gave risky shifts, the risky behavior was socially desirable (e.g., the pulp writer trying the epic novel). The history of this slow discovery was nicely summarized by Roger Brown (1986).

In subjecting the qualitative interaction to close scrutiny, the entire interpretation of the group-induced shifts of attitude was altered. The phenomenon was relabeled as *group polarization*—the tendency for group discussion to develop increased support for attitudes or behaviors initially considered somewhat desirable, whether risky or cautious. It was soon discovered (Myers & Lamm, 1976) that group polarization was generalized beyond the context of risky decisions, applying to dozens of other topics of group discussion. Group discussion increases the extremity of positions initially favored by the bulk of the members.

The Art of Explaining Treatment-by-Context Interactions

In a prior section, we made the distinction between fixed and random context factors. Levels of fixed factors are labeled and particular, constraining generalization; levels of random factors dot the landscape of possibilities, permitting wide (but perhaps vague) generalization if the interactions of effects with contexts are small, and/or the N of contexts is sizable.

Textbooks tell the student that factors are *either* fixed *or* random. If one thinks hard about it, however, it becomes clear that most factors—especially context factors—have aspects *both* fixed *and* random. A specified medical center has intrinsic, relatively constant particularities affecting the success of a treatment, such as the quality of their personnel and equipment. Each center also has extrinsic, transient conditions affecting success—say, a strike of technicians during the period of the experiment, or a defective batch of medication. Specified scenarios in the risky shift experiment or persuasive essays in the communication study are composed of deliberate variations in story plots or topics, and more or less arbitrary embellishments of these themes. In trying to understand significant treatment by context interaction, it is difficult to sort out the relative contributions of stable and transient aspects of contexts, especially when we don't know what *essential* features of contexts influence the magnitude of the treatment effect.

In any case, it is usually misleading to think of context variations strictly in terms of the name of the context factor (see footnote 5 on the "knighthood fallacy"). For example, in the communication study with its variation of topics, we should remember that each persuasive essay is a complex creation, by no means uniquely constrained by the topic name. In the jargon of computer programmers, much of the material in the essay is a "kludge" (pronounced klooge)—a bunch of stuff necessary to implement the experimental task, and meant to be otherwise inessential. The problem is that the supposedly inessential filler in a communication (e.g., an unexpected turn of phrase that puts some readers off) may be the crucial factor producing an expertness by topic interaction, not the topic itself.

What Features of Context Are Essential?   Almost all context variations in psychological experiments represent some mixture of the essential and the inessential.[8] It would be convenient and incisive if we could guarantee that essential variations mapped into fixed levels of a context factor, and transient or inessential variations into assorted versions of random factors. Unfortunately, this is frequently not the case. The context variations (topics, scenarios, centers, etc.) we create or observe are not necessarily the essential variations. Sometimes, if we are lucky, exploratory studies across different contexts provide useful clues as to what context variations matter, should the main effect of treatments prove insufficiently general. The risky shift research is one example of the occurrence of such clues (albeit investigators were slow to realize their importance).

---

[8]The elaborate orchestration of some psychological experiments (particularly in social psychology) raises sharp issues about essentiality. We treat this topic in chapter 9.

Clues From the Data   Another illustration arises from a second look at the information in Table 7.1, on expert versus nonexpert communicators. Notice that the two topics with the biggest effects of expertise—genetic engineering and Puerto Rican statehood—are remote from the personal concerns of the typical undergraduate, whereas the two with near-zero effects—senior exams and parental consent for abortion—have potentially great relevance for college students. Let us call the distinction between the two pairs of topics *ego-involvement* (again, being mindful of the knighthood fallacy). The hypothesis is that the persuasive effect of expertness is lower when the ego-involvement of the audience in the topic is high. The rationale is that when the audience member is personally involved by the topics, he or she will attend closely to the arguments per se, caring little for the credentials of the communicator.

If we cleave the topics factor into two fixed categories, high and low ego-involvement, each represented by a pair of random topics, we can take the means shown in the first part of Table 7.1 and create the more informative display in the first part of Table 7.2.

We notice that the interaction between expertness and ego-involvement is very sharp. There is a substantial effect of communication expertness when involvement is low, and virtually no observed effect when involvement is high. The analysis of variance (ANOVA) of the second part of Table 7.2 shows how neat the results become when topics are categorized by the ego-involvement variable. Involvement (I) is regarded as a fixed factor (with 1 df), and communication topics within involvement level (C(I))—the residual properties of topics—as a random factor (with 2 df). When tested against the MS(Within), the E × I

TABLE 7.2

Analysis of Agreements with Writer's Opinion, Summarized by Ego-Involvement of Topic

Part 1: Mean Agreement with Writer's Opinion			
Ego-Involvement of Topic	*Expert*	*Nonexpert*	*Effect Size*
High (Exam; Abortion)	−.08	−.18	.10
Low (Genetic; Puerto Rico)	1.60	−.38	1.98
Mean	(.76)	(−.28)	(1.04)

Part 2: Expanded Analysis of Variance				
Source	*SS*	*df*	*MS*	*F*	*p*
Expertness(E)	21.53	1	21.53	8.60	< .01
Communication Topic (C)	72.96	3	24.32	9.73	< .01
E × Involvement (I)	17.53	1	17.53	7.01	< .01
E × Residual C (I)	3.57	2	1.78	.71	n.s.
Within cell		72	2.50		

interaction is significant at $p < .01$, and the residual interaction $E \times C(I)$ yields a clearly nonsignificant $F < 1$.

As a consequence, we have cleaned up the noise-creating influence of the $E \times C$ interaction. Random expertness $\times$ topic residual effects no longer inflate the expected value of the Expertness main effect. Thus testing the main effect of expertness against the within-cell error term is now defensible, justifying the F of 8.60 with its decisive $p < .01$. (See Item 2 in the section Minimizing the Dilemma.)

We emerge from the analysis with two ticks concerning the expertness factor: a main effect of expertness, and an interaction between expertness and involvement. The latter is a quantitative, not a qualitative interaction. (Under high involvement, the expertness effect drops near zero, but does not reverse direction.) Nevertheless, it constitutes a but.

This example illustrates a style of exploring treatment by context interactions when a diffuse context factor such as topics is varied within a study. The mean square for Treatments $\times$ Contexts is F tested against its appropriate error term. If the F is significant or suggestive,[9] this indicates a "camel in the tent," that is, some aspect of the context factor that systematically interacts with treatments, but that may be hard to identify amidst the random variation and the multi-aspect nature of the context factor. The detective game is to discern the camel—to point to an essential aspect of context that moderates the treatment effect. When this camel is removed from the tent (i.e., isolated in an analysis such as that of the second part of Table 7.2), the process may be repeated if there is any indication of more camels. (In our example, there was no such indication. The residual interaction was quite nonsignificant.)

Guessing Has Its Downside.   This approach sounds swell, but has drawbacks. As presented earlier, the identification of the essential aspect of context (ego-involvement) was by hunch rather than by theory, and was based on a tiny sample of topics. This is stylistically brash, wide open to criticism as a case of hocus-focus. One can very often search the details of contexts and come up with some cockamamie distinction between those that yield large treatment effects and those yielding no effects or reverse effects. (An experiment is run separately by four different experimenters. Joe and Jane get significant results, whereas Bill and Karen get none. Are we to believe that the experimental phenomenon is contingent upon the experimenter's name beginning with J?)

---

[9]"Suggestive" is meant to indicate a very liberal threshold, as one does not want too readily to dismiss the possibility of systematic treatment $\times$ context interactions. A conventional rule of thumb is to take the interaction seriously if its $F > 2$ (Anscombe, 1967; Green & Tukey, 1960; Hedges, 1983; Tukey et al., 1991).

The possibility of misidentification of the truly essential aspects of context is diminished—but not eliminated—by using a larger number of context levels. By far the best approach to the dilemma of identifying the essential features of contexts lies in the prior development of theoretical hypotheses why particular context variables might amplify, diminish, or reverse the treatment effect. This permits clean variations of fixed context effects, forestalls any hocus-focus, and if the hypotheses are verified, creates a much more compelling story about treatment by context interaction.

Theoretically Predicted Contextual Interactions.   There are many illustrations of theoretical accounts of contextual interactions. One nice example concerns the interaction of communicator expertness with subjects' ego-involvement in persuasion settings, just as in our earlier discussion. In fact, I made up the example of Tables 7.1 and 7.2 to mimic the usual systematic findings from somewhat more complicated experimental designs. Petty and Cacioppo (1979) theorized that there are two essentially different routes to persuasion: the "central route," by which the target of persuasion considers and weighs the content of the arguments in the communication, and the less effortful "peripheral route," whereby the target uses some readily available cue to guess whether the arguments are likely to be sound. Such cues include the expertness of the communicator, the confidence of the tone of the communication, the presence of an enthusiastic audience, and so on. Because mental effort is less likely to be exerted if the target does not really care about the issue, the general prediction is that the presence of a cue such as communicator expertness will make more of a difference for subjects with low ego involvement in the issue.

In a test of this prediction, Petty, Cacioppo, and Goldman (1981) varied expertness by pitting a professor against a high school student as in our example. Ego involvement was manipulated in an elegant way, avoiding the introduction of fuzzy inessentials attached to differences in topics. They used a single topic, the establishment of a comprehensive exam for all seniors, but manipulated the proposed date on which such an exam was to go into effect. In the high-involvement condition, the date was the following year, so that all the subjects in the experiment would have to take it. Under low involvement, the date was set 5 years off, when the subjects would be long gone from the university.

The predicted interaction between expertness and involvement was obtained, such that expertness made more difference under high involvement than low involvement, and (unsurprisingly) the expert communicator was more persuasive than the nonexpert. Score one tick for expertness, and one tick for a quantitative interaction with involvement.

GENERALITY ACROSS STUDIES: META-ANALYSIS

Examples such as the one just given are not as frequent as one would like. Generalizations by individual investigators from single studies are usually rather weak (and the more the effect of interest might interact with many context variables, the weaker the generalization). One might say that isolated claims are not *robust*. Investigators who feel that their results march with full generality into the annals of science are kidding themselves.

Communal Testing of Generality

A research community, however, can do what an individual investigator cannot. Many research teams working on the same phenomenon are capable of manipulating a greater number of context variables, and of testing a variety of theoretical explanations of the phenomenon.

It may seem that the communal advantage over the individual would be maximized if the community were well organized. To caricature such a state of affairs, suppose that there were an Office of Research Governance (ORG) with the authority to specify which context factors should be manipulated, and by whom, in order best to cumulate knowledge of important phenomena.

It hardly needs saying that such centralized control by an ORG would go against the individualistic and democratic grain of American scientists. The stultifying effect of centralized control of research agendas in the social sciences was evident in the dismal state of Soviet social psychology.

It might be argued that federal agencies such as the National Science Foundation and National Institutes of Health do control the research agenda, by funding only those projects judged to be important by a scientific panel. This centralized influence, however, is rather loose, serving mainly to emphasize research directions that look most promising. The majority of researchers are not federally funded, and those that are often deviate in their actual research from what they put forward in their proposals. The net effect of decentralization is to generate in the literature a cacophony of claims for and against the generality of any phenomenon that seizes the imagination of the research community.

Meta-Analysis

Psychology and other social sciences have therefore embraced meta-analysis, a set of techniques for pooling results across different studies of the same phenomenon. Up until 20 years ago or so, the problem of variable, often contradictory results across studies was handled by verbal summaries, perhaps supplemented by a simple count of studies favoring a particular hypothesis, studies favoring the contrary hypothesis, and those with essentially null results. Additionally, the reviewer might suggest context variables that appeared to moderate the size and direction of results. Such reviews were criticized as too subjective and informal, and the careful, quantitative methodology of meta-analysis (Glass, 1978; Hedges & Olkin, 1985; Rosenthal, 1991) evolved as a potentially superior alternative.

We review here neither the history of the gradual acceptance of meta-analysis within the social sciences, nor all the computational ins and outs of the method. Rather, we try to integrate the conceptual basis of meta-analysis—a between-study generalization technique—with our within-study analysis of generalization.

Meta-Analytic Procedures.   Meta-analysis begins with the assembly of all the well-conducted studies of a given effect the meta-analyst can find in the research literature, in press, or in dissertation archives. For each study of acceptable quality, a record is kept of all the interesting variables that characterize it. These would include the methods of experimental manipulation and of response measurement, along with whatever contextual features seem potentially relevant. Effect size measures of the authors' claims (or ticks, in our terms) are transcribed if given, or else calculated from other information. Formulas for effect sizes as a function of ts or Fs or means and standard errors, along with sample ns, can be found in various sources (e.g., Mullen, 1989; Rosenthal, 1991.) The effect size measures are then *combined* across studies, and *compared* between studies.

The combination operation aims to generate an average effect size measure across all studies, and to perform a significance test of its difference from zero (or better, to establish confidence limits on the true average effect size). Comparison of effect sizes across studies has more ambitious goals. If by a chi-square test, the study-by-study effect sizes are significantly heterogeneous—as they almost always are—then a further set of tests is performed on the distinguishing variations characterizing different sets of studies. This is to see if contextual or methodological variables can be identified that will explain some or all of the heterogeneity of effect sizes between studies.

If one or more such variables are found, they may suggest or support particular contextual mechanisms that produce interactions with the effect of interest. This is analogous to the steps we took for Table 7.1, introducing the variable of Ego-Involvement to account in Table 7.2 for the significant Expertness × Topic interaction.

Example: Pygmalion in the Classroom.   Let us consider a meta-analysis, given the following background: Rosenthal and Jacobson

(1968) conducted an experiment to test what they called the "Pygmalion effect in the classroom." They arranged to tell elementary school teachers that some of the children in their classes had been identified by a special test as being likely to display future excellence. These "bloomers" were actually chosen at random. The investigators hypothesized that the useless information supplied to the teachers would set in motion a self-fulfilling prophecy, whereby the teachers would be uncharacteristically attentive to the bloomers. This in turn would increase the classroom involvement and self-confidence of these students, resulting in increased learning and better scores on objective tests. At year's end, several tests of mental ability were administered, and the bloomers compared with control children.

The results supported the prediction, but created considerable controversy. Especially debatable was the authors' finding that the mean IQ scores of bloomers were 4 to 6 points higher than the IQ scores of control subjects. There is a widespread supposition that IQ tests measure intellectual aptitude, not achievement, and therefore that IQ scores should not be sensitive to short-term situational manipulations. Additionally, questions had been raised about some of the details of Rosenthal and Jacobson's (1968) statistical analysis of the IQ data.

The purported phenomenon was so interesting (see chap. 8), however, that an avalanche of replication studies followed, many in other environments such as workplaces, ships at sea, and organizational hierarchies. Meanwhile, the vast majority of classroom studies dealt with possible gains in achievement and comportment, not with IQ. (This neglect was probably due to early failures to replicate the IQ findings, so that attention turned to other measures.)

A meta-analysis of Pygmalion effects on IQ scores was eventually undertaken by Raudenbush (1984). He identified 18 relevant studies with acceptable quality, including the original Rosenthal and Jacobson (1968) experiment. Table 7.3 displays the standardized effect sizes for the set of 18 studies, taken from Table 1 of Raudenbush and rearranged

TABLE 7.3
A Meta-Analysis of Pygmalion Effects on IQ Scores—
Stem-and-Leaf Diagram of Effect Sizes in 18 Studies

.5	2 5
.4	
.3	0
.2	1 7
.1	4 6 8
.0	2 5
−.0	6 4 3 2 2 1
−.1	3 3

Note. Data adapted from Raudenbush (1984).

in a stem-and-leaf diagram (see chap. 5). Each entry represents, for a particular study, the mean difference between the IQ scores of bloomers and controls, divided by the pooled within-group standard deviation. Minus signs indicate results contrary to the predicted direction. For now, ignore the distinctions between standard, bold, and italic fonts in Table 7.3.

Only a bare majority of studies give results in the predicted direction—10 positive effects and 8 negative effects. The median effect size is a mere .035. However, the distribution has positive skewness; that is, when positive results are obtained, their effects are much bigger in absolute size than those for negative results. As a consequence, the algebraic mean effect size—.109—is bigger than the median. Raudenbush (1984) reported standard meta-analytic statistical tests, establishing that the mean effect size is significantly different from zero, and that the spread of effect sizes is much greater than one would expect if only chance variability were operating from one study to another.

It must be said, though, that the mean effect size of .109 is not very consequential. In relative IQ gain, it amounts to a bit more than 1½ points. But what of the cases in the upper tail of the distribution? Could Raudenbush (1984) account for the handful of effect sizes of .20 or more (representing differential IQ gains of some 3 to 8 points) by some distinguishing attribute(s) of the studies from which they came? Indeed he could.

One feature that had been recorded for each study was the number of weeks the teacher had known the children in the class before he or she was told which were the bloomers. In four studies, the teachers had had no contact with the children before receiving information favorable to some of them. The effect size results for these cases are given in bold italics in Table 7.3. In three other cases, prior contact had been for approximately 1 week, and these are indicated in simple italics.

It is evident at a glance, even without a formal statistical test, that the previous contact variable systematically explains a substantial amount of the effect size variation. The six highest effect sizes come from the four no-prior-contact cases and two of the three with 1-week-prior contact. (The original Pygmalion study is one of the latter, with effect size .21.)

Commonsense reasoning supports a clear mediating role for the prior contact variable. If a teacher has had little or no prior contact with a group of students, "information" about which ones have superior potential capabilities will exert an influence on how the teacher behaves toward them. But if he or she already knows the group fairly well, then habits already formed in interacting with these individuals will take precedence over abstract predictions based on some esoteric test.

The inverse relationship between prior contact and a Pygmalion effect can be seen as a particular case of the general social psychological proposition that subjective impressions of people are more manipulable when previous information is ambiguous or missing. This may seem obvious once it is stated, but with all the other variations from one Pygmalion study to the next, it might easily have been missed without the discipline of a meta-analysis.

GENERALITY ACROSS AND WITHIN STUDIES: A PARALLEL

A Thought Experiment

To appreciate the conceptual parallel between contextually qualified generalizations based on meta-analyses and those based on single studies with contextual variations, let us perform a thought experiment.

Pygmalion Again.   Suppose that 18 Pygmalion manipulations had been carried out within a single study, each in a different school. Associate each of the 18 outcomes tabulated in Table 7.3 with a particular school. These 18 pieces of data would represent the differences between the mean IQs of bloomers and of control group children in each of the schools. (To be faithful to the Raudenbush [1984] analysis, we should note that he tabulated standardized, not raw differences. However, the standard deviation of IQ scores is approximately 15 in typical samples, so that the relation between raw and standardized measures can be roughly characterized as simply that of a multiplying constant.)

The 18 schools in our reinterpretation can be divided into two sets: In 4 of them, the teachers had no prior contact with the children involved in the experiment, whereas in the remaining 14 they did have contact. The main variation of interest is the Expectancy (Pygmalion) treatment. Prior contact is a context variable, and the experimental arrangement is an Expectancy by Context design. Contexts are subdivided into a fixed factor—prior Contact—and a random factor, Schools-Within-Contact. We can now subject the 18 data points to an ANOVA, and Table 7.4 displays the results.

TABLE 7.4
Analysis of Variance of Meta-Analytic Data

Source	SS	df	MS	F	p
Expectancy(E)	.1067	1	.1067	7.36	< .05
School (S)	??[a]	17	??	—	—
E × Contact(C)	.1119	1	.1119	7.72	< .05
E × S-Within-C	.2319	16	.0145	—	—

[a]Sum of squares cannot be computed from available information, but variations in school IQ means are of no interest here.

The grand mean of the effect sizes, .1089, serves as the basis for calculating the Expectancy sum of squares.[10] There are 17 df having to do with variation of effect sizes over schools. One of these degrees of freedom corresponds to the potentially systematic interaction of Expectancy with prior Contact. The remaining 16 df include residual interactions, if any, between Expectancy and other aspects of context. The sum of squares for this source of variation is labeled E × Schools-Within-Contact. The corresponding mean square (.0145) serves as the error term for the respective F tests of the overall E effect, and the E × C interaction. These Fs both come out fairly large (above 7), and are significant at the .05 level.

We therefore would end up claiming one tick—a main effect of teacher expectancy, with one but—an interaction between expectancy and prior contact. The summary of the results would be something like:

"The analysis supports the existence of a systematic Pygmalion effect on IQ scores, but we find that this effect interacts with the length of prior contact between teacher and students. With no prior contact, the average standardized effect size is .32. With some prior contact, the average size is .05."[11]

Comparing this ANOVA approach with the meta-analytic techniques applied by Raudenbush (1984), the same conclusions are reached. However, he was able to apply an additional test, to see whether the residual variation in effect sizes exceeded the theoretical chance level. This could be done also in our paradigm, by noting the number of students in each experimental and each control group, and redoing the analysis with Fisher's z (Mullen, 1989) as the effect size measure.

Meta-Analysis in Relation to Treatment-by-Context Designs

That meta-analyses can be framed in terms of a traditional, single-study ANOVA is not meant as a criticism of meta-analysis. Indeed, it is reassuring that the two points of view converge. Meta-analysis can be learned as a more or less self-contained tool kit. It has the advantage that several contextual variables can be examined simultaneously for

---

[10]In an ANOVA on N observations, one ordinarily regards the number of degrees of freedom as $(N-1)$. Here we have 18 observations and 18 df. The "extra" df attaches to the difference of the grand mean from zero, that is, a test of the average effect size.

[11]An interesting exercise here is to set aside the four no-contact cases, and examine the stem-and-leaf of the remaining 14. It turns out that by Tukey's procedure, the effect size of .55 is an outlier (falling not in the "far out" region, but beyond the inner fence as an "outside point"—see chap. 5). If this one case is set aside, the mean of the remaining effect sizes is .01, and we can feel safe in characterizing the phenomenon as having vanished. An alternative is to redo the whole analysis, making a separate context category of the three cases where the teachers had 1 month of prior contact with the students (this includes the outlier from the some-prior-contact distribution). Close scrutiny of the details of the outlier study with the effect size of .55 would be useful.

interactions with the treatment effect, which is awkward to do from a simple ANOVA perspective. Another advantage is that it makes convenient the simultaneous inspection of a large number of studies with different response measures and different significance tests.

On the other side of the ledger, meta-analysis tends to rely on chance models that do not take into account the interactions of treatments with random context effects. Because such interactions are almost always present, the standard significance tests in meta-analysis are too generous, much like the analysis in the second part of Table 7.1. Indeed, this has been recognized by statistical experts in meta-analysis (Hedges, 1983), though not widely appreciated.

Another potential—but avoidable—drawback is that if meta-analysis became a virtually inevitable procedure for any given phenomenon, focused theoretical arguments might be weakened. There might be a temptation for individual experimenters to take a laissez-faire attitude toward contextual influences, reckoning that other people will vary this and that, and meta-analysis will sweep it all up. The result could be a more willy-nilly choice of experimental designs, and a consequent loss of conceptual acumen. To avoid this, social science should still retain the basic functions of a lore sensitive to dialogue among investigators, with meta-analysis waiting in the wings. For unresolved, interesting issues, careful quantitative scrutiny of the record will prove superior to sole reliance on the lore.

FINAL CAVEAT

We have seen that the manipulation or meta-analysis of a context variable can provide good articulation of the interaction of treatments with that context variable. But what of context variables that are not explicitly varied? Clearly there is no end to the list of contextual variations. One cannot explicitly vary more than a couple of context variables in a big experiment, or perhaps half a dozen in a typical meta-analysis. Thus one can only try to deal with the most important of them, that is, the ones that are most theoretically critical, and most likely to produce quantitative or qualitative treatment by context interactions. Our ability to generalize is always weaker than we think.

This seems so obvious as to hardly need stating. Yet it is amazing to what extent investigators hold the illusion that if some context variable has not been tried, it has no effects. One can make reasonable guesses, but the only sure way to have knowledge of the importance of a context variable is to vary it. Thus Abelson's Seventh Law: *You can't see the dust if you don't move the couch.*

8 Interestingness of Argument

In this chapter and the next, we broaden our discussion of the narrative aspects of statistical claims. We ask what makes a statistical claim interesting to a research audience. This is an important issue, because when a statistical story becomes a conversation piece, further research is likely to be generated. If a claim is so blah that no one cares to read or talk about it, the chances are small that it will enter the lore of a field—much less stimulate further investigation. Thus high interest acts as a magnifier, and low interest as a filter, shaping the body of lore in the direction of more interesting claims.

Yet the nature of interestingness is elusive. Philosophers (Davis, 1971), psychologists (Hidi & Baird, 1986; Tesser, 1990), computer scientists (Schank, 1979; Wilensky, 1983), and others have grappled with this concept. After a preliminary discussion, we focus on the question of what makes research claims theoretically interesting, and only make passing reference to popular interest, or pizazz.

CAN STATISTICS BE INTERESTING?

At the outset, we must confront the widespread stereotype of statistics as a dull subject. (When working on this book, friends and acquaintances would ask me what it was about. "Statistics," I would say. "Oh... Yes...", would come the reply. "...And how is your family?")

Interesting Claims and Interesting Methods

The reputed dullness of statistics is often assumed to spread like some musty odor, covering everything statistical with a layer of suffocating tedium. Students burdened with this stereotype fail to realize that the point of a statistical argument can be interesting, even if the technical substance of its rhetoric is somewhat dry. What is more, in some cases a clever statistical analysis can itself be interesting in the way it manages to reveal something not previously known or properly understood.

Example: A Case of Disputed Authorship. A topic may not of itself be of great importance to nonspecialists, but a statistical story about it may be interesting because of the unexpected use of a pattern of clues, much as in a satisfying detective story. In a classic example of a scholarly "whodunit," statisticians Mosteller and Wallace (1964) set out to infer the true authorship of several Federalist Papers long in dispute as between James Madison and Alexander Hamilton. For many years, inconclusive debate had raged about stylistic similarities between the unattributed papers and the Federalist Papers known to have been written by Madison and by Hamilton, respectively. Authorship arguments based on ideological content had gotten nowhere, and scholars had begun to look at quantitative indices such as sentence length or average numbers of subordinate clauses per sentence. After study, Mosteller and Wallace rejected these methods; instead, they counted particular word usages—such as *while* versus *whilst*—in the disputed papers and the known papers of these two authors. With the aid of Bayesian reasoning they came to the conclusion that the contested manuscripts were almost certainly penned by James Madison. It is surprising that idiosyncracy in skilled human expression could be much more readily identified by very concrete details than by general stylistic tendencies.

The Statistician as Grinch. Interest in the authorship example requires academic curiosity. There are many other examples of clever statistical detective work, dealing with hotter topics than Hamilton and Madison, and bearing on beliefs held by the general public. In chapter 1, we mentioned the statistical sleuthing by Carroll (1979) that exposed the flaw in the claim of special longevity for orchestra conductors. In chapter 2 we saw a statistical reinterpretation of the legendary hot hand in basketball, and in chapter 5, the revelation of a statistical peculiarity in some mental telepathy data. Also in chapter 5, we presented an incisive debunking job on the supposed baby boom from the New York blackout.

In many such examples, the statistician is cast in the role of a skeptical investigator who does not readily accept a popular explanation of some newsworthy phenomenon. His statistical reanalysis impugns the credibility of an existing belief, showing that the true magnitude of a hypothesized effect was nil, or its basis artifactual. As we elaborate next, the potential to change belief is characteristic of interesting statistical stories.

In cases where beliefs are spoiled,[1] a regrettable side effect is that statisticians are made to seem like grinches who loiter about, waiting for opportunities to snatch legends from unsuspecting populaces. In practice, the public is protected from such unpleasantness by its imperviousness to statistics, either because skeptical reanalyses are not sufficiently publicized, or because the public is inattentive or disbelieving.

Like the general public, researchers do not readily abandon their pet hypotheses either. But they must face evidence and argument more squarely than the public does. Debate over the interpretation of results is commonplace, and interestingness plays a role in these confrontations.

THEORETICAL INTEREST

Let us turn to the concept of *theoretical interest*. Here we are concerned specifically with the interestingness of research claims based on statistical evidence; thus, we might equally well use the term, *scientific interest*. This might be variously defined, but for our purposes the following conception is appropriate: A statistical story is scientifically interesting when it has the potential to change what scientists believe[2] about important causal relationships.

Change of Belief

The key concept is change of belief, which could consist of strengthening old or creating new beliefs, of weakening existing beliefs, or of modifying beliefs depending on context. New results may create a disparity between observation and expectation, putting pressure on research audience members to re-examine the basis for their expectations, which in turn may change their beliefs. In other words, research must be *surprising* in order to play a role in potential belief change. Thus interest arises from surprising results on an important issue.

Note that we refer to potential belief change. An investigator may make claims that are not accepted, and therefore do not actually change what people believe. If flaws in the conduct and analysis of the research

---

[1]There are examples, of course, in which statistical analysis supports a popular belief. One illustration concerns the "long, hot summer" hypothesis for the urban riots of the late 1960s, namely, that the probability of riot occurrence increased with increasing temperature. The psychological notion here is that the hotter the day, the greater the discomfort of an already frustrated inner-city population, lowering its threshold for an explosion of anger. Baron and Ransberger (1978) examined maximum ambient temperatures for the dates and locations of the occurrence of riots during the turbulent summers of 1967–1971. On the basis of their statistical analysis and a refined reanalysis by Carlsmith and Anderson (1979), one can be quite confident that higher temperatures were systematically associated with greater riot propensity in those summers.

[2]For a discussion of distinctions between knowledge and belief, see Abelson (1979).

are obvious, it might be dismissed out of hand, and never even be seen as interesting. In other cases, acceptance depends on the persuasive force of the statistical evidence. This depends on the magnitude (chap. 3), articulation (chap. 6), generality (chap. 7), and credibility (chap. 9) of the effects. Claims that are highly surprising, and of great theoretical (or applied) consequence excite great interest and great skepticism simultaneously. The claim by Wilson and Herrnstein (1985) that criminality is genetically transmitted is an illustration of a startling proposal that invokes resistance.

Important beliefs are not readily changed in the typical research community. Beliefs acquire their importance by being anchored in networks of interrelated propositions, often as part of a theory. Change in one belief usually entails changes in others, which in turn imply still further changes, foreshadowing an unwelcome cascade of alterations. As a result, even if the surprising claim is persuasive on paper, cycles of argument and counterargument—to say nothing of further research—may be necessary before beliefs change. During the period following the claim, interest hangs in limbo, the research community collectively not knowing whether to take the claim seriously. Attitudes toward the claim during this limbo period could be paraphrased as, "It seems interesting, but...."[3]

The tension might finally be resolved by the acceptance, rejection, or modification of the initial claim. Following the change or reaffirmation of all the relevant beliefs, the claim loses current interest. Alternatively, the research community may divide into camps with rival beliefs, in which case interest may last until both sides exhaust their ideas on how to do further useful research.

Too Incredible to Be True.   In the extreme, if a claim were so totally bizarre that almost anyone hearing it would immediately dismiss it as incredible, then its interest value for all but true believers would be nil. To give a cockeyed geophysical example, I once heard about a theory that the earth was spherical, all right, but with everyone living on the inside of the sphere, and the heavens in the center. This theory is not an interesting topic for empirical research (though it might be interesting as a delusion), because there are many ways to falsify it with existing knowledge. The incredible claim by Philpott (1950) of an infinitesimal mental time unit, discussed in chapter 3, is a case in point from the psychological literature.[4]

---

[3]Anyone who has ever heard old-style Soviet academics argue will recognize the typical opening line of vicious criticisms: "Comrade Potchky's analysis of the problem is very interesting. However,...[whamski, bamski, socko]."

[4]The "thin red line" between implausibility and sheer lunacy is notoriously difficult to locate, unfortunately, so that we encounter here a problem similar to the one we met in chapter 3 in our discussion of Bayesian prior probabilities. From the standpoint of the challenger of orthodoxy, to have one's creative visions dismissed out of hand as mad delusions seems quite unfair. Indeed, once in a blue moon, it is.

SURPRISINGNESS

Our emphasis on surprisingness is consistent with the advice of Leon Festinger and his students that *counterintuitiveness* should be a major criterion for good research hypotheses. He argued that if you performed a piece of research that provided evidence for something your grandmother could have told you already, then you had wasted your time. In this view, for example, it is uninteresting to show that individuals dislike people who disagree with them, or that people will exert greater effort for a larger reward. This doctrine has a weak spot, however: Sometimes what your grandmother (or anyone else) "knows" coexists with knowledge of its opposite. ("Out of sight, out of mind," plus "Absence makes the heart grow fonder.")

I agree, however, that when an unambiguous prediction of a folk theory or a scientific theory is generally believed, it is usually more interesting to cast doubt on it than to provide evidence strengthening it. Also interesting would be research and statistical analysis illuminating the particular circumstances under which the existing theory holds or fails to hold. According to McGuire's (1989) perspectivist view of psychology, conditions can virtually always be arranged under which any given relationship, even the most obvious, can be reversed. It is instructive to take examples and try to dream up what such conditions might be. When, perchance, might people show increased liking for someone who had been critical of them? (When they knew they had performed badly, and deserved criticism. See Deutsch & Solomon, 1959.) The bottom line in all this is that to be interesting, a result has to make you think about the topic—or at least make you want to think.

Surprising Ticks in a New Area

One way to create surprise is with a research initiative on a neglected topic, producing results that bruise our intuitions or seem to defy logic.

Example: Milgram's Study of Obedience.   A sensation was created by Milgram's (1963) obedience study, in which a majority of ordinary people were induced by an "experimenter" to deliver apparently dangerous levels of electric shock to a helpless victim. Hardly anyone predicted this outcome. Every time a new tick surprises us because it contradicts common wisdom, there are actually two interrelated changes of belief we are called upon to make. One is the acceptance of the reality of the new phenomenon, and the other is a diminution in the perceived force of the prior wisdom.

In the Milgram (1963) case, the common assumption is that evil things are done by evil people, not by evil situations. This is a hard assumption to free ourselves from, as it seems to provide a simple explanation of many events in the social world, and it is a tenet that often arises in law, politics, and religion. Milgram argued against the evildoer theory of cruelty by characterizing the people who obediently deliver the shocks as obedient sheep rather than predatory wolves. Even with the intellectual help of this metaphor, however, it is still difficult not to feel repeatedly surprised every time one thinks of the Milgram study.

Example: Comprehension and Belief. In a less dramatic, yet quite important way, the research of Daniel Gilbert (1991) provides another example that promotes the replacement of a lifelong presupposition in favor of a new conception. Gilbert was concerned with the general relationship between one's comprehension of novel statements and one's belief in them.

The usual view of the matter is that when a statement is presented, the first cognitive task for the receiver is to comprehend it. If the statement is understood, a subsequent decision is made whether to believe or disbelieve it. Since the early years of persuasion research (Hovland et al., 1953), investigators have posited that the comprehension of a persuasive passage is followed by a process of acceptance or rejection. In fact, this conception predates psychological research by more than three centuries, going back at least to Descartes.

A radical alternative view, credited to Spinoza, is that comprehension *entails* initial belief, following which there is the possibility of later unbelief. In this way of putting the matter, belief is the default state. Barring an active subsequent process of rejection, "perceiving is believing."

If the Spinozan view is correct, then early interruption of the cognitive processing of each of a mixed set of true and false statements ought to yield a bias toward accepting the false ones as true, compared to a control condition with no interruption. An appropriate experiment by Gilbert (1991) yielded just such a surprising result. This will probably require a great deal of rethinking of the relation between comprehension and belief.[5]

---

[5]If replications support Gilbert's (1991) findings in favor of the Spinozan conception, the implications are extensive. At an informal level, light is shed on several apparently senseless eccentricities of human behavior, such as why people deliberately set their watches 5 minutes fast, and why children are so monumentally upset when repeatedly called by the wrong name. At a theoretical level, a number of phenomena in the literatures on persuasion and propaganda become more intelligible: the surprising effectiveness of the Big Lie in propaganda, the persuasive effects of distraction in communication (Festinger & Maccoby, 1964), and the success of persuasion in fiction (Gerrig & Prentice, 1991), to name three.

Accumulating Buts

In chapter 7, on generality, we discussed the various kinds of replication attempts that may follow on the publication of claims in a new area. Replications are especially likely when the initial study is interesting.

Suppose that almost every replication agrees with the initial claim. If we imagine a cumulative meta-analysis updated after each new replication, the changes in the estimated overall effect size will tend to be smaller and smaller, thus less and less surprising and interesting. After 20 studies, we usually won't know much more than we did after 19 studies.

This decrease of interest with increasing replication is especially pronounced if replications are performed mindlessly, each time with some haphazardly chosen, minor variation. The way to revive interest in an effect is to find contextual factors that qualify it, either by *nullifying* it, or (even more interesting) *reversing* it. Hopefully, such qualifying factors would be meaningfully related to the effect in question. If a particular laboratory effect failed to occur only when the moon was full, that might make an interesting story, but it would be incoherent unless further explicated. (See chap. 9.)

When many replications are carried out, it is quite likely that under some conditions there will be failure to reproduce the original result. If these failures are credible (see chap. 9), then the initial tick will accumulate buts.

Example: Butting an Early Claim of Dissonance Theory.   In the dissonant situation in which someone is rewarded for speaking out contrary to his original beliefs, the claim coming out of the Festinger and Carlsmith (1959) study was that a small reward ($1) is more influential than a large reward ($20) in causing the person to change his beliefs (chap. 2).

Many investigators subsequently performed similar studies (with smaller overall rewards to meet criticism of the $20 amount), and at least three clear buts emerged. Linder, Cooper, and Jones (1967) showed a qualitative interaction in a 2×2 design: When subjects were given a *choice* whether to write an essay counter to their opinions,[6] a group paid 50¢ indeed changed their opinions more than a group paid $2.50, but when subjects had no choice, the relative effects of the rewards reversed. Helmreich and Collins (1968) tested whether public *commitment* by the subject was a necessary condition for replicating the dissonance prediction. They had subjects agree to argue against their own point of view,

---

[6]The subjects really only have an *illusion* of free choice. In the typical high-choice manipulation, the experimenter gives the subject a very effective soft sell, emphasizing that the subject's participation would really be appreciated, but that "It's entirely up to you." Virtually all subjects cooperate.

some to make a videotape with their names and faces prominent, and others to record their statements anonymously on audiotape. Under the public video manipulation, small reward was more effective than large reward, but under the anonymous audio condition, the effect of reward disappeared.

A third limiting condition was the nature of the *consequences* likely to follow from the counterattitudinal performance. Nel, Helmreich, and Aronson (1969) gently persuaded some squeaky clean Texas undergraduates to prepare to speak for the virtues of marijuana to an audience of nonsmoking young high school students, and others to speak to a college audience already favorable to marijuana. The former audience was the more consequential one, because the speech might push the innocents down the path to drug abuse. Dissonance predictions held only for this consequential condition, not for the speech to the already corrupted collegians.

The upshot of these studies (and others—we have simplified matters) was the eventual appearance of summary statements in journals and books, to the effect that opinion or belief change from expressing the other side of an issue is indeed greater when the reward is smaller, *but* only if the behavior is voluntary, publicly committal, and perceived to have negative consequences.

Actually, the first qualification, that subjects should think they had a free choice, had been predicted by dissonance theory (Brehm & Cohen, 1962). The necessity for subjects to be committed to their behavior was strongly implicit in the theory as well. The requirement that the subject's behavior have negative consequences did not flow so readily from the theory, and required some effort to make it fit. The procedures of the Festinger and Carlsmith (1959) experiment, it should be noted, satisfied the three constraints, although only the factor of choice was explicit. This could be considered lucky for the investigators, although I suspect that Festinger knew intuitively what sort of scenario would work.

Interest in a striking phenomenon tends to be maintained when its prevailing explanation does not quite cover all the empirical buts. Typically there is tension between the integrity of a theory and the need to stretch it to accommodate qualifications. If the theory is stretched, it may no longer be the same theory. An often cited example is the addition of ugly epicycles to make Ptolemy's conception of the heavenly bodies fit orbital observations.

In the dissonance case, the account of self-persuasion for a small reward has gradually been bent into a different form. The subject is no longer seen as motivated merely by inconsistency between his beliefs and his behavior. When he voluntarily agrees to exercise a harmful public deception for a payment of 50¢ or $1, he is making a fool of himself. Belief change can be seen as an attempt to justify an otherwise sleazy performance (Aronson, 1969). Under this view, variously articulated by several social psychologists, the subject is motivated by self-esteem maintenance rather than mere inconsistency reduction.

Thesis, Antithesis, Synthesis

In a very thoughtful article, Tesser (1990) discussed the nature of interesting ideas in psychological research. He suggested that ideally, psychological hypotheses should be about processes rather than static abstractions, and that empirical results should tell a story. (As he put it, if you want to avoid boring ideas, tell yourself "process, process, process, plot, plot, plot.")

One of his formulas for producing surprise and interest is this: For any thesis, generate the antithesis, and propose a synthesis. In our lingo, start with a tick, find a but for it, and finally reframe the issue so that the but becomes another tick. In one example Tesser (1990) gave, the thesis is that an outstanding performance by someone produces jealousy in those close to him. But the opposite can also be demonstrated, whereby an excellent performance arouses pride in close others, a "basking in reflected glory" (Cialdini et al., 1976). The resolution of this contradiction (Tesser, 1988) is that what is at stake for the close other is the maintenance of his self-esteem. (The reappearance here of this particular concept is coincidental.) If the outstanding performance is on some activity that is relevant to his self-esteem, he is likely to be jealous; if it is irrelevant, he will bask in reflected glory.

Quantifying Surprisingness

A Basic Formula.   If we attend not merely to ticks and buts, but also to the magnitudes of expected and observed effects, we can roughly quantify our intuitions about surprisingness. In chapter 3 we mentioned a surprisingness coefficient (S); we now formalize it.

That a result is surprising means that it is much stronger or weaker, or even in the reverse direction from what we expected. This suggests that we choose some directional magnitude measure by which expectation and observation can be compared. In the simplest type of Bayesian analysis, the probability of a hypothesis is assessed after the data are gathered, and can be compared with the prior probability. For the reasons given in chapter 3, however, an observed effect size in relation to the expected effect size seems a preferable magnitude concept to use for indexing surprisingness.

The measure of effect size could be a mean difference, raw or standardized; a correlation coefficient (Rosenthal, 1991); or a causal efficacy, objective or subjective. Staunch Bayesians could, if they wished, stick

TABLE 8.1
Potential Values of the Surprisingness Coefficient

Case	Expected Effect Size	Observed Effect Size	Surprisingness Coefficient
A	0	.5	.5
B	.1	.5	.27
C	.3	.5	.05
D	.5	.5	0
E	.5	.3	.05
F	.5	0	.5
G	.5	−.5	1.0
H	.7	−.7	1.4
I	u	−ω	u + v when u,v > 0.

with probability as a measure. Denoting the measure of magnitude by m, our surprisingness coefficient is: $S = (m[o] - m[e])^2 / | m[o] + m[e] |$. Here, $m[o]$ is the *observed* magnitude of effect for the comparison of interest in a specified context, and $m[e]$ is the *expected* magnitude, assuming general consensus for the expectation. A null outcome would set $m[o]$ to zero,[7] and a null expectation would set $m[e]$ to zero. (If the study concerned a novel relationship about which there was no expectation one way or another, then $m[e]$ would be undefined, and the formula inapplicable.) Effect sizes are of course directional; when $m[e]$ and $m[o]$ are opposite in sign, this indicates that the outcome was the reverse of what was expected. The rationale for the formula is that it is the simplest expression intuitively capturing how surprise arises as a function of effect size, with the constraint that we want the measure of surprise to be in the same units as the measures of effect size.

Behavior of the Coefficient.   It proves helpful to play with the aforementioned formula, inserting different hypothetical values for the effect magnitude. For simplicity of illustration, let us take the correlation coefficient[8] as the measure m, potentially ranging from −1 to +1. Table 8.1 specifies the coefficient S for several basic situations.

As the table indicates for Cases A–D, when the observed effect size is .5 (i.e., when the observed correlation between some putative cause and its claimed effect is .5), the surprisingness coefficient S is itself .5 when the expected correlation was zero, but declines very sharply as the expected correlation increases. Of course, if the expected correlation were also .5, there would be no surprise whatever.

In symmetrical fashion, if we fix the expected correlation at .5, and ask how S varies as the observed correlation falls off below .5 (Cases

---

[7]If probability were used as the magnitude measure, the nil value for *directional* hypotheses would be $p = .5$.

[8]Any other measure of effect size, such as d, could be used instead of r in the formula. The measure S is to be interpreted in the scale units of the measure of effect magnitude.

D–G), we find that surprisingness increases. This increase is gradual at first, but when the observed correlation is zero in the face of the expectation that the correlation should be about .5, S is again .5. If we expect .5 and we get minus .5, surprisingness doubles, to 1.0. As Cases H and I indicate, surprisingness can go even higher, if expectation and observation are both strong, and opposite in direction. Using correlation as the effect size measure, the maximum value of S is 2.0.

Blurring of the Coefficient.   According to our formula, the absence of an effect that everybody expected is as surprising as the presence of an effect that nobody expected. This seems to be a reasonable intuition, although we should note a qualification. Expectations can sometimes be sharply focused at the exact value of zero; for example, doubters of ESP can believe that there simply is no such thing. By contrast, *outcomes* are never sharply focused at exactly zero (or at any other exact value, for that matter)—there is always some confidence interval within which the results may be said to lie. (Gilovich et al., 1985, didn't prove the nonexistence of the hot hand in basketball; their results only imply that the effect, if any, is of limited magnitude.) Demonstrations of the absence of an effect are thus apt to be more uncertain than expectations of its absence. Accordingly, allowance should be made for the blurring of an m[o] of zero (or any other fixed central value) throughout some range around zero (or other central value). Actually, if we follow this line of reasoning, we should also allow for the blurring of expected effect magnitudes other than zero. The general case, then, would be one in which m[o] and m[e] had probability distributions, the only fixed case being an occasional m[e] of zero. In all cases, the coefficient S would have a distribution, rather than a single value. However, this analysis carries us beyond the level of sophistication we need or wish to achieve here. When we refer to m[o] and m[e], therefore, we are supposing that central values for each are sufficiently exact for our purposes.

Heterogeneous Initial Beliefs

Although we are choosing not to analyze variations within research observers, we must confront variations between observers. This is because, in any real research situation, different investigators may have different beliefs about the magnitude (or even the very existence) of a given phenomenon.

Consider the simplest case of heterogeneous beliefs, in which there are two groups of scientists, each with a different level of belief in a theoretically important phenomenon. Suppose that for the larger of the two groups, the expected effect size is zero; that is, they disbelieve the existence of the phenomenon. The minority group has some positive expectation, m[e]. Imagine that members of this group want to convince the skeptical majority. They run an experiment on the phenomenon, and observe a positive result with effect size m[o] precisely equal to their expectation m[e]. The surprisingness of this result stands to be different for the two groups: For the skeptical majority, the surprisingness coefficient apparently equals m[o], the magnitude of the unanticipated effect; for the minority group, the coefficient equals zero, because the result is exactly what they expected.

At this point, if the two groups were rivalrous and uncivil, the dialogue between them might be caricatured thus:

Minority: There, you see! *That* result ought to surprise you!
Majority: (Defensively): Doesn't surprise us at all. It's only an illusion. Your experiment is flawed, and we don't accept your claim.
Minority: And why is that?
Majority: Because...[ARGUMENT].
Minority: But...[COUNTERARGUMENT]! And furthermore....
Majority: Don't waste your breath. We're not interested.
Minority: And you call yourselves scientists!

Here, one group tries to command the attention of the other by surprising them with data they don't expect, and—because surprisingness along with importance creates interest—thence to interest them. The second group can appear unsurprised and disinterested by declining to accept the validity of the data.[9] This of course requires the development of an argument criticizing the claim made by the first group, possibly supported by the presentation of a replication that fails to confirm the claim (see chap. 9.) If the majority is unable to damage the claim by the minority, but is not yet willing to give up, their state of mind might be described as reluctant interest: They have to pay attention.

Contextual Qualification of Beliefs

Let us elaborate our analysis of surprisingness to apply to the case in which the expected effect size is of magnitude r, but the observed effect is contingent upon some context variable. In the presence of a particular context variable, the result indeed comes out to be of magnitude r, but in its absence, the effect vanishes. How surprised ought the observer to be?

---

[9]Old-timers in psychology will recall the feisty exchanges between the Hullians, with their behaviorist view of learning, and the cognitivist Tolmanians. Poor Tolman kept inventing ever and ever more colorful attempts to demonstrate the existence of "cognitive maps" in rats, hoping to get a rise out of the Hullians. He never succeeded, although years later, cognitive approaches became respectable in learning theory.

A simple approach to this type of question is to take the mean of the surprisingness coefficients calculated with the context factor present and with it absent, respectively. In the specified case, the coefficients for these two situations are 0 and r, yielding an average surprisingness of r/2. In other words, when an observer expects a general effect, and it fails in half the situations, he will be half as surprised as he would be were the expected effect to fail universally. This is of course a rough way of stating our intuitions.

If the observer were to anticipate that the context variable might make a difference, she could have different expectations about the effect size for the context present and context absent situations. The observer might be somewhat off in one or both of her two expectations, and this would occasion a modicum of surprise. If, on the other hand, she correctly foresaw the two respective effect sizes, her surprise would be zero. Of course, other researchers might be surprised and interested, and their beliefs might change.

The process of introducing further context variables that produce unanticipated differences, and therefore elicit surprise, could in principle continue indefinitely. However, the greater the number of combinations of context factors, the less impact minor contextual refinements would have—which is another way of saying that research areas tend to lose interest when everyone learns to understand approximately what outcomes to expect under the most crucial circumstances.

IMPORTANCE

Interestingness, we have said, depends on importance as well as surprisingness. The importance of any single empirical result is a direct function of the number of consequences it has for relationships between variables pertinent to the issue at hand. The importance of the issue, in turn, depends on its density of connections to other (important) issues. Insights about cancer are more important than insights about callouses, because more people (and more biological and psychological phenomena) are more deeply affected by the former. This example is obvious, and may make it seem that a judgment of importance is easy. In fact this is a hard judgment to make, especially for theoretical rather than applied research, because the ramifications of theories are often difficult to anticipate.

Differences in Importance for Different Investigators

What seems important to some investigators may seem unimportant to others. If I have heard somewhere that all mammals have periods of rapid eye movements (REM) during sleep, and I idly run across a research report that there is an Australian armadillo that does not show REM sleep, I will hardly be riveted with fascination. I care so little one way or the other that as I write this, I'm not even sure I have my facts straight. Of course, there will be researchers or others who have concerned themselves with REM sleep or armadillos, who would find the new fact interesting. For me, the matter is peripheral; for them, it is central.

The Illusion of Importance.   Indeed, scholars of a particular topic are prone to generate dense networks of conceptual relationships within the topic area, thus lending by the sheer weight of number of relationships an aura of apparent importance to each contribution to the topic.[10] But to nonspecialists in the area, the topic might have very little importance, because knowledge gained therein does not shed much light on the understanding of other topics. We refer to this phenomenon as the *illusion of importance.*

This skeptical characterization of narrow, ingrown fields of research may seem unfair, because one cannot confidently anticipate whether connections to other research fields or practical applications will be forthcoming in any given case. In my framing of this phenomenon, I mainly want to emphasize that knowing a lot about a particular subject matter creates subjective importance for it, whether or not it is objectively warranted.

The exhaustive study within cognitive psychology many years ago of the principles of learning of lists of nonsense syllables may be a case in point. Despite the density of knowledge on this topic, the whole enterprise (arguably) lacked major importance because its findings did not extend well to the learning of meaningful prose—or for that matter, to the learning of content material that was not in the form of lists requiring rote memorization.

We do not attempt to develop a formula for importance. That would require a model of knowledge representations carrying us far afield from our core concerns. Nevertheless, the key question to ask in diagnosing the importance of a given result is, "What can I learn from this about other things that are also important?"

---

[10]The tendency for scholars to want to become expert in tiny domains has been lampooned in the old aphorism, "College deans learn less and less about more and more, until they know nothing about everything. Professors learn more and more about less and less, until they know everything about nothing."

With a cosmic metaphor, social psychologist Richard Nisbett (personal communication, April 30, 1994) said of a particular field of psychology, "Sometimes I think that...[this field]... has imploded, and become a white dwarf."

9 Credibility of Argument

To this point, we have discussed four criteria affecting the persuasiveness of arguments based on the statistical analysis and interpretation of empirical data: magnitude, articulation, generality, and interestingness. Failure to satisfy one or more of these criteria will weaken the force of the investigator's argument, increasing the likelihood that the results will be ignored. Indeed, the research may not even be published. A good rule of thumb—the *rule of two criticisms*—is that two deficiencies among these four criteria will result in rejection by journal editors.[1]

By contrast, if these four criteria are apparently met satisfactorily, but the research claim lacks credibility, the reported results will be likely to set off debate. When research presentations advance claims that many or most readers deem incredible, these claims are vulnerable to severe challenge. In response, there will typically be a rebuttal by the investigator, and then a fresh round of criticism. The burden of proof shifts back and forth between the investigator and the critic in what might be called the game of "burden tennis."

WHY RESEARCH CLAIMS ARE DISBELIEVED

There are two different ways in which a research claim may not seem credible to an audience: The claim may be based on poor methodology;

---

[1]The basis for this rule of thumb is that journal reviewers' evaluations of manuscripts usually take the form of informal scorecards, using criteria that can be mapped onto the ones I have proposed. If the research claims are strong, well articulated, and interesting, a reviewer will tend to be tolerant of a lack of generality. Or if the claims are well-articulated, interesting, and general, weakness of magnitude can be tolerated. One limitation is forgivable; after all, nobody is perfect. But it is hard to champion a research report with two unmet criteria. A referee feeling favorable toward such a report would find herself in the unenviable position of the fictional baseball scout whose report on a young prospect read, "Although he is a terrible fielder, he is a lousy hitter."

or it may contradict a strongly held conception—a popular theory, a world view, or even just common sense.

Characteristically, the critic who disbelieves a research claim primarily for conceptual reasons will nevertheless bolster his case by putting forward one or more *methodological objections*, that is, complaints about the research design or the statistical analysis. It is contrary to scientific norms to reject an empirical finding solely because the critic does not believe it. It would seem arrogant for a journal editor to write the investigator, "We are rejecting your manuscript, *The Life Force in Snails*, because we just don't believe it." The editor and the reviewers might feel that way, but protocol restrains such brutal frankness. The editor might politely suggest another journal as more suitable for this manuscript, or—more interesting for our discussion—the editor might follow the rule of two criticisms. That is, there would be some mention of objections to the questionable conceptual status of the result being proposed, but also an elaboration of one or more methodological criticisms. Often there is consensus about poor methodology in a field,[2] so that such criticism can be powerful.

If, however, the methodological attack is persuasively countered by the investigator, there is a chance that a revised manuscript might be reconsidered and accepted, thus opening the matter for general debate. Among other conceivable outcomes, the claim that was once incredible might eventually be vindicated.

Although not always perfect models of objectivity and decorum, debates can be creatively constructive. This is among the reasons why it has lately become fashionable for various disciplines in the behavioral sciences to sponsor journals such as *The Behavioral and Brain Sciences* that welcome—indeed, promote—clashing views. A scholar with a position considered controversial or outrageous is asked to write a target article. A number of critics, supporters, and wise old heads contribute commentaries, to which the target person responds.

Empirical evidence free of methodological flaws is crucial to putting one's best case forward in an extended public debate. Success depends on the details of research design and procedure, and of statistical analysis, in relation to the status of the debate. Good research management includes good debate management. In the examples that follow, we consider how empirical results influence argument, and how argument stimulates new studies.

---

[2]Of course, from time to time there are debates about proper methodology. As we saw in chapter 5, these debates may be touched off by the publication of a number of counterintuitive results, suggesting something fishy about the prevailing methodology or statistical analysis.

THE STRUCTURE OF DEBATES ON DISBELIEVED CLAIMS

When a Positive Universal is Challenged by a Counterexample

The prototypic debate starts with a research result that challenges a strongly held current theory or belief system. Often, the nature of the challenged belief is that of a positive or negative *universal*, a statement with the structure, "All X is Y," or "Under conditions C, phenomenon P is impossible." Challenge comes in the form of an empirical *counterexample* purporting to show an X that is not Y, or an instance of P under conditions C. For example, the universal proposition that all human behavior is self-interested would be challenged by a research demonstration of pure altruism.

To give life to the subsequent dialogue in these scripted debates, we name the character expressing the universal Professor Neat, and the rebel with the counterexample Professor Scruffy. (The former name suggests a preference for orderly, formal statements and procedures; the latter connotes a tolerance for realism and messiness; Abelson, 1981). Their dialogue might go like this:

Neat: Xs are always Y.
Scruffy: In my experiment, subjects high on X were randomly as-
          signed to a foofram or a no-foofram condition. Sixty-three
          percent of the foofram subjects showed no Y whatsoever.
          Thus Y is not inevitably associated with X.
Neat: The so-called refutation by Scroughy[3] of the (X,Y) Law is
          clearly an artifact. Fooframming inhibits the registration of
          Y on the standard measure. Thus it is not surprising that
          many subjects appeared to be at zero.
[or]
          Scruffy's attack on the (X,Y) law is not justified by his
          experiment. His data are irrelevant, for the reason that true
          Xs do not occur in his subject population.

These two possible volleys by Neat are similar in style—they dismiss the challenge—but they differ in nature. The first puts it that the methodology was biased so as to disconfirm the universal. The second states, in effect, that Scruffy lacked conceptual understanding of the universal, as he didn't even use a relevant sample of subjects.

---

[3]It is not altogether rare for Neat to misspell Scruffy's name. As a target of criticism myself, I have been called Adelson, and Ableson, and have acquired new middle initials. I interpret this as motivated inattention to details about the target person, rather than as deliberate gamesmanship.

Scruffy has potential ways to respond to each of these shots. To the accusation of artifact, an effective line of defense is to give statistical or procedural details that undercut the accusation (e.g., by revealing that 34% of the non-foofram group also showed zero Y). To the conceptual criticism, he must respond conceptually (e.g., by arguing why his subjects are indeed Xs).

An entirely different tack may be taken by Scruffy. He or she may produce another counterexample. If the same rejoinders by Neat do not apply to the new study, then Neat is driven into the position of proposing different artifacts and conceptual rationalizations for each example. Extrapolate to a half-dozen counterexamples, and Neat's ability to retort coherently seems to shrink to zero. Yet, as we soon see, Neat has a last-ditch rhetorical weapon.

Example: The Model of the Rational Actor.   The interdisciplinary field of behavioral economics has produced controversy that illustrates the phenomenon of repeated exceptions to a universal. Mainstream economic theory depends heavily on a universalistic model of rational actors all trying to maximize their economic well-being. Political theory, meanwhile, has been massively influenced by the analogue model of political actors seeking to maximize their political self interests. Suitably mathematized and operationalized, this model has the facility to spin out predictions and explanations in a wide variety of economic and political situations.

Neats love the model. If data would conform to its predictions, the model would unify an impressive array of phenomena. When the rational actor model has been tested, however, either the tests have been weak or trite, or the model falsified by anomalous results (Green & Shapiro, 1994). The research on decision heuristics and biases conducted by Tversky and Kahneman (1974) and further elaborated by Nisbett and Ross (1980) has explicated many anomalies of decision and judgment.

When anomalies first appeared, economists were inclined to ignore them as esoteric exceptions to the mainstream model. As counterexamples began to accumulate, however, it became necessary to develop a single, coherent response. A *meta-criticism*, sweepingly applicable to dozens of purported anomalies, is what was needed. The most popular such critique was the complaint that psychological experiments, done in the laboratory (often with paper-and-pencil methods), were not predictive of economic situations in which real money was at stake.

But the size of payoffs did not seem to be much of a predictor of laboratory results (Grether & Plott, 1979). Worse yet for the critics, anomalies in actual market behavior began to appear. Richard Thaler (1991), an economist in the Scruffy role, collected a large number of such anomalies and challenged economists to deal with them.

Defenders of the model are now increasingly forced to rely on the more desperate criticism of acknowledging anomalies, but inviting opponents of the rational actor conception to come up with a better model that would explain more data. As a play in burden tennis, this rejoinder is a high, wind-blown lob sent up with the prayer that the opponent's arm is too weak to smash it back. That is probably true in this case, and the game may continue for some time.

When Counterexamples Are Given Before the Universal Is Explicit

Sometimes in a debate between defenders and opponents of a position, its universality is initially implicit, that is, not directly articulated in its strongest form. But when apparently challenging evidence is presented, supporters of the universal may feel compelled to articulate it explicitly as an absolute.

Neat: To study X, we should model Y.

Scruffy: To study X in my experiment, I found it more profitable to ignore Y and model Z.

Neat: A poor choice. All Xs are Y. And in fact no X is based on Z.

Scruffy: Then how do you account for my data?

Neat: Your method contains artifacts.

[or]

What you are calling Z is really Y in disguise.

Example: All Knowledge is Propositional.   Since the 1960s, psychology has been massively influenced by information processing models of cognition. Human reasoning, problem solving, and language processing have all been simulated by computer programs operating on some knowledge base. Typically, bits of knowledge were represented as propositions linking elements in the base.

It was not asserted in the literature on computer models of human cognition that propositions were the only possible way of representing human knowledge. Typically, computer programs worked only within a given specialized domain, such as chess playing, and there was no commitment to representations outside that content area. That chess knowledge is conveniently considered propositional does not suggest whether or not knowledge of the Mona Lisa is propositional.

In the 1970s, two independent results appeared that seemed to demonstrate striking processes of mental imagery qualitatively different from the manipulation of propositions. Shepard and Metzler (1971) asked subjects to judge whether paired geometric figures with different orientations, each made up of a set of cubes arranged in a knobby L-shaped configuration, were actually the same or were mirror images of each other. This task appears to require subjects to imagine the rotation of one diagram to superimpose it on the other diagram. The interesting result was that the average time taken to verify the identity of paired figures was proportional to the angle of the required rotation. This finding suggested a cognitive process isomorphic with the physical rotation of a visual object.[4]

Meanwhile, Kosslyn (1975) tested hypothesized consequences of instructing subjects to form mental images of objects with implicitly different sizes. For example, subjects were asked to imagine a rabbit sitting beside an elephant, or alternatively, beside a fly. Questions about details of the target objects were then posed, such as, "Does a rabbit have whiskers?" The time to answer was longer when the target image (the rabbit) was paired with the larger companion (the elephant). This prediction supposes that subjects refer to their mental images, and "read off" the answers from details "seen" in the image. If images are constrained within boundaries like scenes in a camera window, then to accommodate an elephant in the same image as a rabbit, the rabbit must be shrunk. The existence of whiskers (and other small details) should take longer to identify on a shrunken than on a big rabbit, as indeed they did.

Such a result would not naturally follow from a propositional view of knowledge, which would presume that knowledge of the whiskeredness of bunny rabbits would consist of a single affirmative proposition. The size of the rabbit would have no bearing on the question—which makes it hard for a propositionalist to explain the result. However, a disbeliever in mental imagery might still find bizarre the notion that subjects construct mental pictures and read information from them, and would argue that the mind does not need an imagery capacity, because anything visual could somehow be represented propositionally.

Of critics of this type, one of the most vocal and persistent was Pylyshyn (1973). The image theorists were only trying to advance understanding of a seemingly nonpropositional type of knowledge, but Pylyshyn took these experiments as a kind of hostile take-over of the field of information processing. He declared that all knowledge is propositional. The experimental results of these renegades were to be explained without reference to mental imagery.

Pylyshyn's (1973) account of the Shepard and Metzler (1971) mental rotation result involved a hypothetical recoding of the spatial information in the figures as a network of propositions, with the property that the more different the angles of orientation, the longer it would take to compare the networks for figural identity. The argument that Zs are really Ys—that images are just networks of propositions—is a common

---

[4]Note here the vital importance of a quantitative tick. It would be weak to state only that the time taken to answer the question was significantly different for different angles of rotation.

defense of universals against counterexamples. (If you can't beat them, incorporate them.) Images can in fact be represented propositionally.[5] The moot point is whether any such representation would mimic the properties of the experimental results.

Indeed, the response of the proponents of imagery was to produce demonstrations of ever and ever more specialized properties of mental images, anchored by neurophysiological findings (Kosslyn, 1994). By now, the debate has subsided. It was evident that imagery was a coherent set of processes, with lawful experimental consequences. Therefore, even if it was "really" only a brand of network processing, it was different enough to require separate analysis.

The grounds for deciding on the true essences of ill-fitting subcategories have been at one time or another a source of debate in the arts ("Is computer-composed music really music?") and the physical sciences ("Is light really a particle, or is it a wave?"), as well as in psychology. I find such debates insipid and pointless. The sensible questions have to do with the coherence of the properties of the subcategory. Does the subcategory have what might be called a recognizable *signature*? In the imagery debate, the answer is yes. In the rational actor argument, the answer might be yes, but the signature is not yet clear.

For the investigator in a field afflicted with a case of the "reallies," the moral is clear: Do not take the debate very seriously. Work on the coherence of the set of counterexamples to the universal.

When a Claim Runs Counter to Common Sense

Scientific disciplines are supposed to be self-contained, with formal definitions of their primitive constructs, and theories based on formal relationships between them. There is ultimate reference to the real world, but it is constrained by particular rules and operations. What is not supposed to happen is for commonsense intuitions to sneak ad hoc into explanations of particular phenomena.

Physicists are rather good at following this precept. Most of their observations and theories deal with things that are totally out of the realm of human experience. Common sense does not have anything to say about distances as small as 10^{-8} cm, or as large as a million light-years. Ditto for time intervals as short as nanoseconds or as long as ten billion years. In fact, common sense rebels at small and large magnitudes far less extreme than these. (That is one reason why ordinary citizens have so much trouble understanding federal budgets and the theory of evolution.) By contrast, psychologists are lax about screening ordinary intuitions out of their subject matter. Psychology is

---

[5]Modern technology has thoroughly digitized sound and sight. Images can of course be digitized, which in a formal sense propositionalizes them.

far from adequately formalized, and most psychologists can't prevent common sense explanations of human behavior from implicitly suggesting themselves. One entry point for common sense is in judging the credibility of research claims; if a result seems to violate common sense, it is likely to be as much criticized as a result that violates a modest psychological theory. Our next example is one in which both theory and common sense are violated.

Example: Do Infants Understand Simple Numerosity?   In developmental and educational psychology, quarrels often occur concerning the earliest age at which children are capable of such and such. The Neats tend to believe in an orderly sequence of unfolding abilities, each with its appropriate age. In his highly celebrated theory, Jean Piaget (1954) postulated a series of stages of mental ability from the most concrete to the most abstract, each step in the progression occurring at a roughly specifiable age.

Such views were inviting targets for countertheories. Bruner (1971) maintained that any child could learn anything at any given age, given appropriate instruction. Specific counterexamples to Piaget's strictures were proposed. Gelman (e.g., Gelman & Mack, 1983) claimed that children aged 3 and 4 years could master all the logical tasks necessary for counting, even though children of this age were not supposed to be ready for the appropriate Piagetian stage. In what became a scruffy game of "Can you top this?," researchers tried to extend potentialities to earlier and earlier ages.

In what seems to be the ultimate stretch, Wynn (1992) claimed to have demonstrated that infants as young as 5 months old understood concepts of simple numerosity—that is, they can distinguish oneness from twoness, and in some abstract sense, understood addition and subtraction. Further, she postulated that such competence is innate. Her claim was so astonishing that it provoked a flurry of reactions (and was even covered in the mass media). Here was a claim that not only ran counter to formal theory (however tattered that had become), but also flew in the face of common sense.

In her complex and novel experimental procedure, one or two identical puppetlike dolls were exposed to the child's view on one side of a little arena like a puppet stage, and then a screen was raised in front of that side, blocking the child's view of the puppets. Next, a clearly visible adult hand appeared on the other side of the stage. For one group of infants, the hand held a puppet, which it then put behind the screen. For a second group of infants the hand was initially empty, but it reached behind the screen, emerging with a puppet that it took off stage. The former operation was called *addition*, and the latter, *subtraction*. Finally, the screen was lowered to reveal either an arithmetically correct or incorrect number of dolls.

Specifically, starting with one puppet on stage, the addition of one should reveal two puppets when the screen is lowered. On half the trials, two puppets correctly appeared, whereas for the other half, only one could be seen—the other having been sneaked out through a trapdoor by the experimenter. For the subtraction condition, two puppets initially appeared on stage, and the final presentation revealed either one (correct), or two (incorrect)—the extra one having been sneaked in through the trapdoor. Six trials were run per infant, alternating correct and incorrect trials.

The dependent variable was the time in seconds the infant spent gazing at the stage after the screen was lowered. This measure has often been used with infants to index surprise, a reaction akin to an adult double take. Here, the assumption was that the incorrect condition would elicit longer gazing times. After t testing the mean differences across infants between correct and incorrect trials for both the addition and subtraction conditions, Wynn (1992) concluded that the infants were indeed differentially responsive to correct and incorrect arithmetic.

This is the sort of complicated experiment with an unlikely claim that gives its research community the shakes. It becomes a conversation piece, and there arises a "find the artifact" challenge. As I write this, all sorts of artifacts and objections have been proposed, including unreliable time measurement, biased hands, squeaky trapdoor, the questionable feature of alternating correct and incorrect trials, and the marginality of the p values (.03-ish at best). By the time the reader reads this, some clarity may have been achieved—but more likely, it will take more time for the dust to settle.

When a Seemingly Impossible Effect Is Claimed

When systematic research purports to demonstrate a phenomenon completely outside the boundaries of prevailing science, the reaction of the audience is even sharper than in examples such as the one just discussed, and this creates a vexing conflict. The debate over extrasensory perception, referred to in several sections of this book, is a prototypic example. Here, we briefly give a related illustration.

Example: Can Group Meditation Affect Behavior at a Distance?
At Maharishi University training centers around the world, students are taught transcendental meditation, alone or in groups. One consequence of shared mental activity is said to be the emergence of a "field of unified consciousness." This field can, according to its proponents, inhibit deaths and accidents at other locations, hundreds of miles away.

In an effort to establish empirical support for this seemingly bizarre claim, Orme-Johnson et al. (1988) performed an elaborate statistical study of the effects of group meditation sessions, held daily at a hotel in East Jerusalem in the summer of 1983. The independent variable was the number of meditators, and the dependent variables were crime rates, auto accidents, and fires in Jerusalem, and war fatalities in Lebanon, among others. Each variable comprised a day-by-day time series over the 61 days of the study.

The statistical analysis was complex, but the heart of the matter is that significant correlations over days were found. On days when more meditators were meditating, there were fewer crimes, auto accidents, and war fatalities. A causal interpretation was given to these connections, and the research report was submitted to a journal.

If you were the journal editor, how would you handle this? There is no known physical principle that could account coherently for direct causation of such an effect. Nor is there any articulation of how the unified field, if somehow active on its target people and institutions, would translate itself into the necessary psychological and political behaviors. In Bayesian terms (chap. 3), the prior probability of a "Maharishi effect" is practically zero. Yet, if the study appears to be methodologically sound, it would be contrary to the ideal of scientific openness to give it no hearing whatever, no matter how seemingly cockamamie its claims. The editor has a problem.

The Bayesian argument is of course rejected by Maharishi adherents, for whom the prior probability is close to 1.0. In response to claims that the effect is impossible, its supporters quote yoga traditions in India to the effect that transcendent states of mind achieve a level of pure consciousness like a "wave settling to become the silent, unbounded surface of the ocean...[creating]...fieldlike effects...said to quell animosity in its vicinity" (Orme-Johnson et al., 1988, p. 779). Such a mystical metaphor comes from a world view so different from that of Western empirical science that it is hard to imagine a meaningful translation from one to the other.

In critiques (Duval, 1988; Schrodt, 1990) and defense (Orme-Johnson et al., 1990) of the eventually published Orme-Johnson et al. (1988) study, disputes about what was and was not believable were of no avail. The comprehensible part of the argument came down to a methodological point: Could the apparent relationship between the size of the meditating group and the lessening of various tragedies be due to a coincident time pattern followed by each? On weekends, for example, the number of meditators might be higher (because it was most convenient for them to arrive at the hotel on Wednesday or Thursday night, and leave on Sunday morning), and traffic deaths might be lower (because religious Jews would refrain from Sabbath travel). Had the daily numbers of meditators been randomly assigned by the investigators, this would have ruled out such artifacts.

Orme-Johnson et al. (1988) claimed that the day-to-day variation in number of meditators was virtually random, but this statement is disingenuous. The number rose systematically throughout the first month, and then settled into a clear weekly cycle during the second month. On whom does the burden of proof fall in this situation? The critic says there could have been an artifactual time patterning due to a variety of unknown factors. The investigators might say yes, but you have not demonstrated that any particular factor is responsible.

The standards in such a dispute are clear: The burden of proof is on the investigator. Research claims are regarded as guilty of obvious artifactual possibilities unless these are explicitly and adequately dealt with. In the Maharishi study, the observation of a correlation over time between the number of meditators and various dependent variables is a very weak datum. Correlations over time are notoriously subject to artifacts. The authors tried to upgrade their study to the level of a quasi-experiment, in which levels of the independent variable happen to occur at random in time. The failure of random occurrence demotes the study back to mere correlational status, and the burden ball is back in Maharishi's court. In the nature of such cases, furthermore, the less credible the results, the greater the burden falling on the claimant.

METHODOLOGICAL ARTIFACTS

When the smoke clears in the previous examples, criticism motivated by a challenge to a conceptual universal gets played out at the methodological level. In many less dramatic cases, debate may be almost entirely methodological from the start.

We have seen that the category of methodological artifacts is a broad one.[6] Here we discuss three general categories that come up repeatedly: the influence of *third variables*; the presence of *impurities* in the variables; and *procedural bias*. Cases involving third variables typically apply to correlational studies, procedural bias to experimental studies, and impurities to both types of studies.

Third Variables

We go back to basics and begin our discussion by considering an elementary claim from a correlational study that two variables are related as cause and effect. We saw in chapter 1, in our discussion of the purported longevity of conductors, how misleading such claims can be.

---

[6]Campbell and Stanley (1963) gave an excellent treatment of some very specific sources of artifact in the class of studies known as *quasi-experiments*. It is must reading for any serious student planning to do applied research in which there is little control over the crucial independent variables.

Every student in the social sciences is to a greater or lesser degree taught to be reluctant to draw causal conclusions from correlations, but it is surprising how causal implications nonetheless sneak insidiously into interpretations of correlations.

An investigator who takes her correlational results as indicating a causal relationship is subject to a plentiful source of criticisms—the artifact of the third variable. If it be asserted from a significant correlation of A with B that A causes B, the critic can usually rebut forcefully by proposing some variable C as the underlying causal agent[7] for both A and B.

In fact, the investigator typically starts out so much on the defensive in making claims from correlations that critics don't often feel compelled to present empirical evidence in favor of their proposed artifacts. They simply trot out the usual suspects: "How do you know," they challenge the investigator, "that the relationship is not just an artifact of social class? Of education? Of age?" and so forth. Because the burden of proof is considered to be on the investigator, she typically loses if she presents little or no further data or analysis. Causal conclusions from correlations do not get accepted at face value by the trained research community.

Power Dressing: A Whimsical Example.   As a hypothetical example, consider a relationship for high school seniors between the sizes of their wardrobes and scores on the Scholastic Aptitude Test (SAT). Let us imagine that a significant correlation of .40 between these two variables is announced by an investigator, who weaves a tale about the importance of power dressing for success in life.

A critic cries humbug, noting that the relation could easily be explained as an artifact of income differences. Socially advantaged kids have lots of clothes, and by and large do well on standardized tests, whereas disadvantaged kids have fewer clothes, and perform less well on tests.

The critic may make this shot overpowering by reanalyzing the investigator's data (or by analyzing new data), showing that when income differences are partialed out, or when income is held constant, the relationship between wardrobe size and SAT scores disappears. One way to look for such an outcome—awkward in practice but conceptually clear—is to sort cases on the income variable into class intervals, and then for the cases within each class interval, see whether there is any

---

[7]A further ambiguity with correlational results is that cause and effect might be in the reverse direction from the one the investigator favors. For example, consider the empirical finding that children with pet dogs are more well-behaved than those without them. The investigator might go on to say that the responsibility of caring for an animal is a maturing influence on the child. In an equally plausible, reverse interpretation of cause and effect, however, the association could come about because ill-behaved children are not allowed to have dogs.

relationship between the original two variables. If there is very little or none, the third variable can be said to explain the relation between the other two. The investigator will usually be left without any satisfactory rejoinder.[8] Presumably this is what would happen in the hypothetical example of the wardrobes.

Thus far, I have given a stock analysis of the lack of credibility of simple interpretations of correlations. Actually, the epistemological situation is somewhat more complicated, as there are examples of highly believable inferences from correlational data. Single, isolated correlations are always doomed to ambiguity, but *patterns* of covariation can offer some hope for a reasonable rejoinder by the investigator. For one thing, multiple regression techniques can damage the plausibility of some artifacts a critic might dredge up, provided the investigator has had the foresight to get reliable data on each such possibility. The presumed artifact, say, age or gender, is partialed out of the relationship of interest. If a significant correlation still remains, the artifactual factor may be discredited as a sufficient explanation.

Even more general than multiple regression, there is a class of techniques known as structural equations modeling or "path analysis" (Kenny, 1979), specifically designed to test alternative models of networks of influence within a set of correlated variables. The influences are hypothesized to flow from independent (exogenous) to dependent (endogenous) variables, with mediating variables in between. Different models are distinguished by the particular variables taken to influence other particular variables in a network of relationships. Each plausible model can be subjected to a statistical goodness-of-fit test, and the poorly fitting models weeded out. Successful models are not unique, but the set of viable models can be considerably narrowed.

Another possibility for turning leaden correlations into golden causal statements lies in testing several implications of a postulated mechanism explaining the correlation at hand. This possibility is easier to understand than the somewhat arcane applications of structural equations modeling. We illustrate this in our next, quite consequential, example.

Example: Does Smoking Cause Lung Cancer?   Picture the situation when it was first authoritatively claimed that heavy smokers more

---

[8]Occasionally, an investigator might be able to prepare a shrewd retort to an anticipated stock criticism. I remember a colloquium many years ago at which Hyman Witkin presented his research on the personality characteristic of field independence (Witkin et al., 1954). He made much of his result that so-called field independent subjects, categorized on the basis of their ability to find hidden figures in complex designs, had little difficulty locating a true vertical position when seated in a tilted chair in a tilted room. Feeling a bit sheepish to make such an obvious criticism, I said, "Have you partialed out intelligence?" "Partialed it out?" he snorted. "Field independence *is* intelligence!"

frequently contract lung cancer than do nonsmokers (U.S. Surgeon General, 1964). What could critics, many of them apologists for the tobacco industry or smokers trying to rationalize their habit, come up with in the way of other explanatory variables? Here are some samples: Maybe smokers are on the average more tense than nonsmokers, and it is tension that disposes toward getting cancer; maybe smokers tend to drink a lot of coffee when smoking, and it is coffee that causes cancer; maybe it's just that men happen to smoke more than women, and men also happen to be more vulnerable to lung cancer.

In each of these speculations, the critic names a factor, fortuitously correlated with smoking, that could perhaps itself cause lung cancer. However, one can't just name any old variable as a possible artifact. It would be a very weak criticism to propose that the smoking–cancer link is an artifact of astrological signs. There is no reason to believe that smokers tend disproportionately to have particular astrological signs, even if one could manage to persuade one's audience that those particular signs are more deadly than others. In the game of burden tennis, this shot wouldn't make it over the net.

Confining attention to plausible third-variable artifacts, many of these can be rebutted by showing that controlling for them does not eliminate the relationship between smoking and cancer. For example, gender is a totally insufficient explanatory variable: The cancer rates are substantially higher for smokers than nonsmokers, within both the male population and the female population.

The limitation on such rebuttals is that a new third variable of the month can be proposed by critics. Even with the motivation and the resources to meet each new criticism, the process would be foiled by variables for which no good data were available—levels of nervous tension, for example.

A more powerful strategy is to spell out the details of the proposed causal mechanism implicating smoking, and then test the consequences this mechanism would entail. Such a strategy was indeed followed by the cancer research community.

The postulated mechanism for the causal link, in simplified, nontechnical form, is that tobacco smoke contains substances that are toxic to human tissue when deposited by contact. The more contact, the more toxicity. Now, what are some empirical implications of such a mechanism?

1. The longer a person has smoked cigarettes, the greater the risk of cancer.
2. The more cigarettes a person smokes over a given time period, the greater the risk of cancer.
3. People who stop smoking have lower cancer rates than do those who keep smoking.

4. Smokers' cancers tend to occur in the lungs, and to be of a particular type.
5. Smokers have elevated rates of other respiratory diseases.
6. People who smoke cigars or pipes, the smoke usually not being inhaled, have abnormally high rates of lip cancer.
7. Smokers of filter-tipped cigarettes have somewhat lower cancer rates than do other cigarette smokers.
8. Nonsmokers who live with smokers have elevated cancer rates (presumably by passive exposure to smoke).

All of these implications have moderate to strong empirical support in U.S. Surgeon General (1964) and a succession of later reports. All of them[9] were established correlationally (by comparing cancer rates in different population subgroups). Yet the case is extremely persuasive because it is so coherent, with so many consequences implied by the toxic smoke mechanism supported by strong evidence. Furthermore, no additional explanatory mechanism seems required, as there are no anomalous results that remain to be explained. If smokers were found to have four times the rate of fallen arches as nonsmokers, this would create a nagging bit of incoherence when included along with items 1–8 listed earlier, and keep the search for causes open to new ideas.

Note that the smoke toxicity explanation of the evidence has a comparative advantage over alternative explanations. If a factor associated with a smoking habit, such as coffee drinking or an anxious personality were the true cancer cause, it would be very difficult to explain results 3, 4, 5, 6, and 7.

Thus a tight bundle of strong, plausible correlational results can indeed be causally compelling. A set of ticks connected by a single hypothesized underlying process is its *signature*, so to speak. Thus we call this rebuttal strategy the *method of signatures.*[10] The specification of a recognizable signature enhances the credibility of claims that particular underlying processes are operative, much as would a coroner's report (Scriven, 1974) of seven different signs of a heart attack (and no signs of any other cause of death). This simple idea is quite important, and justifies a second example, one in which the claim sounds quite implausible at the outset.

Example: Suicides and Motor Vehicle Fatalities.   Phillips (1977) claimed a systematic connection between the dates of widely publicized

---

[9]Implication 8, concerning "passive smoking," has been independently disputed by some who otherwise concede the direct dangers of smoking. The interchange between Gross (1994) and Rockette (1994) is a prototypic statistical argument on this point.

[10]This same idea is part of good test development practice, too, often under the name of *construct validity*. Experienced experimental psychologists employ this type of strategy as well.

suicides, such as those of eminent people, and the number of motor vehicle fatalities within the 7-day periods following these particular dates. The hypothesis behind this mysterious connection is that publicized suicides encourage people with suicidal inclinations to take a self-destructive action, one form of which is to deliberately crash a car.

His analysis (Phillips, 1977) covered the period from 1966 through 1973, and was carried out with data from California. (The reason for the latter choice was that the California Highway Patrol had very detailed automobile fatality data, and not, as the reader might have conjectured, because every conceivable craziness can be found out there.) Phillips compiled an exhaustive list of the front-page suicide stories covered by one or more leading metropolitan newspapers in the state during the 8-year period. The 20 dates associated with these suicides were noted, along with the total number of motor vehicle fatalities in the week following each critical date.

Phillips (1977) faced a difficult comparison problem in proceeding with his analysis. How was he to tell whether the fatality rates were especially high in those critical weeks? Appropriate nonsuicide weeks were necessary for comparison. What Phillips did was to pick weeks from years before and after the critical weeks, located at nearly identical positions on the calendar, and starting on the same day of the week. The presence or absence of a holiday in each critical week was matched in the choice of a comparison week.

Finally, for each critical week, the percentage by which its fatality rate exceeded or fell short of the comparison fatality rate was calculated. The 20 resulting percentages, rounded to the nearest whole number, are shown in the stem-and-leaf of Table 9.1 (a minus indicates a lower rate in the suicide week). Fifteen of these 20 comparisons were in the direction of the hypothesis, and the mean of all 20 was +9.12, significantly different from zero by a t test. (With a one-tailed t test, the p value is .01.)

The claim, then, was that in California for the years indicated, highly publicized suicide stories systematically produced an average increase in motor vehicle fatalities of about 9% in the week following. This seems

TABLE 9.1
Excess Automobile Fatalities 2 Days After Publicized Suicides

3	056
2	09
1	248
0	0445778
−0	422
−1	
−2	00

Note. Data are in percentage over and under baseline. $N = 20$.

a surprising effect on motor vehicle fatalies from such an apparently irrelevant influence as suicide stories. One can mitigate one's sense of incredulity somewhat by noting that the 9% increase in fatality rates amounted to only 7.5 extra deaths per suicide week, as the comparison death rate ran to about 88 per week. One can further cushion the surprise by realizing that the 9% figure is merely an estimate, subject to chance variation. Ninety-five percent confidence limits on this estimate run from 1.7% to 16.5%, and values in the lower part of this interval don't seem jarringly implausible.

Still, the proposed mechanism may seem far-fetched. As we have seen, one should be especially suspicious of correlations between variables over time, because all kinds of events that have nothing to do with each other can co-occur in yearly, monthly, or weekly synchrony, like leap years and presidential elections, or church attendance and betting on professional football games. Candidates for third variables that would create an artifactual appearance of a suicide–motor accident relationship come readily to mind. Perhaps certain days of the week have more suicides, and 2 days later in the week, more traffic accidents. Maybe there is some connection with holiday weekends. Another line of explanation would invoke short periods of national or international crisis: When war is threatened, or terrorism strikes, or the stock market declines precipitously, mass stress induces more suicides and worse driving.

The list could go on, but skeptics can do quite nicely without one. In the language of our tennis metaphor, the toughest critics wouldn't even acknowledge that the ball was in their court. If they saw only the allegation that publicized suicides were systematically followed by traffic accidents, they would call the author's shot out of bounds, and not respond until the opponent produced a better serve. (This case is similar to the Maharishi example, albeit less extreme.)

Therefore, it behooved the investigator to present a *signature*—a bundle of evidence consistent with the hypothesis that suicidal crashes are activated by suicide publicity, and inconsistent with other explanations. Such evidence was indeed adduced. For starters, Phillips (1986) found that suicides that received heavier publicity were followed by more automobile fatalities.

As Phillips and Bollen (1985) argued, the most compelling kind of supporting evidence for an initially implausible relationship involves selective variations in the focus of the analysis, such that the relationship should go away if the investigator's hypothesized mechanism for the relationship is correct. (Recall Lazarsfeld's dictum from chap. 7.) If Phillips' (1986) analysis is on the mark, one ought to find that if time were reckoned backwards, with auto fatalities tallied in the week before the suicides, there would be no relationship. Indeed, there was none. A subtler point pertaining to the original data is that the increase in fatal traffic accidents should be confined to cases with a lone driver. There is no reason to expect an increase in fatal accidents involving vehicles with passengers, and in fact, there was no relation between publicized suicides and such crashes. These three ancillary results begin to fill in a signature characterizing a genuine link between publicized suicides and passengerless auto crashes.

The authors of the Maharishi study can be faulted for not sufficiently pursuing this type of conceptual protection against artifacts. Keeping the sequence of number of meditators as the day-by-day independent variable, they could have taken as dependent variables the daily crime, accident, fire, and war death figures from summers before and after the year of the study. Nonzero relationships would be inexplicable as other than calendar-related artifacts, and would damage the original claim of a Maharishi effect. Another test of this nature would be to take as independent variable some other measure of daily activity by intellectuals, such as attendance at music festivals or coffee houses. If an appropriate data series of this kind showed a mock Maharishi effect, that too would undercut the hypothesis that the meditators as such were causing benign effects. One can imagine many other tests as well. The failure to run such self-skeptical analyses leaves the investigation without an intelligible signature.

Impurities in Correlations

An important variant of the third-factor type of criticism of correlational results occurs when the artifactual variable is *attached* to one of the explicit variables as an impurity, like barnacles to rocks, or MSG in food. This category produces subtleties of causal interpretation, illustrated next with fanciful and serious examples sharing the following formal structure: The investigator asserts that X causes Y; the critic replies that it is not X that causes Y, it is unmentioned Q, attached to X, that causes Y. Variable Q thus *mediates* the relation between X and Y. This mediation can be extrinsic or intrinsic.

First, consider the results proclaimed by the imaginary Professor I. B. Fenstermacher, based on his extensive studies of the health consequences of frequent picnicking. Although he found no significant difference in cholesterol count between frequent and infrequent picnickers, he did find a significant and strong difference in the average number of itchy red spots on exposed skin surfaces. He concluded that picnics systematically cause this peculiar malady. Objection was raised by the critic M. Neffer, who had immediately recognized that these red spots were in fact mosquito bites. He went on to argue that despite the systematic relationship between the event of picnicking and the occurrence of mosquito bites, it makes more sense to say that mosquitoes cause mosquito bites, and it just so happens that mosquitoes show up with annoying frequency at picnics.

A similar, but far less frivolous example arises from the claim that there is an association between peanut butter consumption and increased risk of cancer. Yes, peanut butter! The mechanism is that a small subset of peanut shipments to peanut processers are contaminated with a mold containing aflatoxin, a substance known to be highly carcinogenic for animals (National Research Council, 1978). Here, a critic might say that it is not peanut butter that causes higher vulnerability to cancer, it is aflatoxin—the more proximate cause. However, insisting that peanut butter is not the real cause is small comfort to the person who loves peanut butter and fears cancer. A de facto risk (small though it may be) lurks in the long line of Skippy® jars consumed in a lifetime. Thus the bald assertion that peanut butter is cancer causing may not be all that silly.

For our third example, let us return to the imaginary Professor I. B. Fenstermacher. Having been embarrassed by Neffer's scathing criticism of the conclusions he drew from his picnic study, Fenstermacher tries to get revenge. Neffer has published an article claiming that smoking causes lung cancer. Fenstermacher has by this time learned the structure of the argument for artifactual causation. He submits a rejoinder stating, "Smoking doesn't cause lung cancer. Tar and nicotine in the lungs cause cancer."

It appears that Fenstermacher has made another stupid mistake, because the tar and nicotine deposits are themselves caused by, rather than being fortuitously associated with smoking. This seems to be a case where the proposed artifact is the phenomenon itself. The critic citing the artifact speaks unintentionally in favor of the phenomenon (see footnote 8).

Let us take a closer look at these three examples. All three refer to dangers attaching to pleasurable substances or activities, but the danger is more and more irrevocable—that is, intrinsic to the activity—as we progress from the first example to the third.

There are practical ways to minimize the presence or the bites of mosquitoes at picnics: insect repellant, for example. It is not necessary to suffer mosquito bites at picnics, though it may be statistically frequent. Similarly, there are conceivable ways to eliminate aflatoxin from peanut butter, albeit they may be impractical and/or extremely expensive with available technology. (Both reasons have been advanced against the idea of universal inspection of peanut crops.) In any case, there is no absolute necessity for peanuts to be carcinogenic.

Purification of the causal variable in these two cases removes its association with negative consequences. In the smoking case, the connection between cause and effect seems more unavoidable, as all cigarettes contain tar and nicotine. Still, from a logical point of view, one might suggest that if these two substances were removed from cigarettes, then smoking might no longer cause cancer. Lord knows, cigarette companies have thought of and worked on this scenario.

The difficulty is that nicotine removal, in particular, would spoil an essential aspect of the smoking experience. The dangerous impurity is inseparable from the pleasure of smoking, and thus smoking takes the rap for the danger. (This would change if some new tobacco substitute gained currency, were proven safe, and became labeled as a new activity—call it *schmoking*. Then one could say that whereas smoking causes cancer, schmoking doesn't. The cancer-causing agents lie in some or all of the features distinguishing schmoking from smoking.) At the root of arguments about impurities as artifacts, therefore, lie quarrels about the true essences of things. (This is reminiscent of the argument on whether or not mental images are essentially different from networks of propositions.)

We next consider impurities in experimentally manipulated variables, which sometimes also spur murky debates about psychological essences.

Impurities in Experiments

Experiments with random assignment of subjects to experimental conditions have a deservedly better reputation for avoiding artifacts than do correlational studies. This is because random assignment rules out all third-variable explanations of results. The subjects experiencing a particular condition cannot be said to differ systematically on some third variable (say, intelligence, or family income) from subjects not placed in the condition. The experimenter, not the real world, causes subjects to be assigned to conditions, and random assignment assures the absence of systematic biases. (Recall the hypothetical orchestra conductor experiment in chap. 1.)

However, though this has not been well advertised, experiments are as vulnerable to artifacts of *impurity* as are correlational studies. Something about the experimental treatments can create the results, rather than the treatments per se. The impurity could in principle be removed (like aflatoxin from peanuts), but in a given experiment may not have been. Criticisms of experimental investigations and rebuttals by investigators very frequently revolve around whether supposed impurities were present, and if so, whether they are intrinsic to the experimental variable or only gratuitously attached.

This type of issue is likely to arise when specific experimental manipulations and measurements are designed to represent broader concepts. The interpretation of results is then meant to be general, not literal. The experimenter wants to examine the connection between a class of causes and a class of effects, and in order to do this, he has to operationalize cause and effect with particular procedures and measurements. One might say that general cause and general effect are each *instantiated* by particular cause and particular effect. The critic may claim that there were extraneous influences—impurities, if you will—in the operations used by the investigator to achieve the intended concepts. We consider the character of debate surrounding possible operational impurities, using two quite different types of example.

Example: Impurity in Manipulation of Perceived Gender.   A very clever, simple method for detecting gender bias was initiated somewhat casually by Goldberg (1968). He presented a group of subjects with identical essay material, but randomly varied the author's name at the top to be, for example, either John Smith or Jane Smith. After reading an essay, subjects were asked to evaluate its quality in several respects (whether it was well written, persausive, etc.). These quality ratings were higher when the author had a male, rather than a female name—even for female subjects.

A very large number of investigators have since used experimental devices akin to Goldberg's (1968) in all sorts of contexts. The results are quite variable, but many of them demonstrate the attribution of superior intellectual competence to the male figure, and stereotypic, largely negative attributes to the female figure.

The method seems to eliminate the possibility of experimental impurities. The change of name is a minimal manipulation, of the kind that warms the hearts of experimental design mavens. Nothing is varied except the name. One is hard put to imagine a cleaner, more artifact-free manipulation.

Guess what? An impurity was recently discovered (Kasof, 1993)! This critic's argument was that all names, male or female, have evaluative connotations. A Waldo is viewed less favorably than a William or a Walter, and a Donna compares poorly with a Diana. Kasof had subjects rate the attractiveness of each of a large corpus of names, and then he inspected the attractiveness of names used in the gender bias type of experiment.

In selecting pairs of names (or sometimes, lists of names), one male, the other female, experimenters had unwittingly used less attractive names for their female figures. This is particularly obvious in pairs constructed by appending the suffix "a" to feminize a male name—Robert/Roberta, Paul/Paula, Donald/Donna, and so forth. The suffixed versions are generally less appealing names. Therefore, experiments purporting to show sexism might instead be illustrations of *nameism*—the tendency to attribute incompetence to people with klutzy names. Kasof (1993) concluded that this artifact was indeed generally operative in the literature, as studies using equally attractive male and female names tended to show relatively small or zero gender effects.

The objection might be raised that if female names tend on average to be more negatively viewed than male names, this is another manifestation of sexism. Female names like Roberta, and so on, might carry negative connotations because they are female names. Thus, the artifact would be the phenomenon.

Kasof (1993) anticipated this objection. He noted that there is no mean difference in the rated attractiveness of male and female names in the entire corpus of available names. There is, however, an attractiveness difference (on average) between the sets of male and female names used by experimenters. It looks as though experimenters unwittingly tended to choose names that would (artifactually) demonstrate apparent gender effects.

Like any overview of a many-sided literature, Kasof's (1993) analysis may be modified by later scrutiny. For our purposes, it is a very striking demonstration of the lurking impurities that can contaminate even apparently pure experimental manipulations.

Example: The Dissonance Theory of the Effects of Incentives.   In contrast to the elegant argument in the previous example of experimental impurity, our next example is somewhat murky. Recall the essence of the Festinger and Carlsmith (1959) study: Subjects offered $1 to publicly misrepresent the interestingness of a task they had just performed came to agree that it was indeed somewhat interesting, more so than did subjects paid $20. The theoretical reasoning from dissonance theory is that the $1 incentive seems to subjects insufficient for them to have agreed to say that the dull task was interesting. To reduce the dissonance (discomfort) of these thoughts, subjects persuade themselves that the task was really somewhat interesting after all, and judge it to be so in making task ratings. By contrast, those promised $20 consider themselves more than amply compensated, give the matter little further thought, and subsequently rate the task as not having been interesting.

There were many critiques of this experiment (Chapanis & Chapanis, 1964; Elms & Janis, 1965). After all, the experimental procedure was quite complicated (see chap. 2), with many seeming opportunities for impurities and biases to creep in. In one critique, Rosenberg (1965) argued that there was an artifact contaminating the $20 condition. He had expected—for reasons that need not concern us—that the effect of incentive on self-persuasion would increase with increasing incentive, not decrease. Thus subjects in the $20 condition ought to have judged the task as having been more interesting than did the $1 subjects. Why didn't they?

According to Rosenberg (1965), it was not because they were in a state of low dissonance. It was because a $20 incentive seemed excessive, and the subjects in the $20 condition wanted to show the experimenter that they couldn't be bought so easily. Sure, they would agree to take the money and go through their act, but their later ratings of the interesting-ness of the task would show the experimenter that his bribe had been resisted.

This criticism established a clear disagreement over the essence of the $20 condition. For Festinger and Carlsmith (1959), $20 was a sufficient justification for an inauthentic performance; for Rosenberg (1965), it was a bribe. Rosenberg was pointing to a possible impurity, that is, an unintended, misleading feature of the offer of $20. He tried to sharpen his criticism by showing in a study of his own that if self-persuasion effects were compared for a $1 and a $5 condition, subjects offered the larger incentive would show the greater self-persua-sion.

In his experiment (Rosenberg, 1965), he asked Ohio State students to write essays on why the Ohio State football team should refuse to go to the Rose Bowl, should an invitation come. Some subjects chosen at random were offered $1, others $5. After writing the essays, the $5 subjects indicated a greater average degree of opposition to the attrac-tive Rose Bowl bid. Rosenberg interpreted his results as showing that when precautions are taken to remove the gratuitous influence of *excessive* incentive, the dissonance prediction fails.

There was an oversight in Rosenberg's (1965) experimental design, however. With his $1 and $5 conditions, he had shown that a larger incentive produced more self-persuasion. To make his case complete, he should have included a $20 condition. If self-persuasion against going to the Rose Bowl had been weaker here than in the $5 condition, it would have established that too much reward produces a backlash, just as he had predicted. On the other hand, more Rose Bowl opposition for $20 than for $5 would have undercut his criticism of $20 as a perceived bribe.

To argue convincingly that there was an artifactual feature in some-one else's experiment, therefore, one should not simply do one's own study with the offending feature removed. It is important also to replicate the original, with the feature included. This way, you can be clear about whether the feature seems truly to produce artifactual results, or whether there is some other difference between the compet-ing experiments (such as whether the subjects were asked to speak out, or to write an essay against their own opinions).

It is astonishing how often this replication procedure is not followed. This may be because critics convince themselves that the original investigator did something wrong, and they know how to do it right, and get the right result. It does not occur to the critic to repeat the experi-ment the "wrong" way.

As postscript on the argument over the $20 payment, we note that in the subsequent dissonance theory literature, the issue was simply avoided by using a smaller range of payments or by manipulating other justifications for action than monetary incentives. The dissonance theory prediction was massively confirmed in later experiments, though not without theoretical modification (see chap. 8; see also Cooper & Fazio, 1984).

Procedural Bias

Impurities as artifacts are generally unintended by the experimenter. Somewhat distinct from this are cases in which bias is associated directly with the role played by the experimenter—who typically has a preference for one outcome over others. Rather than using single, focal examples, we treat this category of potential artifacts by general discussion.

Experimenter Bias. Investigators typically want the results of their experiments to come out in a particular way. At a minimum, they wish to make one of the elementary arguments of chapter 2, say, that a particular causal factor is responsible for a systematic difference between experimental groups. If their wishes became experimental realities, they would be happy. But short of sheer fraud, carelessly slanted data tabulation, or a brash style of analysis and presentation, can experimenters bias, knowingly or unknowingly, the outcomes of their experiments?

The answer appears to be yes. Robert Rosenthal (1963), in a series of studies some years ago, showed that different experimenters induced to believe in different experimental hypotheses tended to come up with results supporting their particular sides. He called this tendency the "experimenter expectancy effect." It might be due to the increased enthusiasm or attention lavished on subjects in the experimental group, as opposed to the control group. Or the bias could be mediated by subtle, nonlinguistic cues given off by the experimenter. (For reviews of the evidence for, and explanations of experimenter expectancy effects, see Rosenthal, 1976; and Rosenthal & Rubin, 1978.)

There are standard precautions to forestall critics waiting to pounce on the mere possibility of experimenter bias effects. The best rhetorical protection is provided by having the experimenter be unaware of, or *blind*, to which condition each individual subject is in. The most foolproof way to do this is to confine the experimenter's contact with the subject to the time period before the subject is randomly assigned to a condition. The experimenter might give the general instructions applying to all subjects, and then have the specific instructions, varying by condition, administered by computer.

A less than absolutely perfect, but still very good precautionary method is to divide the administration of the experiment between two experimenters, one who introduces the critical experimental manipulation, and the other who obtains the final response measures (whatever else the two of them do). The second experimenter should be blind to the condition the first experimenter has introduced.

There are many cases in which such less than perfect protection against experimenter bias is the best one can do, because any attempt to keep the main experimenter blind to the experimental conditions produces an awkward or even bizarre situation. Suppose a therapist were comparing two kinds of therapy, each kind to be tried on a random half of her patients. We could not reasonably demand of the therapist that she not know what kind of therapy she was providing to each individual patient. However, we could ensure that evaluation of clinical benefits be done by someone else who was kept blind to the therapy.

Despite its ready availability as a criticism, there is uncertain rhetorical force behind the assertion that the experimenter might have biased the results in such and such a way. In questions of potential experimenter bias, what seems to tip the balance of debate is whether or not the experimenter took every reasonable precaution. An investigator who overlooks the need to keep the experimenter blind to condition, or an assistant blind to the hypothesis, is especially vulnerable when it would have been relatively simple to take these steps. As we have seen in cases of potential experimental impurities, prevention is the best defense—although sometimes it is not simple to maintain investigator blindness. An alternative, albeit weaker line of defense is to show that though an experimenter bias effect was a conceptual possibility, it in fact was not likely to have occurred. This requires that some written or filmed record of the experimenter's (or assistant's) behaviors has been kept, and that judges cannot distinguish the sets of behaviors toward different experimental groups.

Demand Characteristics. When an investigator puts forward a claim that a particular experimentally manipulated factor produced a systematic difference between groups of randomly selected individuals, critics may point out that human subjects are capable of deliberate, strategic responses to the experimental situation. Subjects may wonder what is going on, they may be suspicious,[11] they may try to please the experimenter, and so on. The term *demand characteristics* is used to evoke the possibility that subjects ask themselves, "What does the experimenter want me to do? What demands are being made upon me?" and then they behave so as to satisfy (or in some cases, resist) those perceived demands. Other variants of this criticism are that subjects try

---

[11]In psychological experimentation, the preponderance of studies have been run using college undergraduates as subjects (see Sears, 1986), usually through recruitment procedures that remain constant year after year. Word about tricky experimental procedures has gotten around, and nowadays undergraduate subjects are chronically suspicious, or at least skeptical of experiments.

to respond in the most socially desirable way, or that they regard the experiment as some kind of a test of character.

Potential artifacts in the demand characteristics category do not concern the direct influences of the experimenter; rather, they depend on subjects' *interpretations* of the experimenter's behavior and purposes. Such interpretations, judging by what subjects say afterward, are commonly highly inaccurate.

The demand characteristic argument is quite difficult to meet. Investigators have very limited access, at best, to subjects' states of mind. In fact, subjects may have very limited access to their own states of mind, especially concerning why they may have acted in a certain way (Nisbett & Wilson, 1977). The most secure protection against demand characteristics arises in experimental designs that can be arranged so that subjects are blind to condition, or where the response is not under conscious control. The first condition often is mitigated in between-group experiments. Each subject experiences the critical manipulation along with a lot of other procedural stuff, and ordinarily does not know which feature of the design is the one that subjects in other groups will experience differently. The second condition, lack of conscious control, obtains for many physiological response measures, and arguably can be achieved using reaction time as the measure. For experiments lacking such fortunate circumstances, procedural precautions against demand characteristics may be hard to devise, and they are best employed severally.[12]

Among the steps a reasonable experimenter might take are the following:

1. Emphasize to the subjects their personal anonymity.
2. Deemphasize testlike aspects of the procedure.
3. Make the instructions straightforward and credible.
4. Interview pilot subjects about their interpretations.
5. If necessary, redesign the study to alleviate suspicions.
6. Separate response measures from treatment manipulations.
7. Use unobtrusive or nonreactive response measures.
8. Use procedures to diagnose demand characteristics.

Example: Attitude Extremity and Biased Processing.   Most of the precautions in the previous list are self-explanatory. The device (Item 8) of creating extra materials to diagnose attempts to conform to experimental demands can be illustrated by the Lord et al. (1984) study of the stubbornness associated with strong attitudes. In this study as well

---

[12]No single rejoinder by itself may be very compelling, yet the totality may be persuasive. This circumstance is satirized by the tailor's boast: "We lose money on each suit, but we sell so many we make a profit."

as in previous research (Lord et al., 1979), people with extreme attitudes for or against capital punishment were found to twist mixed evidence concerning its deterrent effects so much that people on the two sides were more polarized in their attitudes after exposure to the evidence than before.

In a consider-the-opposite condition, all the partisans were told prior to seeing the evidence that most people find more flaws in data critical of their point of view than in data supporting it. They were urged to ask themselves when examining each bit of evidence whether they would have had the same evaluation of it if the results had favored the other side of the issue. As the investigators predicted, the consider-the-opposite instruction produced almost even-handed treatment of the evidence, and eliminated the polarization effect. However, this is the sort of finding that is most vulnerable to a demand characteristics explanation. A critic might say that the investigators flatly told the subjects what to do—treat all evidence equally critically—and by golly, the subjects did it.

Anticipating both the finding and the criticism, Lord et al. (1984) ran a third group, a be-unbiased condition, with instructions to the subjects to be as objective and unbiased as possible, like a judge or juror weighing evidence fairly and impartially. The results for this condition showed as much bias and polarization as in the condition with no special instruction. Just telling subjects to be impartial does not work. Moreover, an independent group of people, when shown the consider-the-opposite and be-unbiased instructions, rated the latter as more likely to apply pressure to subjects to do what the experimenters wanted. From this, the authors argued that the whole pattern of results of the experiment was not plausibly explained by demand characteristics.

Because the demand characteristics explanation is so often available and applicable in principle, it is an easy criticism to make. However, if the experimenter has employed reasonable preventive devices, one might hope that critics would refrain from automatically jerking their demand-characteristics knee.

Bias Associated With Stimulus Materials: An ESP Example.
There are possibilities for a number of other extraneous influences to creep into psychological experiments. We will cover just one more, chosen because of its relevance to the thematic mental telepathy experiments discussed in chapter 2 and 5.

In all experiments on ESP, it is of course a presumption that cues from normal sensory channels have been ruled out. Stage magicians often rely on the devious use of ordinary information channels in demonstrations of mind reading, such as having an accomplice eavesdrop in the lobby as the audience files in. (I was once the butt of a classroom demonstration in which the "psychic" told the class exactly what I had eaten for dinner the night before. He obtained this information in a telephone conversation with my wife, who promised to go along with the gag.)

Responsible experimenters in parapsychology, of which there are many, sincerely try to eliminate ordinary information channels. Yet on occasion information is unintentionally conveyed in some subtle but normal way. One example of this possibility arises in *Ganzfeld* studies of mental telepathy (see Bem & Honorton, 1994).

In this paradigm, the isolated receiver is cut off from visual information by a ping-pong ball, halved and cupped over his eyes, and from auditory information by white noise in his earphones. The sender has 30 minutes to try to convey by telepathy the essence of a visual scene from a picture that has been randomly chosen from a set of four pictures. The sender is permitted to hold the chosen picture. Subsequently, the receiver is given the set of four pictures from which the target was chosen, and (in the simplest version of the procedure) is asked to name the target picture.

A meta-analysis of Ganzfeld studies (Bem & Honorton, 1994; Honorton, 1985) produced claims of hit rates significantly above the chance level of .25. Several of the skeptics who pored over the details of the early Ganzfeld experiments, however, noticed a possible channel of sensory leakage: The receiver, given a set of four pictures including the target—the only picture handled by the sender—can be correctly cued by smudges, fingerprints, or even a temperature difference.

This critique was like the $20 critique of the Festinger and Carlsmith (1959) study in that it had *face credibility*, with the upshot of throwing the investigator on the defensive. The best way to handle this was (as in the $20 case) to avoid the problem procedurally in later studies. What was subsequently done in the Ganzfeld protocol was to have duplicate sets of pictures, so that the copy of the target in the receiver's set had not been handled or even seen by the sender. This effectively eliminates the purported artifact.

Interestingly, there is no evidence that hypothetical smudges on target pictures actually helped receivers to score more highly. Hyman (1985), a persistent critic of parapsychology, reported no correlation between opportunity for sensory leakage and telepathic hit rate. Yet, protective measures against leakage, including duplicate sets of pictures, are now included in the design of any Ganzfeld study.

THE INFLUENCE OF CRITICISM ON METHODOLOGY

In two of our examples of criticism of experiments, one based on an impurity in a manipulation (the $20 incentive) and one based on a procedural bias (sensory leakage), we saw that the subsequent strategy of researchers in the particular domain was to change the design to avoid the potential impurity. This was the case even though there was no evidence in either case that the experimental results were affected in any way by the supposed artifacts.

I believe that this peculiar phenomenon obtains rather generally, not only in science, but in other arenas such as politics. When a particular criticism is widely raised, and the rebuttal seems insufficient, the criticism will tend to become even stronger and more fashionable, and be used again in similar circumstances. Targets of such criticisms may conclude that the only way to survive is to accept the criticism as valid (even though it may not be), and avoid precipitating it in the future. Thus, any celebrated flurry of criticism is likely to provoke a methodological change in future studies of the same type—especially if it is as easy to implement as was the introduction of duplicate picture sets in the Ganzfeld paradigm.

In any discipline aspiring to excellence in its research methods, the long-run consequence of measures designed to protect against criticism will be the accretion of a body of practices that become habitualized in its methodology. Today's complaint becomes tomorrow's precaution. In the words of Abelson's Eighth Law, *Criticism is the mother of methodology.* This is a major feature of my thesis that argument is intrinsic to statistical and conceptual analysis of research outcomes, and is good for the health of science.

We have come full circle. Research results are articulated with particular arguments, supported by disciplined research procedures and statistical analyses. As research cumulates under pressure from the exchange of counterarguments, previous theoretical generalizations will be supported, modified, or abandoned, and new generalizations may emerge. Beyond the development of theories and general findings, wisdom accumulates on the pitfalls and benefits of particular research and statistical methods. Over time, albeit slowly, methodological criticism becaomes more trenchant and demanding, and investigators must conduct research with more intelligence and care. Each new generation of research workers in the social sciences, therefore, is exposed to a more sophisticated scientific culture than the previous cohort. Thus, principled statistical argument is not only unavoidable, it is fundamental.

References

Abelson, R. P. (1953). *Spectral analysis as a method for analyzing time-ordered psychological data.* Unpublished doctoral dissertation, Princeton University, Princeton, NJ.

Abelson, R. P. (1979). Differences between belief systems and knowledge systems. *Cognitive Science, 3,* 355–366.

Abelson, R. P. (1981). *Constraint, construal, and cognitive science.* Invited address at the Third Annual Conferencve of the Cognitive Science Society, Berkeley, CA.

Abelson, R. P. (1985). A variance explanation paradox: When a little is a lot. *Psychological Bulletin, 97,* 128–132.

Abelson, R. P., & Miller, J. (1967). Negative persuasion via personal insult. *Journal of Experimental Social Psychology, 3,* 321–333.

Adams, D. (1980). *A hitchhiker's guide to the galaxy.* New York: Harmony Books.

Adams, W. J. (1974). *The life and times of the central limit theorem.* New York: Kaedmon.

Anscombe, F. J. (1967). Topics in the investigation of linear relations fitted by the method of least squares. *Journal of the Royal Statistical Society* (Series B), *29,* 1–52.

Aronson, E. (1969). The theory of cognitive dissonance: A current perspective. In L. Berkowitz (Ed.), *Advances in experimental social psychology* (Vol. 4, pp. 1–34).

Aronson, E., Brewer, M., & Carlsmith, J. M. (1985). Experimentation in social psychology. In E. Aronson & G. Lindzey (Eds.), *Handbook of social psychology* (Vol. 1, pp. 431–483). New York: Random House.

Atlas, D. H. (1978). Longevity of orchestra conductors. *Forum on Medicine, 1*(9), 50–51.

Bailar, J. C., & Mosteller, F. (1988). Guidelines for statistical reporting in articles for medical journals: Amplifications and explanations. *Annals of Internal Medicine, 108,* 266–273.

Banaji, M. R. & Crowder, R. G. (1989). The bankruptcy of everyday memory. *American Psychologist, 44,* 1185–1193.

Baron, R. A. & Ransberger, V. M. (1978). Ambient temperature and the occurrence of collective violence. The "long, hot summer" revisited. *Journal of Personality and Social Psychology, 36,* 351–360.

Bayes, T. (1764). An essay towards solving a problem in the doctrine of chances. *Philosophical transactions of the Royal Society of London 53,* 370–418 (for 1763). Reprinted in E. S. Pearson & M. G. Kendall (Eds.).(1970). *Studies in the history of statistics and probability.* London: Charles Griffin.

Beall, A. (1994). *Gender and the perception of emotion.* Unpublished doctoral dissertation, Yale University, New Haven, CT.

Bem, D. J., & Honorton, C. (1994). Does psi exist? Replicable evidence for an anomolous process of information transfer. *Psychological Bulletin, 115,* 4–18.

Bem, D. J., Wallach, M. A., & Kogan, N. (1965). Group decision making under risk of aversive consequences. *Journal of Personality and Social Psycholgy, 1,* 453–460.

Blackwell, T., Brown, C., & Mosteller, F. (1991). Which denominator? In D. C. Hoaglin, F. Mosteller, & J. W. Tukey (Eds.), *Fundamentals of exploratory analysis of variance* (pp. 252–294). New York: Wiley.

Brehm, J. W., & Cohen, A. R. (1962). *Explorations in cognitive dissonance.* New York: Wiley.

Brody, J. E. (1991, March 14). Personal health. *The New York Times,* p. B8.

Brown, R. (1986). *Social psychology the second edition.* New York: The Free Press.

Browne, M. W. (1993, January 12). Coin-tossing computers found to show subtle bias. *The New York Times,* p. C1.

Bruner, J. (1971). *The relevance of education.* New York: Norton.

Burt, C. (1955). The evidence for the concept of intelligence. *British Journal of Educational Psychology, 25,* 158–177.

Burt, C. (1966). The genetic determination of differences in intelligence: A study of monozygotic twins reared together and apart. *British Journal of Psychology, 57,* 137–153.

Bush, L. K., Hess, U., & Wohlford, G. (1993). Transformations for within-subject designs: A Monte Carlo investigation. *Psychological Bulletin, 113,* 566–579.

Campbell, D. T. (1960). Recommendations for APA test standards regarding construct, trait, or discriminant validity. *American Psychologist, 15,* 546–553.

Campbell, D. T., & Stanley, J. C. (1963). Experimental and quasi-experimental designs for research. In N. L. Gage (Ed.), *Handbook of research on teaching.* (pp. 171–246). Chicago: Rand McNally.

Carlsmith, J. M., & Anderson, C. A. (1979). Ambient temperature and the occurrence of collective violence: A new analysis. *Journal of Personality and Social Psychology, 37,* 337–344.

Carroll, J. D. (1979, January 23). Music and age. *The New York Times,* p. C2.

Chapanis, N. P., & Chapanis, A. (1964). Cognitive dissonance: Five years later. *Psychological Bulletin, 61,* 1–22.

Cherlin, A. (1990). The strange career of the "Harvard–Yale study". *Public Opinion Quarterly, 54,* 117–124.

Cialdini, R. B., Borden, R. J., Thorne, A., Walker, M. R., Freeman, S., & Sloan, L. R. (1976). Basking in reflected glory: Three (football) field studies. *Journal of Personality and Social Psychology, 34,* 366–375.

Ciminera, J. L., Heyse, J. F., Nguyen, H. H., & Tukey, J. W. (1992). *Tests for qualitative treatment-by-center interaction using a "pushback" procedure.* Unpublished manuscript, Merck, Sharp, & Dohme Research Laboratories, Whitehouse Station, NJ.

Clark, H. H. (1973). The language-as-fixed-effect fallacy. *Journal of Verbal Learning and Verbal Behavior, 12,* 335–359.

Clark, H. H., Cohen, J., Smith, J. E. K., & Keppel, G. (1976). Discussion of Wike & Church's comments. *Journal of Verbal Learning and Verbal Behavior, 15,* 257–266.

Cleveland, W. S. (1993). *Visualizing data.* Summit, NJ: Hobart.

Cliff, N. (1993). Dominance statistics: Ordinal analyses to answer ordinal questions. *Psychological Bulletin, 114,* 494–509.

Cohen, J. (1962). The statistical power of abnormal-social psychological research: A review. *Journal of Abnormal and Social Psychology, 65,* 145–153.

Cohen, J. (1988). *Statistical power analysis for the behavioral sciences* (2nd ed.). Hillsdale, NJ: Lawrence Erlbaum Associates.

Cohen, J. (1990). Things I have learned (so far). *American Psychologist, 45,* 1304–1312.

Cohen, J. (in press). The earth is round ($p < .05$). *American Psychologist.*

Cohen, J., & Cohen, P. (1983). *Applied multiple regression and correlation analysis for the behavioral sciences* (2nd ed.). Hillsdale, NJ: Lawrence Erlbaum Associates.

Cook, T. D., & Campbell, D. T. (1979). *Quasi-experimentation: Design and analysis issues for field settings.* Chicago: Rand McNally.

Cooper, H., DeNeve, K. M., & Mosteller, F. (1992). Predicting professional sports game outcomes from intermediate game scores. *Chance, 5*(3–4), 18–22.

Cooper, J., & Fazio, R. H. (1984). A new look at dissonance theory. In L. Berkowitz (Ed.), *Advances in experimental social psychology* (Vol. 17, pp. 229–266). New York: Academic Press.

Cowles, M. (1989). *Statistics in psychology: An historical perspective.* Hillsdale, NJ: Lawrence Erlbaum Associates.

Crano, W. D., & Brewer, M. (1986). *Principles and methods of social research.* Boston: Allyn & Bacon.

Davis, J. A., & Smith, T. W. (1991). *The NORC General Social Survey: A user's guide.* Newbury Park, CA: Sage.

Davis, M. S. (1971). That's interesting! *Philosophy of the Social Sciences, 1,* 309–344.

Dawes, R. M., Mirels, H. L., Gold, E., & Donahue, E. (1993). Equating inverse probabilities in implicit personality judgments. *Psychological Science, 4,* 396–400.

DeBondt, W., & Thaler, R. (1990). Do security analysts overreact? *American Economic Review, 80,* 52–58.

Deutsch, M., & Solomon, L. (1959). Reactions to evaluations by others as influenced by self-evaluation. *Sociometry, 22,* 93 112.

Diaconis, P. (1985). Theories of data analysis: From magical thinking through classical statistics. In D. C. Hoaglin, F. Mosteller, & J. W. Tukey (Eds.), *Exploring data tables, trends, and shapes.* (pp. 1–36). New York: Wiley.

Diaconis, P., & Mosteller, F. (1989). Methods for studying coincidences. *Journal of the American Statistical Association, 84,* 853 861.

Dorfman, D. D. (1978). The Cyril Burt question: New findings. *Science, 201,* 1177–1186.

Duncan, D. B. (1955). Multiple range and multiple F tests. *Biometrics, 11,* 1–42.

Duncan, O. D., Sloane, D. M., & Brody, C. (1982). Latent classes inferred from response consistency effects. In K. G. Jöreskog (Ed.), *Systems under indirect observation* (Part I). Amsterdam, Netherlands: North-Holland.

Duval, R. (1988). TM or not TM?: A comment on "International Peace Project in the Middle East." *Journal of Conflict Resolution, 32,* 813–817.

Dworkin, B. R., & Miller, N. E. (1986). Failure to replicate visceral learning in the acute curarized rat preparation. *Behavioral Neuroscience, 100*(3), 298–314.

Eagly, A. H. (1978). Sex differences in influencibility. *Psychological Bulletin, 85,* 86–116.

Edgington, E. S. (1987). *Randomization tests* (2nd ed.). New York: Marcel Dekker.

Edwards, W., Lindman, H., & Savage, L. J. (1963). Bayesian statistical inference for psychological research. *Psychological Review, 70,* 193–242.

Efron, B. (1982). *The jacknife, the bootstrap, and other resampling plans.* Philadelphia: SIAM.

Eggplant flavor peaks in 42 days. (1992, July 25). *Science News,* p. 60.

Einhorn, H., & Hogarth, R. (1986). Judging probable cause. *Psychological Bulletin, 99,* 3–19.

Ekman, P. (1980). *The face of man: Expressions of universal emotions in a New Guinea village.* New York: Garland STPM Press.

Ekman, P. (1994). Strong evidence for universals in facial expressions: A reply to Russell's mistaken critique. *Psychological Bulletin, 115,* 268–287.

Elms, A. C. & Janis, I. L. (1965). Counter-norm attitudes induced by consonant vs. dissonant conditions of role-playing. *Journal of Experimental Research in Personality, 1,* 50–60.

Emerson, J. D. (1991a). Graphical display as an aid to analysis. In D. C. Hoaglin, F. Mosteller, & J. W. Tukey (Eds.), *Fundamentals of exploratory analysis of variance* (pp. 165–192). New York: Wiley.

Emerson, J. D. (1991b). Introduction to transformation. In D. C. Hoaglin, F. Mosteller, & J. W. Tukey (Eds.), *Fundamentals of exploratory analysis of variance* (pp. 365–400). New York: Wiley.

Evans, G. (1991). The problem of analyzing multiplicative composites: Interactions revisited. *American Psychologist, 46,* 6–15.

Falk, R., & Greenbaum, C. W. (in press). Significance tests die hard: The amazing persistence of a probabilistic misconception. *Theory and Psychology.*

Fernald, A. (1993). Approval and disapproval: Infant responsiveness to vocal affect in familiar and unfamiliar languages. *Child Development, 64,* 657–674.

Ferrenberg, A. M., Landau, D. P., & Wong, Y. J. (1992). Monte Carlo simulations: Hidden errors from "good" random number generators. *Physical Review Letters, 69*(23), 3382–3384.

Festinger, L. (1957). *A theory of cognitive dissonance.* Evanston, IL: Row, Peterson.

Festinger, L., & Carlsmith, J. M. (1959). Cognitive consequences of forced compliance. *Journal of Abnormal and Social Psychology, 58,* 203–210.

Festinger, L., & Maccoby, N. (1964). On resistance to persuasive communication. *Journal of Abnormal and Social Psychology, 68,* 359–366.

Feynman, R. P. (1965). *The character of physical law.* Cambridge, MA: MIT Press.

Fienberg, S. E. (1980). *The analysis of cross-classified categorical data* (2nd ed.). Cambridge, MA: MIT Press.

Fischhoff, B., Slovic, P., & Lichtenstein, S. (1977). Knowing with certainty: The appropriateness of extreme confidence. *Journal of Experimental Psychology: Human Perception and Performance, 3,* 552–564.

Fisher, R. A. (1936). Has Mendel's work been rediscovered? Annals of Science, 1, 113–137.

Fisher, R. A. (1946). *Statistical methods for research workers* (10th ed.). London: Oliver & Boyd.

Fisher, R. A. (1955). Statistical methods and scientific induction. *Journal of the Royal Statistical Society* (Series B), *17,* 69–77.

Food and Drug Administration. (1973). *Histopathologic evaluation of tissues from rats following continuous dietary intake of sodium saccharin and calcium cyclamate for a maximum of two years* (Final report, Project No. P 169-170). Washington, DC: U. S. Government Printing Office.

Forster, K. I. & Dickinson, R. G. (1976). More on the language-as-fixed-effect-fallacy: Monte Carlo estimates of error rates for F_1, F_2, F', and min F'. *Journal of Verbal Learning and Verbal Behavior, 15,* 135–142.

Fu, J. C., & Koutras, M. V. (1994). Distribution theory of runs: A Markov chain approach. *Journal of the American Statistical Association, 89,* 1050–1058.

Gangestad, S. W., & Snyder, M. (1991). Taxonomic analysis redux: Some statistical considerations for testing a latent class model. *Journal of Personality and Social Psychology, 61,* 141–146.

Gelman, R., & Mack, E. (1983). Preschoolers' counting: Principles before skill. *Cognition, 13,* 343–359.

Gergen, K. J. (1973). Social psychology as history. *Journal of Personality and Social Psychology, 26,* 309–320.

Gerrig, R. J. & Prentice, D. A. (1991).The representation of fictional information. *Psychological Science, 2,* 336–340.

Gigerenzer, G. (1993). The superego, the ego, and the id in statistical reasoning. In G. Keren & C. Lewis (Eds.), *A handbook for data analysis in the behavioral sciences: Methodological issues* (pp. 311–339). Hillsdale, NJ: Lawrence Erlbaum Associates.

Gilbert, D. (1991). How mental systems believe. American *Psychologist, 46,* 107–119.

Gilovich, T. (1991). *How we know what isn't so: The fallibility of human reasoning in everyday life.* New York: The Free Press.

Gilovich, T., Vallone, R., & Tversky, A. (1985). The "hot hand" in basketball: On the misperception of random sequences. *Cognitive Psychology, 17,* 295–314.

Glass, G. V. (1978). Integrating findings: The meta-analysis of research. *Review of Research in Education, 5,* 351–379.

Goldberg, P. (1968, April). Are women prejudiced against women? *Transaction,* pp. 28–30.

Goldstein, A. (1964). *Biostatistics: An introductory text.* New York: Macmillan.

Goodman, L. A. (1970). The multivariate analysis of qualitative data: Interactions among multiple classifications. *Journal of the American Statistical Association, 65,* 226–256.

Green, B. F. (1992). Exposé or smear?: The Burt affair. *Psychological Science, 3,* 328–331.

Green, B. F. & Tukey, J. W. (1960). Complex analysis of variance: General problems. *Psychometrika, 25,* 127–152.

Green, D. P., Goldman, S. L., & Salovey, P. (1993). Measurement error masks bipolarity in affect ratings. *Journal of Personality and Social Psychology, 64,* 1029–1041.

Green, D. P., & Shapiro, I. (1994). *Pathologies of rational choice theory: A critique of applications in political science.* New Haven, CT: Yale University Press.

Greenwald, A. G. (1975). Consequences of prejudice against the null hypothesis. *Psychological Bulletin, 82,* 1–20.

Greenwald, A. G., Gonzalez, R., Harris, R. J., & Guthrie, D. (1993). *Using p values and effect sizes to evaluate novel findings: Significance vs. replicability and demonstrability.* Unpublished manuscript, University of Washington, Seattle.

Grether, D., & Plott, C. (1979). Economic theory and the preference reversal phenomenon. *American Economic Review, 69,* 623–638.

Grice, H. P. (1975). Logic and conversation. In P. Cole & J. Morgan (Eds.), *Syntax and semantics 3: Speech acts* (pp. 41–58). New York: Academic Press.

Gross, A. J. (1994). Does exposure to second-hand smoke increase lung cancer risk? *Chance, 6,* 11–14.

Hansel, C. E. M. (1980). *ESP and parapsychology: A critical reevaluation.* Buffalo, NY: Prometheus Books.

Hartigan, J. A., & Hartigan, P. M. (1985). The dip test of unimodality. *Annals of Statistics, 13,* 70–84.

Harville, D. A., & Smith, M. H. (1994). The home-court advantage: How large is it, and does it vary from team to team? *American Statistician, 48,* 22–28.

Hedges, L. V. (1983). A random effects model for effect sizes. *Psychological Bulletin, 93,* 388–395.

Hedges, L. V., & Olkin, I. (1985). *Statistical methods for meta-analysis.* New York: Academic Press.

Helmreich, R., & Collins, B. E. (1968). Studies in forced compliance IV: Commitment and incentive magnitude as determinants of opinion change. *Journal of Personality and Social Psychology, 10,* 75–81.

Hidi, S., & Baird, W. (1986). Interestingness—A neglected variable in discourse processing. *Cognitive Science, 10,* 179–194.

Hill, B. (1977). *A short textbook of medical statistics* (10th ed.). Philadelphia: Lippincott. (Original work published 1937)

Hoaglin, D. C., Iglewicz, B., & Tukey, J. W. (1986). Performance of some resistant rules for outlier labeling. *Journal of the American Statistical Association, 81,* 991–999.

Hoaglin, D. C., Mosteller, F., & Tukey, J. W. (Eds.).(1983). *Understanding robust and exploratory data analysis.* New York: Wiley.

Hoaglin, D. C., Mosteller, F., & Tukey, J. W. (Eds.).(1985). *Exploring data trends tables and shapes.* New York: Wiley.

Hoaglin, D. C., Mosteller, F., & Tukey, J. W. (Eds.).(1991). *Fundamentals of exploratory analysis of variance.* New York: Wiley.

Hochberg, Y., & Tamhane, A. C. (1987). *Multiple comparison procedures.* New York: Wiley.

Honorton, C., Berger, R. E. Varvoglis, M. P., Quant, M., Derr, P., Schechter, E. I., & Ferrari, D. C. (1990). Psi communication in the Ganzfeld: Experiments with an automated testing system and a comparison with a meta-analysis of earlier studies. *Journal of Parapsychology, 54,* 99–139.

Hovland, C. I., Janis, I. L., & Kelley, H. H. (1953). *Communication and persuasion.* New Haven, CT: Yale University Press.

Hovland, C. I., & Weiss, W. (1951). The influence of source credibility on communication effectiveness. *Public Opinion Quarterly, 15,* 635–650.

Huff, D. (1954). *How to lie with statistics.* New York: Norton.

Hyman, R. (1985). A Ganzfeld psi experiment: A critical appraisal. *Journal of Parapsychology, 49,* 3–49.

Hyman, R. (1991). Comment. *Statistical Science, 6,* 389–392.

Hyman, R. (1994). Anomaly or artifact? Comments on Bem and Honorton. *Psychological Bulletin, 115,* 19–24.

Isen, A. M., & Levin, P. F. (1972). The effect of feeling good on helping: Cookies and kindness. *Journal of Personality and Social Psychology, 21,* 384–388.

Iyengar, S., & Greenhouse, J. (1988). Selection models and the file drawer problem (with discussion). *Statistical Science, 3,* 109–135.

Jaynes, J., & Bressler, M. (1971). Evolutionary universals, continuities, alternatives. In J. F. Eisenberg & W. S. Dillon (Eds.), *Man and beast: comparative social behavior.* (pp. 333–344). Washington, DC: Smithsonian Institution Press.

Jones, E. E. (1985). Major developments in social psychology during the past five decades. In G. Lindzey & E. Aronson (Eds.), *Handbook of social psychology* (Vol. 1, 3rd ed., pp. 47–107). New York: Random House.

Jöreskog, K. G. (1978). *LISREL: Analysis of linear structural relationships by the method of maximum likelihood.* Chicago: National Education Resources.

Judd, C. M., & McClelland, G. H. (1989). *Data analysis: A model comparison approach.* San Diego: Harcourt Brace.

Judd, C. M., McClelland, G. H., & Culhane, S. E. (in press). Continuing issues in the everyday analysis of psychological data. *Annual Review of Psychology.*

Kahneman, D., & Tversky, A. (1972). Subjective probability: A judgment of representativeness. *Cognitive Psychology, 3,* 430–454.

Kasof, J. (1993). Sex bias in the naming of stimulus persons. *Psychological Bulletin, 113,* 140–165.

Kenny, D. A. (1979). *Correlation and causation.* New York: Wiley.

Kenny, D. A., & Judd, C. M. (1986). Consequences of violating the independence assumption in analysis of variance. *Psychological Bulletin, 99,* 422–431.

Keppel, G. (1991). *Design and analysis: A researcher's handbook* (3rd ed.). Englewood Cliffs, NJ: Prentice-Hall.

Keuls, M. (1952). The use of studentized range in connection with an analysis of variance. *Euphytica, 1,* 112–122.

Kihlstrom, J. (1987). The cognitive unconscious. *Science, 237,* 1445–1452.

King, G. (1986). How not to lie with statistics: Common mistakes in quantitative political science. *American Journal of Political Science, 30,* 666–687.

Kirk, R. E. (in press). *Experimental design: procedures for the behavioral sciences* (3nd ed.). New York: Brooks/Cole.

Kosslyn, S. (1975). Information representation in visual images. *Cognitive Psychology, 7,* 341–370.

Kosslyn, S. (1994). *Image and brain: The resolution of the imagery debate.* Cambridge, MA: MIT Press.

Kunda, Z., & Nisbett, R. E. (1986). The psychometrics of everyday life. *Cognitive Psychology, 18,* 195–224.

Langer, E. J. (1975). The illusion of control. *Journal of Personality and Social Psychology, 32,* 311–328.

Langer, E. J., & Abelson, R. P. (1974). A patient by any other name: Clinician group differences in labeling bias. *Journal of Consulting and Clinical Psychology, 24,* 26–32.

Langer, E. J., & Rodin, J. (1976). The effects of choice and enhanced personal responsibility for the aged: A field experiment in an institutional setting. *Journal of Personality and Social Psychology, 34,* 191–198.

Larkey, P. D., Smith, R. A., & Kadane, J. B. (1989). It's okay to believe in the hot hand. *Chance, 2*(4), 22–30.

Lehnert, W. G. (1978). *The process of question answering.* Hillsdale, NJ: Lawrence Erlbaum Associates.

Linder, D. E., Cooper, J., & Jones, E. E. (1967). Decision freedom as a determinant of the role of incentive magnitude in attitude change. *Journal of Personality and Social Psychology, 6,* 245–254.

Loftus, G. R. (1991). On the tyranny of hypothesis testing in the social sciences. *Contemporary Psychology, 36,* 102–105.

Lord, C. G., Lepper, M., & Preston, E. (1984). Considering the opposite: A corrective strategy for social judgment. *Journal of Personality and Social Psychology, 47,* 1231–1243.

Lord, C. G., Ross, L., & Lepper, M. (1979). Biased assimilation and attitude polarization: The effects of prior theories on subsequently considered evidence. *Journal of Personality and Social Psychology, 37,* 2098–2109.

Madansky, A. (1988). *Prescriptions for working statisticians.* New York: Springer-Verlag.

Maier, M. H. (1991). *The data game: Controversies in social science statistics.* Armonk, NY: M. E. Sharpe.

Mandlebrot, B. (1965). A class of long-tailed probability distributions and the empirical distribution of city sizes. In S. Sternberg, V. Capecchi, T. Kloek, & C. T. Leenders (Eds.), *Mathematics and social sciences.* (pp. 257–279). Paris: Mouton.

Mann, H. B., & Whitney, D. R. (1947). On a test of whether one of two random variables is stochastically larger than the other. *Annals of Mathematical Statistics, 18,* 50–60.

Marshall, G. D., & Zimbardo, P. G. (1979). Affective consequences of inadequately explained physiological arousal. *Journal of Personality and Social Psychology, 37,* 970–985.

Mayer, J. D., & Bower, G. H. (1985). Mood-dependent retrieval: Commentary on Wetzler. *Psychological Reports, 57,*(3, Pt. 1), 1000–1002.

McGuire, W. J. (1983). A contextualist theory of knowledge: Its implications for reform and innovation in psychological research. In L. Berkowitz (Ed.), *Advances in Experimental Social Psychology* (Vol. 16, pp. 1–47). New York: Academic Press.

McGuire, W. J. (1989). A perspectivist approach to the strategic planning of programmatic scientific research. In B. Gholson, W. R. Shadish, Jr., R. A. Neimeyer, & A. C. Houts (Eds.), *Psychology of science: Contributions to metascience* (pp. 214–245). New York: Cambridge University Press.

Mesquita, B., & Frijda, N. (1992). Cultural variation in emotions: A review. *Psychological Bulletin, 112,* 179–204.

Meyer, D. E., & Schvaneveldt, R. W. (1971). Facilitation in recognizing pairs of words: Evidence of a dependence between retrieval operations. *Journal of Experimental Psychology, 90,* 227–234.

Micceri, T. (1989). The unicorn, the normal curve, and other improbable creatures. *Psychological Bulletin, 105,* 156–166.

Milgram, S. (1963). Behavioral study of obedience. *Journal of Abnormal and Social Psychology, 67,* 371–378.

Miller, N. E. (1972). Interactions between learned and physical factors in mental illness. *Seminars in Psychiatry, 4,* 239–254.

Miller, N. E., & Banuazizi, A. (1968). Instrumental learning by curarized rats of a specific visceral response, intestinal or cardiac. *Journal of Comparative and Physiological Psychology, 65,* 1–7.

Miller, R. G. (1981). *Simultaneous statistical inference* (2nd ed.). New York: Springer-Verlag.

Mosteller, F., & Bush, R. R. (1954). Selected quantitative techniques. In G. Lindzey (Ed.), *Handbook of social psychology, Vol. 1. Theory and method.* (pp. 289–334). Cambridge, MA: Addison-Wesley.

Mosteller, F., & Tukey, J. W. (1991). Purposes of analyzing data that come in a form inviting us to apply tools from the analysis of variance. In D. C. Hoaglin, F. Mosteller, & J. W. Tukey (Eds.), *Fundamentals of exploratory analysis of variance* (pp. 24–39). New York: Wiley.

Mosteller, F., & Wallace, D. L. (1964). *Inference and disputed authorship: The Federalist.* Reading, MA: Addison-Wesley.

Mullen, B. (1989). *Advanced BASIC meta-analysis.* Hillsdale, NJ: Lawrence Erlbaum Associates.

Myer, D. L. (1991). Misinterpretation of interaction effects: A reply to Rosnow and Rosenthal. *Psychological Bulletin, 110,* 571–573.

Myers, D. G., & Lamm, H. (1976). The group polarization phenomenon. *Psychological Bulletin, 83,* 602–627.

Na, E.-Y. (1992). *Resistance of identity-relevant beliefs under threat from an antagonistic outgroup.* Unpublished doctoral dissertation, Yale University, New Haven, CT.

National Research Council. (1978). Saccharin: Technical assessment of risks and benefits. *Report of the Committee for a Study on Saccharin and Food Safety Policy (Panel I: Saccharin and Its Impurities).* Washington, DC: Institute of Medicine and National Science Foundation.

National Research Council. (1979). Food safety policy: Scientific and societal considerations. *Report of the Committee for a Study on Saccharin and Food Safety Policy (Panel II: Saccharin and Food Safety Policy).* Washington, DC: Institute of Medicine and National Science Foundation.

Neisser, U., & Winograd, E. (Eds.).(1988). *Remembering reconsidered: Ecological and traditional approaches to the study of memory.* New York: Cambridge University Press.

Nel, E., Helmreich, R., & Aronson, E. (1969). Opinion change in the advocate as a function of the persuasibility of his audience: A clarification of the meaning of dissonance. *Journal of Personality and Social Psychology, 12,* 117–124.

Newman, D. (1937). The distribution of the range in samples from a normal population, expressed in terms of an independent estimate of standard deviation. *Biometrika, 31,* 20–30.

Nisbett, R. E., & Ross, L. (1980). *Human inference: Strategies and shortcomings of social judgment.* Englewood Cliffs, NJ: Prentice-Hall.

Nisbett, R. E., & Wilson, T. D. (1977). Telling more than we can know: Verbal reports on mental processes. *Psychological Review, 84,* 231–259.

Oakes, M. (1986). *Statistical inference: A commentary for the social and behavioral sciences.* New York: Wiley.

Okun, M. A., Olding, R. W., & Cohn, C. M. G. (1990). A meta-analysis of subjective well-being interventions among elders. *Psychological Bulletin, 108,* 257–265.

Olby, R. (1985). *Origins of Mendelism* (2nd ed.). Chicago: University of Chicago Press.

Oliver, M. B., & Hyde, J. S. (1993). Gender differences in sexuality: A meta-analysis. *Psychological Bulletin, 114,* 29–51.

Orme-Johnson, D. W., Alexander, C. N., & Davies, J. L. (1990). The effects of the Maharishi technology of the unified field: Reply to a methdological critique. *Journal of Conflict Resolution, 34,* 756–768.

Orme-Johnson, D. W., Alexander, C. N., Davies, J. L., Chandler, H. M., & Larimore, W. E. (1988). International peace project in the Middle East: The effects of Maharishi technology of the unified field. *Journal of Conflict Resolution, 32,* 776–812.

Overstated risks, understated benefits. (1979, June 2). *New York Times,* p. 22.

Pearson, E. S. (1962). Some thoughts on statistical inference. *Annals of Mathematical Statistics, 33,* 394–403.

Pearson, E. S., & Kendall, M. G. (Eds.).(1970). *Studies in the history of statistics and probability.* London: Charles Griffin.

Petty, R. E., & Cacioppo, J. T. (1979). Issue involvement can increase or decrease persuasion by enhancing message-relevant cognitive responses. *Journal of Personality and Social Psychology, 37,* 1915–1926.

Petty, R. E., Cacioppo, J. T., & Goldman, R. (1981). Personal involvement as a determinant of argument-based persuasion. *Journal of Personality and Social Psychology, 41,* 847–855.

Phillips, D. P. (1977). Motor vehicle fatalities increase just after publicized suicide stories. *Science, 196,* 1464–1465.

Phillips, D. P. (1986). Natural experiments on the effects of mass media violence on fatal aggression: Strengths and weaknesses of a new approach. In L. Berkowitz (Ed.), *Advances in experimental social psychology* (Vol. 19., pp. 207–250). New York: Academic Press.

Phillips, D. P., & Bollen, K. A. (1985). Same time last year: Selective data dredging for negative findings. *American Sociological Review, 50,* 364–371.

Philpott, S. J. F. (1950). Apparent relations between psychological and physical constants. *British Journal of Psychology, 39,* 123–141.

Piaget, J. (1954). *The construction of reality in the child.* New York: Basic Books.

Polich, J., Pollock, V. E., & Bloom, F. L. (1994). Meta-analysis of P-300 amplitude from males at risk for alcoholism. *Psychological Bulletin, 115,* 55–73.

Pool, R. (1988). Similar experiments, dissimilar results. *Science, 242,* 192–193.

Pratkanis, A. R., Greenwald, A. G., Leippe, M. R., & Baumgartner, M. H. (1988). In search of reliable persuasion effects III: The sleeper effect is dead: Long live the sleeper effect. *Journal of Personality and Social Psychology, 54,* 203–218.

Prentice, D. A., & Miller, D. T. (1992). When small effects are impressive. *Psychological Bulletin, 112,* 160–164.

Price-Williams, D. R. (1985). Cultural psychology. In G. Lindzey & E. Aronson (Eds.), *Handbook of social psychology* (Vol. 2, pp. 993–1042). New York: Random House.

Pylyshyn, Z. W. (1973). What the mind's eye tells the mind's brain. *Psychological Bulletin, 80,* 1–24.

Ramsey, P. H. (1981). Power of univariate pairwise multiple comparison procedures. *Psychological Bulletin, 90,* 352–366.

Ratcliff, R. (1993). Methods for dealing with reaction time outliers. *Psychological Bulletin, 114,* 510–532.

Raudenbush, S. W. (1984). Magnitude of teacher expectancy effects on pupil IQ as a function of the credibility of expectancy induction: A synthesis of findings. *Journal of Educational Psychology, 76,* 85–97.

Rhine, J. B., & Pratt, J. G. (1954). A review of the Pearce–Pratt distance series of ESP tests. *Journal of Parapsychology, 18,* 165–177.

Richardson, L. F. (1952). Dr. J. S. F. Philpott's wave theory. *British Journal of Psychology*, *43*, 169–176.

Rockette, H. E. (1994). What evidence is needed to link lung cancer and second-hand smoke? *Chance, 6*, 15–18.

Rodin, J. (1986). Aging and health: Effects of the sense of control. *Science, 233*, 1271–1276.

Roese, N. J., & Jamieson, D. W. (1993). Twenty years of bogus pipeline research: A critical review and meta-analysis. *Psychological Bulletin, 114*, 363–375.

Rosenberg, M. J. (1965). When dissonance fails: On eliminating evaluation apprehension from attitude measurement. *Journal of Personality and Social Psychology, 1*, 28–42.

Rosenberger, P. B. (1992). Dyslexia—is it a disease? *The New England Journal of Medicine, 326*, 192–193.

Rosenthal, R. (1963). On the social psychology of the psychological experiment: The experimenter's hypothesis as unintended determinant of experimental results. *American Scientist, 51*, 268–283.

Rosenthal, R. (1976). *Experimenter effects in behavioral research* (enlarged ed.). New York: Irvington.

Rosenthal, R. (1978). Combining results of independent studies. *Psychological Bulletin, 85*, 185–193.

Rosenthal, R. (1979). The "file drawer" problem and tolerance for null results. *Psychological Bulletin, 86*, 638–641.

Rosenthal, R. (1991). *Meta-analytic procedures for social research* (rev. ed.). Newbury Park, CA: Sage.

Rosenthal, R., & Jacobson, L. (1968). *Pygmalion in the classroom: Teacher expectation and children's intellectual development*. New York: Holt, Rinehart & Winston.

Rosenthal, R., & Rosnow, R. L. (1985). *Contrast analysis: Focused comparisons in the analysis of variance*. New York: Cambridge University Press.

Rosenthal, R., & Rubin, D. B. (1978). Interpersonal expectancy effects: The first 345 studies. *The Behavioral and Brain Sciences, 3*, 377–386.

Rosenthal, R., & Rubin, D. B. (1979). A note on percent variance explained as a measure of the importance of effects. *Journal of Applied Social Psychology, 9*, 395–396.

Rosnow, R. L., & Rosenthal, R. (1991). If you're looking at the cell means, you're not looking at only the interaction (unless all main effects are zero). *Psychological Bulletin, 110*, 574–576.

Ross, L. (1977). The intuitive psychologist and his shortcomings: Distortions in the attribution process. In L. Berkowitz (Ed.), *Advances in experimental social psychology* (Vol. 10, pp. 173–220). New York: Academic Press.

Russell, J. A. (1994). Is there universal recognition of emotion from facial expression? A review of the cross-cultural studies. *Psychological Bulletin, 115*, 102–141.

Russett, B. (1988). Editor's comment. *Journal of Conflict Resolution, 32*, 773–775.

Salovey, P., & Rodin, J. (1984). Some antecedents and consequences of social-comparison jealousy. *Journal of Personality and Social Psychology, 47*, 780–792.

SAS Institute, Inc. (1988). *SAS / Stat* user's guide, Release 6.03 Edition*. Cary, NC: Author.

Sawilowsky, S. S., & Blair, R. C. (1992). A more realistic look at the robustness and Type II error properties of the t test to departures from population normality. *Psychological Bulletin, 111*, 352–360.

Schachter, S., & Singer, J. E. (1962). Cognitive, social, and physiological determinants of emotional state. *Psychological Review, 69*, 379–399.

Schaffer, J. P. (1977). Reorganization of variables in analysis of variance and multidimensional contingency tables. *Psychological Bulletin, 84*, 220–228.

Schaffer, J. P. (1991). Probability of directional errors with disordinal (qualitative) interaction. *Psychometrika, 56*, 29–38.

Schank, R. C. (1979). Interestingness: Controlling inferences. *Artificial Intelligence, 12,* 273–297.

Scheffé, H. (1959). *The analysis of variance.* New York: Wiley.

Schmid, C. F. (1983). *Statistical graphics: Design principles and practices.* New York: Wiley.

Schmid, C. H. (1991). Value-splitting: Taking the data apart. In D. C. Hoaglin, F. Mosteller, & J. W. Tukey (Eds.), *Fundamentals of exploratory analysis of variance* (pp. 72–113). New York: Wiley.

Schmidt, F. L. (1992). What do data really mean?: Research findings, meta-analysis, and cumulative knowledge in psychology. *American Psychologist, 47,* 1173–1181.

Schrodt, P. A. (1990). A methodological critique of a test of the effects of the Maharishi technology of the unified field. *Journal of Conflict Resolution, 34,* 745–755.

Schwartz, S. H. (1992). Universals in the content and structure of values: Theoretical advances and empirical tests in 20 countries. In M. P. Zanna (Ed.), *Advances in experimental social psychology* (Vol. 25, pp. 1–65). New York: Academic Press.

Scriven, M. (1974). Evaluation perspectives and procedures. In W. J. Popham (Ed.), *Evaluation in education: Current applications* (pp. 68–84). Berkeley, CA: McCutchan.

Sears, D. O. (1986). College sophomores in the laboratory: Influences of a narrow data base on social psychology's view of human nature. *Journal of Personality and Social Psychology, 51,* 515–530.

Shavelson, R. J., & Webb, N. M. (1991). *Generalizability: A primer.* Newbury Park, CA: Sage.

Shaywitz, S. E., Escobar, M. D., Shaywitz, B. A., Fletcher, J. M., & Makuch, R. (1992). Evidence that dyslexia may represent the lower tail of a normal distribution of reading ability. *The New England Journal of Medicine, 326,* 145–150.

Shepard, R. N., & Metzler, J. (1971). Mental rotation of three-dimensional objects. *Science, 171,* 701–703.

Shils, M. E., & Young, V. R. (1988). *Modern nutrition in health and disease* (7th ed.). Philadelphia: Lea & Fabinger.

Siegel, S. (1956). *Nonparametric statistics.* New York: Wiley.

Skinner, B. F. (1963). Operant behavior. *American Psychologist, 18,* 503–515.

Snyder, M. (1974). The self-monitoring of expressive behavior. *Journal of Personality and Social Psychology, 30,* 526–537.

Tajfel, H., & Turner, J. C. (1986). The social identity theory of intergroup behavior. In W. Austin & S. Worchel (Eds.), *The social psychology of intergroup relations* (pp. 7–24). Monterey, CA: Brooks/Cole.

Tesser, A. (1988). Toward a self-evaluation maintenance model of social behavior. In L. Berkowitz (Ed.), *Advances in experimental social psychology* (Vol. 21, pp. 181–227). New York: Academic Press.

Tesser, A. (1990, August). *Interesting models in social psychology: A personal view.* Invited address presented at the meeting of the American Psychological Association, Boston.

Thagard, P. (1989). Explanatory coherence. *Behavioral and Brain Sciences, 12,* 435–467.

Thaler, R. H. (1991). *Quasi-rational economics.* New York: Russell Sage.

Thomas, D. (1954). *Quite early one morning.* New York: New Directions.

Too late for Prince Charming? (1986, June 2). *Newsweek,* pp. 54–61.

Tuckel, P. S., & Feinberg, B. M. (1991). Answering machines and telephone surveys. *Public Opinion Quarterly, 55,* 200–217.

Tucker, L. A., & Bagwell, M. (1992). Relationship between serum cholesterol levels and television viewing in 11,947 adults. *American Journal of Health Promotion, 6*(6), 437–442.

Tufte, E. R. (1983). *The visual display of quantitative information.* Cheshire, CT: Graphics Press.

Tukey, J. W. (1953). *The problem of multiple comparisons.* Unpublished manuscript, Princeton University, Princeton, NJ.

Tukey, J. W. (1955). A quick, compact two-sample test to Duckworth's specifications. *Technometrics, 1,* 31–48.

Tukey, J. W. (1962). The future of data analysis. *Annals of Mathematical Statistics, 33,* 1–67.

Tukey, J. W. (1969). Analyzing data: Sanctification or detective work? *American Psychologist, 24,* 83–91.

Tukey, J. W. (1977). *Exploratory data analysis.* Reading, MA: Addison-Wesley.

Tukey, J. W. (1991). The philosophy of multiple comparisons. *Statistical Science, 6,* 100–116.

Tukey, J. W., Mosteller, F., & Youtz, C. (1991). Assessing changes. In D. C. Hoaglin, F. Mosteller, & J. W. Tukey, (Eds.), *Fundamentals of exploratory analysis of variance* (pp. 295–335). New York: Wiley.

Tversky, A., & Gilovich, T. (1989). The "hot hand": Statistical reality or cognitive illusion? *Chance, 2*(4), 31–34.

Tversky, A., & Kahneman, D. (1971). Belief in the "law of small numbers." *Psychological Bulletin, 75,* 105–110.

Tversky, A., & Kahneman, D. (1974). Judgment under uncertainty: Heuristics and biases. *Science, 185,* 1124–1131.

U. S. Surgeon General. (1964). Smoking and health. *Report of the Advisory Committee to the Surgeon General of the Public Health Service.* Washington, DC: U. S. Government Printing Office.

Utts, J. (1991). Replication and meta-analysis in parapsychology. *Statistical Science, 6,* 363–378.

Wachter, K. W., & Straf, M. L. (Eds.).(1990). *The future of meta-analysis.* New York: Russell Sage.

Wagenaar, W. A. (1972). Generation of random sequences by human subjects: A critical survey of the literature. *Psychological Bulletin, 77,* 65–72.

Wainer, H., & Schacht, S. (1978). "Gapping." *Psychometrika, 43,* 203–212.

Wainer, H., & Thissen, D. (1993). Graphical data analysis. In G. Keren & C. Lewis (Eds.), *A handbook for data analysis in the behavioral sciences: Statistical issues* (pp. 391–457). Hillsdale, NJ: Lawrence Erlbaum Associates.

Wallach, M. A., & Kogan, N. (1965). The roles of information, discussion, and consensus in group risk taking. *Journal of Experimental Social Psycholgy, 1,* 1–19.

Whitten, D. J. (1977). Some alternative approaches to investigations in telepathy. *Journal of the Society for Psychical Research, 49,* 644–647.

Wickens, T. D. (1989). *Multiway contingency table analysis for the social sciences.* Hillsdale, NJ: Lawrence Erlbaum Associates.

Wike, E. L., & Church, J. D. (1976). Comments on Clark's "The language-as-fixed-effect-fallacy." *Journal of Verbal Learning and Verbal Behavior, 15,* 249–256.

Wilcox, R. R. (1987). New designs in analysis of variance. *Annual Review of Psychology, 38,* 29–60.

Wilcox, R. R. (1992). Why can methods for comparing means have relatively low power, and what can you do to correct the problem? *Current Directions in Psychological Science, 1,* 101–105.

Wilcoxon, F. (1945). Individual comparisons by ranking methods. *Biometrics Bulletin, 1,* 80–83.

Wilensky, R. (1983). Story grammars versus story points. *Behavioral and Brain Sciences, 6,* 579–623.

Wilson, J. Q., & Herrnstein, R. J. (1985). *Crime and human nature.* New York: Simon & Schuster.

Wilson, T. D., DePaulo, B. M., Mook, D. G., & Klaaren, K. J. (1993). Scientists' evaluations of research: The biasing effects of importance of topic. *Psychological Science, 4,* 322–325.

Winer, B. J. (1971). *Statistical principles in experimental design* (2nd ed.). New York: McGraw-Hill.

Winkler, R. L. (1972). *An introduction to Bayesian inference and decision.* New York: Holt, Rinehart & Winston.

Witkin, H. A., Lewis, H. B., Hertzman, M., Machover, K., Meissner, P. B., & Wapner, S. (1954). *Personality through perception.* New York: Harper.

Worth, L. T., & Mackie, D. M. (1987). Cognitive mediation of positive affect in persuasion. *Social Cognition, 5,* 76–94.

Wynn, K. (1992). Addition and subtraction by human infants. *Nature, 358,* 749–750.

Zajonc, R. B. (1965). Social facilitation. *Science, 149,* 269–274.

Author Index

A

Abelson, R. P., 7, 61, 77, 121, 158, 172
Adams, D., 63
Adams, W. J., 19
Alexander, C. N., 45, 77, 178, 179, 180
Anderson, C. A., 158
Anscombe, F. J., 147
Aronson, E., 13, 34, 50, 135, 163
Atlas, D. H., 2, 4

B

Bagwell, M., 2
Bailar, J. C., 52
Baird, W., 13, 156
Banaji, M. R., 134
Banuazizi, A., 106
Baron, R. A., 158
Baumgartner, M. H., 133
Bayes, T., 18
Beall, A., 115
Bem, D. J., 11, 82, 143, 197
Berger, R. E., 66
Blackwell, T., 138
Blair, R. C., 31, 60
Bloom, F. L., 89
Bollen, K. A., 186
Borden, R. J., 164
Bower, G. H., 133
Brehm, J. W., 163
Bressler, M., 134
Brewer, M., 13, 30, 34, 103, 135
Brody, C., 66
Brody, J. E., 4
Brown, C., 138
Brown, R., 144
Browne, M. W., 21
Bruner, J., 174
Burt, C., 101, 102
Bush, L. K., 61, 69
Bush, R. R., 66

C

Cacioppo, J. T., 148
Campbell, D. T., 11, 12, 13, 180
Carlsmith, J. M., 13, 34, 35, 36, 98, 99,
    100, 113, 135, 158, 162, 163,
    191, 192, 197
Carroll, J. D., 4, 157
Chandler, H. M., 45, 77, 178, 179, 180
Chapanis, A., 191
Chapanis, N. P., 191
Cherlin, A., 3
Church, J. D., 141
Cialdini, R. B., 164
Ciminera, J. L., 142
Clark, H. H., 70, 141
Cleveland, W. S., xi
Cliff, N., 60
Cohen, A. R., 163
Cohen, J., 8, 10, 12, 37, 39, 40, 46, 50, 52,
    68, 74, 76, 84, 141
Cohen, P., 50, 68, 84
Cohn, C. M. G., 6
Collins, B. E., 162
Cook, T. D., 12
Cooper, H., 22
Cooper, J., 162, 193
Cowles, M., 2
Crano, W. D., 30, 103
Crowder, R. G., 134
Culhane, S. E., 50

D

Davies, J. L., 45, 77, 178, 179, 180
Davis, J. A., 2, 88
Davis, M. S., 13, 156
Dawes, R. M., 40
DeBondt, W., 25
DeNeve, K. M., 22
DePaulo, B. M., 50
Derr, P., 66
Deutsch, M., 160

Subject Index